# Computational Linguistics: Studies in Natural Language Processing

# Computational Linguistics: Studies in Natural Language Processing

**Edited by
Elsa Harrington**

MURPHY & MOORE
www.murphy-moorepublishing.com

Published by Murphy & Moore Publishing,
1 Rockefeller Plaza,
New York City, NY 10020, USA

ISBN: 978-1-63987-123-0

**Cataloging-in-Publication Data**

Computational linguistics : studies in natural language processing / edited by Elsa Harrington.
    p. cm.
Includes bibliographical references and index.
ISBN 978-1-63987-123-0
1. Computational linguistics. 2. Speech processing systems. 3. Applied linguistics.
4. Cross-language information retrieval. I. Harrington, Elsa.
P98 .C66 2022
006.35--dc23

For information on all Murphy & Moore Publications
visit our website at www.murphy-moorepublishing.com

**ⓂⓂ MURPHY & MOORE**

# Contents

# Preface

Computational linguistics refers to the scientific study of language from a computational perspective. It is an interdisciplinary field the makes use of concepts from computer science, linguistics, logic, artificial intelligence, philosophy and cognitive science. Natural language processing deals with the study of interactions between human language and computers. It also involves the programming of computers for the processing and analysis of large amounts of natural language data. There are theoretical and applied components of linguistics. Theoretical computational linguistics involves the development of formal theories related to grammar and semantics. Within applied computational linguistics, the statistical methods and machine learning algorithms are applied to natural language processing tasks. This book studies, analyses and upholds the pillars of computational linguistics and its utmost significance in modern times. It provides significant information of this discipline to help develop a good understanding of computational linguistics and related fields. This book will provide comprehensive knowledge to the readers.

The researches compiled throughout the book are authentic and of high quality, combining several disciplines and from very diverse regions from around the world. Drawing on the contributions of many researchers from diverse countries, the book's objective is to provide the readers with the latest achievements in the area of research. This book will surely be a source of knowledge to all interested and researching the field.

In the end, I would like to express my deep sense of gratitude to all the authors for meeting the set deadlines in completing and submitting their research chapters. I would also like to thank the publisher for the support offered to us throughout the course of the book. Finally, I extend my sincere thanks to my family for being a constant source of inspiration and encouragement.

**Editor**

# Handling equivalence classes of Optimality–Theoretic comparative tableaux

*Igor Yanovich*
Universität Tübingen

Keywords: Optimality Theory, ERC set, tableau equivalence, normal form, equivalence-preserving transformations

## ABSTRACT

Many Optimality-Theoretic tableaux contain exactly the same information, and equivalence-preserving operations on them have been an object of study for some two decades. This paper shows that several of the operations proposed in the earlier literature together are actually enough to express *any* possible equivalence-preserving transformation. Moreover, every equivalence class of comparative tableaux (equivalently, of sets of Elementary Ranking Conditions, or ERC sets) has a unique and computable normal form that can be derived using those elementary operations in polynomial time. Any equivalence-preserving operation on comparative tableaux (ERC sets) is thus computable, and normal form tableaux may therefore represent their equivalence classes without loss of generality.

Optimality Theory (OT) is a grammatical formalism based on constraint competition, formulated by Prince and Smolensky (1993) (later published as Prince and Smolensky (2004)). OT is especially popular in phonology, and is used to some extent in other branches of linguistics. In OT, a set of competing output forms $\{Output_1, Output_2, \ldots\}$ is generated by machine **Gen** for the underlying form *Input*. Each pair $\langle Input, Output_N \rangle$ is then evaluated against a set of constraints **Con**. The grammar of a particular language is modeled as an ordering of the universal set of constraints **Con** which determines the winning input-output pair for each *Input*: an input-output pair $\alpha = \langle Input, Output_N \rangle$ wins over another pair $\beta = \langle Input, Output_M \rangle$ when $\alpha$ incurs fewer violations than $\beta$ in the most highly ranked constraint where $\alpha$ and $\beta$ differ. The input-output pairs that do not lose to any other pair are declared grammatical.

The OT formalism expresses two important intuitions regarding how languages might function. First, it easily captures conditions of the form "try A; if impossible, try B; if also impossible, resort to C", which seem to frequently occur in natural language. Second, OT allows for elegant modeling of cross-linguistic variation and language change in terms of re-ranking of a universal set of constraints.

The information that a given dataset contributes constrains the possible rankings of constraints. Such information may be represented in the form of a comparative tableau (Prince 2000) or the corresponding set of Elementary Ranking Conditions, or ERC set (Prince 2002). In this paper, I present an incremental step completing the development of a full theory of equivalence classes of comparative OT tableaux, or, equivalently, ERC sets.

Earlier work, especially that of Hayes (1997), Prince (2000), Prince (2002), Brasoveanu and Prince (2011)[1], and Prince (2006), has established a number of results concerning how one may transform the information in an OT tableau without loss. What has not yet been done in this line of research is to establish the limits of operations that preserve equivalence. For example, the following natural question has not been answered: given two arbitrary comparative tableaux or ERC sets, can we determine whether they contain identical information?[2]

The present paper fills this gap: I show that any (finite) comparative tableau may be (computably, and actually quite efficiently) transformed into a normal form, which is unique for the whole equivalence class. Moreover, this transformation is possible by applying a sequence of a set of five elementary operations and their inverses

---

[1] An earlier version (Brasoveanu and Prince 2005) was circulated through Rutgers Optimality Archive (ROA) http://roa.rutgers.edu/

[2] For a finite constraint set, there is only a finite number of possible rankings, so strictly speaking, brute-force testing for equivalence is possible: one may simply build every possible ranking and test whether the two tableaux/ERC sets are compatible with it. However, the number of logically possible rankings of $n$ constraints is $n!$, so the complexity of brute-force testing is factorial in the number of constraints. This should be compared with the merely polynomial time complexity of our new test for equivalence through normalization given in Theorem (16).

already introduced in the literature. Only two of those are non-trivial, so a very small and simple set turns out to be sufficient to capture all the diversity of possible equivalence-preserving operations on tableaux. Normalization gives us a handle on equivalence classes of tableaux/ERC sets, as we show that each equivalence class contains exactly one normal form tableau. The normal form may therefore serve as the class's representative. A test for equivalence of arbitrary tableaux (computable for finite tableaux) involves normalizing the input tableaux and comparing the resulting normal form tableaux. The original tableaux are equivalent if and only if their normal forms are identical. Thanks to the normal form theorem proved in the present paper, the space of all possible equivalence-preserving operations may be enumerated, and the same is true of the members of which equivalence class.

## 1                     INTRODUCTION

As a concrete example of how OT works, consider the pattern of final obstruent devoicing in Dutch.[3] Underlyingly, Dutch morphemes may have both voiced and voiceless obstruents: the morpheme for 'bed' is /bɛd/, surfacing faithfully in [bɛd-ən] 'beds', while the morpheme for 'dab' is /bɛt/, surfacing faithfully in [bɛt-ən] '(we) dab'. But when the final obstruent of either morpheme closes the syllable, it is realized on the surface by the same voiceless [t]: both 'bed' /bɛd/ and '(I) dab' /bɛt/ surface as [bɛt]. The following OT tableau demonstrates the violation patterns for several potential outputs corresponding to the underlying form /bɛd/:

(1)

| UR: /bɛd/ | *VOICED-OBS-CODA | IDENT-VOICE | *VOICED-OBS |
|---|---|---|---|
| a. [bɛd] | * | | ** |
| b. [bɛt] | | * | * |
| c. [pɛd] | * | * | * |
| d. [pɛt] | | ** | |

According to the OT conventions, solid vertical lines in the tableau indicate that the left-to-right order of the constraints corresponds to their ranking in the grammar: *VOICED-OBS-CODA ≫ IDENT-VOICE

---

[3] My description of the Dutch pattern is based on Kager (1999).

≫ *VOICED-OBS. The constraint *VOICED-OBS penalizes any voiced obstruent. Its specialized cousin *VOICED-OBS-CODA only penalizes voiced obstruents in the coda position of a syllable. Finally, IDENT-VOICE penalizes mismatches in voice between underlying and output consonants. The ranking in the tableau ensures that [bɛt] is the winning output form: [bɛd] and [pɛd] lose to [bɛt] in the highest constraint *VOICED-OBS-CODA, and [pɛt] loses to it in the next constraint IDENT-VOICE. Overall, the ranking says: "avoid voiced obstruents in the coda, but preserve them elsewhere".[4] We worked through this example already knowing the ranking. Normally the work of an OT analyst proceeds in the opposite direction: she would know the constraints, the violation profiles, and the designated winner, and would need to uncover the ranking that selects the winner correctly. For that procedure, it is more convenient to use a comparative OT tableau, Prince (2000). The comparative counterpart of Tableau (1) is given in Tableau (2). Each row of a comparative tableau corresponds to a pair of the winner output and one of the loser outputs of the regular OT tableau as in Tableau (1). For a specific row corresponding to a specific winner-loser pair, if the winner incurs less violations than the loser in a given constraint, the relevant cell is marked with a W; if the loser incurs less violations, the cell is marked with an L. If there is a tie, it is marked with an *e*.

(2)

| UR: /bɛd/ | *VOICED-OBS-CODA | IDENT-VOICE | *VOICED-OBS |
|---|---|---|---|
| [bɛt]~[bɛd] | W | L | W |
| [bɛt]~[pɛd] | W | *e* | *e* |
| [bɛt]~[pɛt] | *e* | W | L |

It is easy to see that converting a traditional OT tableau into a comparative tableau loses information about the number of violations. But the lost information is irrelevant for recovering the ranking. Moreover, the characterization of rankings which select the correct winner becomes very simple with comparative tableaux: a ranking selects the right winner iff in every row, all L-constraints are dominated by a W-

---

[4] It is easy to check that the ranking in 1 predicts correct results for Dutch [bɛd-ən] 'beds', [bɛt-ən] '(we) dab', and /bɛt/-[bɛt] '(I) dab'. It is also the only ranking selecting the correct winner in 1, though there exist tableaux whose winner can be correctly selected by more than one ranking.

constraint. A specific condition selecting the rankings compatible with a fixed row is called the Elementary Ranking Condition, or ERC, by Prince (2002). In Tableau (2), we can see for instance that the pair [bɛt]~[pɛt] necessitates the inclusion of a pairwise ranking IDENT-VOICE ≫ *VOICED-OBS into our grammar. On the other hand, another pair [bɛt]~[pɛd] does not add any useful information: without any Ls in the row, [pɛd] is going to lose to [bɛt] on any possible ranking of our three constraints (i.e., the ERC corresponding to this comparative row is trivial, as it is compatible with any ranking.) In what follows, I will be largely talking in terms of comparative rows and tableaux, but it is easy to translate this into talk about ERCs and ERC sets.

Turning to definitions, a **comparative tableau** is a possibly empty 2-dimensional matrix with labelled columns where each cell contains a W, an L or an $e$. The column labels of a given tableau form the **constraint set**. A **comparative row** is a comparative tableau with one row. The tableau with zero rows is special: it is compatible with any ranking whatsoever; we refer to it as $T_\top$. A **(total) ranking** is a total order of a constraint set. In what follows, we always assume that tableaux and rankings use the same fixed constraint set.

The following terminology, mostly borrowed from Prince (2002), will also be useful. A ranking $M$[5] is **(OT-)compatible** with a comparative tableau $T$ iff for every row, every L-constraint is dominated by some W-constraint. We say that ranking $M$ **covers** an L in constraint $C$ in row $r$ when $M$ orders one of the W-constraints of $r$ higher than the L-constraint $C$. We also say that a W in any constraint $C'$ that dominates $C$ under ranking $M$ **covers** the L in $C$. If every ranking compatible with tableau $T$ is also compatible with tableau $U$, we say that $T$ **entails** $U$. When $T$ and $U$ are compatible with exactly the same rankings, they are called **OT-equivalent**. It is trivial to extend the notions to ERC sets.

Once a comparative tableau is computed, the actual input-output pairs are no longer needed for the task of determining the correct ranking. Thus we may freely combine several tableaux stemming from different input forms into a single bigger tableau: the input informa-

---

[5] Prince (2002) introduces the logical perspective on OT compatibility wherein rows/ERCs are formulas, and rankings are essentially models. Hence $M, N$ as designations for rankings.

tion in it may be viewed as being about the grammar of the language rather than about particular linguistic forms. In this paper, we will be working exclusively with comparative tableaux.

Tableaux directly computed from particular linguistic forms are often suboptimal in how they represent information. For example, the second row of 2 may be omitted without any loss of information; similarly, the W in *VOICED-OBS in the first row is "false", because replacing it with an $e$ will not change which ranking selects the right winner. It thus becomes important to study equivalence relations between comparative tableaux/ERC sets. To name just a few examples, Hayes (1997) (cf. also a follow-up in Prince (2006)) seeks to find transformations for tableaux allowing for better information extraction; Prince (2000) introduces the notion of entailment between rows and tableaux; Brasoveanu and Prince (2011) define an algorithm transforming an arbitrary tableau into a small-size "basis" conveniently representing the same information.

The current paper continues that line of investigation. Namely, I prove that the equivalence-preserving operations introduced in the earlier literature are already enough to handle equivalence classes of comparative tableaux/ERC sets, once we add the necessary proofs. By definition, any (comparative) tableau $T$ belongs to an equivalence class $\mathscr{C}$ such that any tableau in $\mathscr{C}$ is compatible with exactly the same rankings. Whenever there are such non-trivial equivalence classes, there is a problem of handling them: in geometry, there are congruence classes of geometrical figures; in proof theory, there often exist many proofs of the same statement; in lambda-calculus, there are plenty of equivalent lambda-terms. In all those cases we want to be able to obtain results common for the equivalence class. Our strategy for getting a handle on equivalent classes of OT tableaux will be fairly standard: we will find a special representative which exists in every equivalence class, and is unique in it — in other words, a normal form that can represent the class.

The plan is as follows. In Section 2, I review several elementary equivalence-preserving transformations of tableaux from the earlier literature, adding their inverses where needed. Later it will be shown that the introduced set of operations is functionally complete (that is, any equivalence-preserving transformation can be decomposed into a sequence of elementary transformations from the set). In Section 3 I define a normal form for OT tableaux, and prove the central result of the paper: a normal form is unique in its equivalence class. This means that the normal form may be used as the representative of a class, or its *name*. Finally, in Section 4 I provide several easy corollaries following from the normal form theorems. For example, we obtain a test of equivalence for OT tableaux, and a proof that bases of Brasoveanu and Prince (2011) are unique in their equivalence classes and thus can serve as class representatives (just as normal-form tableaux can).

## 2        FIVE ELEMENTARY EQUIVALENCE–PRESERVING TRANSFORMATIONS

In this section, we provide the definitions for five operations with inverses that will be shown in the next section to form a functionally complete set. The operations are either trivial (Operations (3) and (4)) or have been described and proven correct before (Operations (5) and (6) are either explicitly discussed by, or immediately follow from Prince (2002); Operation (7) is studied in Prince (2006)). The proofs of equivalence-preservation are provided here mainly for completeness' sake, so the readers familiar with the operations may wish to skip them. The novelty of the present paper is not in the operations themselves, but in the fact that together they form a functionally complete set that is enough to represent any possible equivalence-preserving operation whatsoever.

The order of columns in example tableaux below does *not* correspond to any ranking, unlike in the previous section.[6] Constraint names are chosen to be $C1$, $C2$, ..., rather than the usual meaningful names, to underscore the fact that the transformations are completely blind to actual linguistic content, and only concern the formal information encoded in a tableau.

We use variables $M$, $N$, ...for OT rankings; variables $T$, $U$, ...for comparative OT tableaux; and $r$ and $q$ for comparative OT rows. $W(r)$, for row $r$, denotes the set of constraints that have a W in $r$. Similarly for $L(r)$. This short notation allows us to define new rows compactly: e.g.,

---

[6] Sometimes the absence of order is marked by using dashed vertical lines. We refrain from this practice at the request of a reviewer.

if we say that $W(r) = \{C3\}$ and $L(r) = \{C1\}$, and CON is the 5-constraint set $\{C1, C2, C3, C4, C5\}$, then row $r$ is the row $(L, e, W, e, e)$.

The first two operations we will consider are trivial. First, row swaps defined in Operation (3) never affect OT-equivalence, as the order of the rows is not significant for determining whether a ranking $M$ is compatible with the tableau. (If we think in terms of corresponding ERC sets, the very concept of row order becomes irrelevant.) Row swap is its all inverse. Second, if a tableau is not compatible with any ranking whatsoever (that is, if it puts contradictory requirements on the ranking of constraints), there is no useful information in it anyway, so as long as the tableau remains contradictory, any changes to it do not offend equivalence (Operation (4)).

(3)   **Row swaps**: swapping any two rows preserves OT equivalence.

| C1 | C2 | C3 | C4 |
|----|----|----|----|
| e  | W  | L  | L  |
| W  | e  | L  | e  |

$\Longleftrightarrow$

| C1 | C2 | C3 | C4 |
|----|----|----|----|
| W  | e  | L  | e  |
| e  | W  | L  | L  |

*Proof*: trivial.

(4)   **Contradictory jumps**: for a contradictory tableau (that is, a tableau not compatible with any ranking), any row can be added, or, inversely, subtracted as long as the resulting tableau is still contradictory.

| C1 | C2 | C3 | C4 |
|----|----|----|----|
| W  | L  | e  | e  |
| L  | W  | e  | e  |

$\Longleftrightarrow$

| C1 | C2 | C3 | C4 |
|----|----|----|----|
| W  | L  | e  | e  |
| L  | W  | e  | e  |
| e  | e  | W  | L  |

*Proof*: trivial.

Row splitting and its inverse, row merging, are also nearly trivial. Given the ERC theory of Prince (2002), it is easy to show that a row with several Ls is equivalent to a set of single-L rows. In ERC terms, such single-L rows have been called Primitive Ranking Conditions by Prince (2006, p. 4). The correctness of row splitting and row merging shows that covering each L in a multiple-L row is independent from covering the other Ls. Working with single-L rows, or PRCs, is often more convenient, especially when we turn all rows in a tableau into this single-L/PRC form.

(5) **Row splittings and mergings**: a row $r$ is equivalent to any set of rows $r_1, \ldots, r_n$ such that $\forall r_i : W(r_i) = W(r)$, and $\bigcup_i L(r_i) = L(r)$. That is, $r, r_1, \ldots, r_n$ must have exactly the same Ws, and the combined Ls of $r_1, \ldots, r_n$ must form the same set as the Ls of $r$.

| $C1$ | $C2$ | $C3$ | $C4$ |
|------|------|------|------|
| W | W | L | L |

$\Leftrightarrow$

| $C1$ | $C2$ | $C3$ | $C4$ |
|------|------|------|------|
| W | W | L | $e$ |
| W | W | $e$ | L |

*Proof*: Suppose a ranking $M$ puts on top of each L in $r$ one of $r$'s Ws. As any $r_i$ has the same Ws, any L in any $r_i$ will also be covered by a W under ranking $M$.

Conversely, suppose a ranking $N$ is compatible with all rows $r_1, \ldots, r_n$. Consider some L of row $r$. Some $r_i$ must have an L in the same constraint, and ranking $N$ covers it with a W in one of $W(r_i)$. That W-constraint in $r_i$ also has a W in $r$, by definition. Thus $N$ covers the arbitrary L in $r$ just as well.

Thus a ranking is compatible with $r$ iff it is compatible with $r_1, \ldots r_n$. $\qquad\square$

The remaining two pairs of operations are the non-trivial part of the set. Some OT rows may be superfluous in their tableaux: even if we delete them, the amount of information in the tableau does not change (e.g., the second row in Tableau (2) is superfluous.) By definition, subtraction or addition of such rows does not offend OT equivalence. What is non-trivial, though, is determining the exact formal conditions under which a row is superfluous. In the proof, I use the criterion by Prince (2002), featuring his operation of fusion.[7] One can provide an alternative characterization of superfluousness based on

---

[7] The operation of fusion on rows is defined by Prince (2002, page 8, Equation (12)). For tableau $U$, the fusion row $fU$ has an $e$ in the $Ci$ cell iff all rows in $U$ have an $e$ in $Ci$; has an L iff some row in $U$ has an L in $Ci$; and has a W otherwise, that is, when at least one row in $U$ has a W in $Ci$, and all other rows have either Ws or $e$s, but not Ls.

domination chains of constraints, but the proof based on such chains is more cumbersome.[8]

Using the fact that row order is not significant in a tableau, cf. Operation (3), we can safely use set notation for tableaux, understood as being parasitic on the notation for ERC sets: $T \setminus r$ denotes tableau $T$ with row $r$ subtracted; $T \cup U$ is a concatenation of tableaux $T$ and $U$; and so forth.

(6)  **Inference eliminations and introductions**: a row $r$ entailed in tableau $T$ by the rest of the tableau (that is, by $T \setminus r$) can be subtracted from $T$, or added back to tableau $T \setminus r$.

| $C1$ | $C2$ | $C3$ | $C4$ |
|------|------|------|------|
| W | L | $e$ | $e$ |
| $e$ | W | L | $e$ |
| W | $e$ | L | $e$ |

$\Leftrightarrow$

| $C1$ | $C2$ | $C3$ | $C4$ |
|------|------|------|------|
| W | L | $e$ | $e$ |
| $e$ | W | L | $e$ |

*Proof*: Trivial. What is non-trivial is how to determine if $r$ is entailed by $T \setminus r$. By Prop. 2.5 of (Prince 2002, p. 14), $r$ is entailed by $T \setminus r$ iff there exists a subtableau $U$ of $T \setminus r$ s.t. the fusion $q$ (cf. Footnote (7)) of $U$ entails $r$. In turn, $q$ entails $r$ either when $r$ has no L-s and thus is compatible with any ranking, or when $W(q) \subseteq W(r)$ and $L(q) \supseteq L(r)$.                                                                   □

---

[8] I provide the definitions of possible and maximal domination chains in (i), and the criterion of superfluousness based on them, without proof, in (ii):

(i)  For a tableau $T$, a row $r_i \in T$, and a $Cj \in L(r_i)$, a **possible domination chain** is a sequence of constraints $\langle C_{k_1}, \ldots, C_{k_n} \rangle$ s.t. $C_{k_n} = Cj$, a single constraint never occurs twice in the chain, and for each $C_{k_l}$, $C_{k_{l+1}}$ there is a row $r_m \in T$ for which $C_{k_l} \in W(r_m)$, $C_{k_{l+1}} \in L(r_m)$. A **maximal possible domination chain** is a possible domination chain for which there is no $r_m \in T$ s.t. $C_{k_1} \in L(r_m)$.

(ii)  **Superfluous row theorem.** A tableau $T = \langle r_1, \ldots, r_n \rangle$ entails a row $q$ iff for each $Ci \in L(q)$, there exists such a row $r \in T$ in every maximal domination chain for $Ci$, $r$, and $T$, that there is a constraint $C_{k_l}$ in it s.t. $C_{k_l} \in W(q)$.

Checking the criterion based on maximal chains does not require computing new rows, as the fusion criterion does. But it is easy to see from the cumbersomeness of the definitions that proving the criterion's correctness from first principles requires a bit of work. Therefore I simply reuse Prince's fusion-based result in the main text, referring the reader to Prince (2002) for proofs of its correctness.

To reduce the computational complexity of inference elimination, an RCD-based method is proposed by (Prince 2002, Sec. 5). Prince shows that instead of checking the fusions of all subtableaux, one may check whether $T \setminus r$ is consistent with the negative $\neg r$ of $r$, obtained by replacing all $r$'s Ws with Ls and vice versa. For $m$ rows, we need $m$ such RCD-based checks. As Magri (2009) explains, RCD requires $m^2n$ operations for a tableau with $m$ rows and $n$ constraints. The complexity of RCD-based inference elimination is thus polynomial, in contrast to subtableau-fusion version which is exponential in the number of constraints $n$.

Finally, not all Ws in an OT tableau are necessarily equal: there may be rows with "false Ws" such that there is no ranking compatible with the tableau which puts that W on top of any Ls in the row. As shown by (Prince 2006, p. 12), such false Ws may be replaced with an $e$ without affecting the set of rankings the tableau is compatible with. An example of such a W is the W in the first row in $C3$ in the left tableau in Operation (7). The third row of the tableau necessitates ordering $C4$ over $C3$ in any compatible ranking $M$, and because of that the L in the first row may never be covered by the W in $C3$ in $M$. Therefore replacing that W with an $e$, as in the right tableau, does not offend OT-equivalence. The operation for doing such changes is called **Generalized Removal of W**, or GRW. We also introduce its inverse, **Generalized Introduction of W**, or GIW.

(7)  **Generalized Removal of W (GRW) and Introduction of W (GIW)**: informally, a "false" W is a W whose replacement with an $e$ does not change which rankings the tableau is compatible with. Thus a false W does not do any actual work. The example tableaux below may help visualize the phenomenon.

<table>
<tr><td>$C1$</td><td>$C2$</td><td>$C3$</td><td>$C4$</td><td></td><td>$C1$</td><td>$C2$</td><td>$C3$</td><td>$C4$</td></tr>
<tr><td>W</td><td>W</td><td>W</td><td>L</td><td rowspan="3">$\Longleftrightarrow$</td><td>W</td><td>W</td><td>$e$</td><td>L</td></tr>
<tr><td>W</td><td>L</td><td>$e$</td><td>$e$</td><td>W</td><td>L</td><td>$e$</td><td>$e$</td></tr>
<tr><td>$e$</td><td>$e$</td><td>L</td><td>W</td><td>$e$</td><td>$e$</td><td>L</td><td>W</td></tr>
</table>

Turning to the formal definition: for rows $r$ and $r'$ such that instead of $r$'s W in a fixed $Ci$, row $r'$ has an $e$, consider a pair of $T$ including $r$ that is not entailed by the rest of $T$, and $T' := (T \setminus r) \cup r'$.

(That is, $T'$ that is exactly like $T$, but with the W in $Ci$ in row $r$ replaced with an $e$.)

The claim is: $T$ and $T'$ thus defined are equivalent iff $T \setminus r$ entails the row $q$ such that $W(q) := L(r) \cup (W(r) \setminus Ci)$, and $L(q) = \{Ci\}$.

*Proof:* Just as with inference eliminations, the fact that a false W can be replaced with an $e$ is trivial. What is non-trivial is the criterion for false Ws: a W is false iff the row $q$ as described above is entailed by $T \setminus r$. Prince (2006, p. 12) proves essentially that criterion in his (31) using fusion.[9] Yanovich (2011) provides a different proof in his (125) using partial OT rankings. The proof below is based on the idea of the proof in Yanovich (2011), but does not use either fusion or the apparatus of partial rankings.

Consider row $r$ with a W in $Ci$, and row $q$ defined as in the criterion above: $W(q)$ contains all W- and L-constraints of $r$ except $Ci$, and the only L-constraint of $q$ is $Ci$. We need to show that the W in $Ci$ in $r$ is false in tableau $T$ precisely when the rest of the tableau, $T \setminus r$, entails the row $q$ so constructed.

Without loss of generality, assume that $r$ has only one L, in constraint $Cj$. (We have the right to assume that because we proved in 5 that any multiple-L row may be split into several single-L rows that are together equivalent to it.)

Suppose $q$ is entailed by $T \setminus r$. We will prove that $T$ is then equivalent to $T'$, and thus the W $Ci$ in $r$ is false. Assume towards a contradiction that there is a ranking $M$ which is compatible with $T$, but not with $T'$. That ranking $M$ must be compatible with $r$, but not with $r'$ which differs from it in that it has an $e$ in $Ci$ instead of a W. Then $M$ must say that $Ci \gg Cj$ and that for every $Ck$ from $W(r) \setminus Ci$, $Cj \gg Ck$: otherwise it would be compatible not only with $r$, but also with $r'$. But then $M$ is incompatible with $q$: the L-constraint $Ci$ dominates $Cj$ in $M$, and then by transitivity any W-constraint $Ck$. This is contrary to assumption, and therefore there cannot be such an $M$. Furthermore, any ranking compatible with $T'$ is bound to be compatible with $T$,

---

[9] Prince's theorem is slightly weaker compared to our formulation: Prince requires all rows in $T$ to be not entailed by the rest of the tableau. His actual proof, though, only employs the fact that $r$ is not entailed by $T \setminus r$, just as our proof does.

and thus we derive that if $q$ is entailed by $T \setminus r$, then $T$ and $T'$ are OT-equivalent.

For the other direction, suppose $q$ is not entailed by $T \setminus r$. We show that then there is a ranking compatible with $T$, but not $T'$. We need to show that there exists ranking $M$ compatible with $T \setminus r$ that says $Ci \gg Cj \gg Ck$ for all $Ck \in W(r')$: such a ranking will be compatible with $r$, but not with $r'$. Towards a contradiction, suppose there is no such $M$. That is only possible if no ranking compatible with $T \setminus r$ says $Ci \gg Cj \gg Ck$. For the $Ci \gg Cj$ part, $T \setminus r$ cannot necessitate the opposite ordering $Cj \gg Ci$: if it did, then it would have entailed $q$, contrary to assumption. For $Cj \gg Ck$, suppose towards a contradiction that every ranking compatible with $T \setminus r$ says for some $Ck \in W(r')$ or other that $Ck \gg Cj$. That can only be if there is a row $s$ in $T \setminus r$ with an L in $Cj$, and $W(s) \subseteq W(r')$. But if that is so, then the row $s$, and thus $T \setminus r$ as a whole, entail $r$: the L is in the same place in $s$ and $r$, and $W(s) \subseteq W(r') \subset W(r)$. That is contrary to assumption, so if $T \setminus r$ does not entail either $q$ or $r$, then there must be a ranking $M$ compatible with $T \setminus r$ saying $Ci \gg Cj \gg Ck$ for all $Ck \in W(r')$. That $M$ is compatible with $T$, but not with $T'$, and thus witnesses that $T$ and $T'$ are not OT-equivalent: $T$ is compatible with a larger number of rankings, thanks to the non-false W for which the criterion based on a specially constructed row $q$ fails.                     □

We have now defined and proved correctness of five pairs of elementary operations preserving OT-equivalence of comparative tableaux. Those operations as such have been known before. What has not been known is that those five pairs form a *functionally complete* set: any transformation preserving OT-equivalence can be performed by applying a sequence of those elementary operations, as we will show in the next section.

The following easy-to-prove fact will become useful later:

(8)    All operations in (3)–(7) have inverses: row swap is self-inverse; for the other four pairs, the two members of the pair are inverses.

What (8) means is that each sequence of applications of our elementary operations may be inverted: if we can derive from tableau $T$ another tableau $U$ using those operations, then we can also derive from $U$ the original tableau $T$ by applying the inverted form of the same sequence.

## 3          NORMAL FORM FOR OT TABLEAUX

In this section, we present core novel results of this paper: two theorems regarding the existence and uniqueness of normal form for comparative OT tableaux. Namely, we define a specific tableau format in Definition (9), and then prove that for each equivalence class $\mathscr{C}$, there exists exactly one tableau in such format, and moreover, that the normal form of a (finite) tableau is computable. Normal forms thus can serve as true representatives of their equivalence classes, giving us a handle on those.

It should be stressed that there is nothing particularly special about normal forms — in fact, as we will see in the next section, other forms may be proven to be usable as normal forms just as well. The reason we define the normal form in Definition (9) the way we do is simply that it is convenient for proof purposes. Nor is the form we chose new: Prince (2006, p. 6) defines essentially the same form in terms of ERCs, called the Minimal Primitive Generator, or MPG. Thus in this section we show that (the tableau counterpart of) an MPG is a true normal form for OT equivalence classes.

(9)  **Normal form for OT tableaux:**

  1.  The only contradictory tableau in the normal form is the one-row tableau with a single L in the first constraint. We can refer to this special tableau as $T_\perp$.

  2.  Each row has at most a single L.[10]

  3.  There are no rows which can be inference-eliminated (see Operation (6)).

  4.  In multiple-W rows, there are no false Ws (see Operation (7)).

---

[10] Such single-L rows correspond to Primitive Ranking Conditions of Prince (2006).

5. The rows are ordered according to some strict total order of the set of all possible rows.[11] (For corresponding ERC sets, the notion of row order becomes irrelevant.)

Here is an example of a normal form tableau:

(10)

| $C1$ | $C2$ | $C3$ | $C4$ | $C5$ |
|------|------|------|------|------|
| W | $e$ | L | $e$ | $e$ |
| W | $e$ | $e$ | L | $e$ |
| W | $e$ | $e$ | $e$ | L |
| $e$ | W | $e$ | L | $e$ |

Just calling something a normal form does not make it one. The results in (11)–(14) establish the fact that the class of tableaux defined in Definition (9) indeed has normal form properties.

(11) **Normal Form Existence Theorem**
An arbitrary (finite) tableau $T$ can be transformed into an equivalent normal form tableau by a (finite) sequence of equivalence-preserving transformations in Operations (3)–(7).

(12) **Corollary to Theorem (11).** Each non-empty equivalence class of tableaux contains at least one normal form tableau.

*Proof of Theorem (11).* We give an explicit procedure for transforming an arbitrary tableau so that it satisfies the requirements in Definition (9). For contradictory tableaux, we just add the row (L, $e$, $e$, ...), and subtract all others. If the tableau is not contradictory, we apply row splittings until all rows have at most one L (and are thus PRC-rows). Assuming the tableau is finite, we can eliminate all entailed rows by testing whether the fusions of subtableaux satisfy Prince's condition on entailment, see Operation (6). After that, we can similarly eliminate all false Ws from the resulting tableau by testing if the conditions for GRW, see Operation (7), are met (as all entailed rows were eliminated by that point, the row independence precondition of the criterion in Operation (7) is met). We finish the procedure by applying row swaps to get the ordering right. □

---

[11] The actual choice of ordering is irrelevant as long as all conceivable rows are strictly ordered. I will use the following: 1) let the first constraint where only one of $r$ and $q$ has a W be $Ci$; then the row with the W in $Ci$ goes first; 2) for rows which have identical W-sets, the row which has an L in the first constraint where only one of them has an L goes first.

*Proof of Corollary (12).* Trivial: if there were no normal form tableau in a non-empty equivalence class, then Theorem (11) could not have been valid.       ☐

Note that if the tableau is finite, the normalization procedure described in our proof of Theorem (11) is computable. This is important because if the normal form were not computable, we could not use it without restrictions in place of any other tableau in its equivalence class: we would not have been able to ensure we can actually derive one from the other in a finite amount of time. In fact, complexity analysis shows that normalization is not only computable, but quite efficient:

(13)    Tableau normalization as defined in the proof of Theorem (11) runs in time polynomial in the number of rows $m$ and the number of constraints $n$.

*Proof of Theorem (13).* Consider tableau $T$ with $m$ rows and $n$ constraints. Consistency check may be performed through fusing all subtableaux of $T$ and checking if any resulting fused row has only Ls — or equivalently and faster using RCD, as shown by Prince (2002, Section 4). To perform RCD, we need $m^3 n$ operations (Magri 2009, p. 371). Next, we do row splittings, which for any of the $m$ rows cannot result in creating more than $n$ rows of $n$ constraints each, so this requires at most $mn^2$ operations. The number of rows in the resulting split tableau is not greater than $mn$. Next, we check for entailed rows to eliminate. As we discussed above regarding Operation (6), rather than doing subtableau fusion, exponential in the number of rows $m$, we can do instead $m$ RCD-based checks as described by Prince (2002, Section 5). We have $mn$ rows, and each RCD involves $(mn)^3 n$ operations, so overall we need $m^3 n^4$ operations for this step. Finally, we need to check for false Ws. For that we check every W in $mn$ rows, so at most this would be $mn^2$ checks (actually, much less, as the same row cannot contain both $n$ Ls and $n$ Ws, but we can ignore this.) Each test involves checking whether the rest of the tableau entails a specially constructed row for each particular W. Again, the cost of an entailment check for a single row and a tableau with $mn$ rows is $m^3 n^4$, so overall we have at most $m^4 n^6$ operations. This will be the dominating term in our complexity estimate. The time complexity of normalization is thus polynomial, which is very good.                    □

From Theorems (11) and (12), we know that each equivalence class has at least one normal form tableau. But can a class contain more than one normal form? Theorem (14) shows that it cannot, and thus a normal form tableau *defines* its class: it is its unique representative. To prove that fact, we will need to use relatively complex ranking-construction techniques.

(14)   **Normal Form Uniqueness Theorem**

In each equivalence class of OT tableaux, there is at most one normal form tableau.

*Proof of Theorem* (14). We show that any two distinct normal form tableaux $T$ and $U$ belong to different equivalence classes.

Pick some row $r$ from $T$ which is not shared by $U$ (in case $T \subset U$, we immediately derive the conclusion by considering a row from $U$ that is not in $T$, and the fact that $T$ cannot entail that row). Either our pick $r$ is entailed by $U$, or it is not. In case $r$ is not entailed by $U$, there is some ranking $M$ compatible with $U$, but not with $r$, and thus not with $T$, so $U$ and $T$ are not OT-equivalent.

The interesting case is when $U$ entails the row $r$ we picked. We will show that in that case, there must be some ranking compatible with $T$, but not with $U$. We pick a minimal subtableau $V$ of $U$ that still entails $r$. As $V$ entails $r$, every ranking compatible with $V$ must also put one of $r$'s Ws on top of $r$'s L. That can only be if there is a row $q \in V$ which has an L in the same constraint where $r$ has an L. Let's call that constraint $Ci$.

Suppose towards contradiction that $T$ and $U$ are equivalent, that is, compatible with exactly the same rankings. Consider some $M$ compatible with $T$, and accounting for $V$ "in the minimal possible manner": let $M$ contain the domination chain $Ck_1 \gg Ck_2 \gg \ldots \gg Ci$ where each pairwise ranking $Ck_1 \gg Ck_2, \ldots, Ck_n \gg Ci$ accounts for one of the rows in $V$, but no other pairwise rankings accounting for any of $V$'s rows. As $V$ is in normal form and all its Ws are not false, it must be possible to construct such an $M$. As $V$ entails $r$, constraint $Ck_1$ is a W-constraint in $r$.

$T \setminus r$ cannot entail $V$: if it did, it would have entailed $r$ by transitivity, which is contrary to the normal form assumption. Therefore it must be possible to lower one of $Ck_i$ constraints below $Ci$ building a ranking $M'$ which is still compatible with $T \setminus r$, but not with $V$. As $V$ entails $r$ by assumption, $M'$ must also be incompatible with $r$. But that can only be if the lowered constraint has to be $Ck_1$, a W-constraint in $r$, for otherwise $M'$ would have still said $Ck_1 \gg Ci$.

We modify $M'$ as follows: raise $Ck_1$ just on top of $Ci$, but below $Ck_n$, resulting in $M'' = \ldots Ck_2 \gg Ck_3 \gg \ldots \gg Ck_n \gg Ck_1 \gg Ci$. That ranking $M''$ is incompatible with $V$, because by construction there must have been a row in $V$ for which we needed the pairwise ranking $Ck_1 \gg Ck_2$, and $M''$ says $Ck_2 \gg Ck_1$. But at the same time $M''$ is compatible with $r$, as it puts one of its Ws on top of its L. Now compare $M'$ and $M''$, and consider their compatibility with $T \setminus r$. $M'$ was compatible with $T \setminus r$. $M''$ differs from it in that it says $Ck_1 \gg Ci$ instead of $Ci \gg Ck_1$. That change could not make $M''$ incompatible with $T \setminus r$: the initial ranking $M$ also said $Ck_1 \gg Ci$ and was compatible with $T \setminus r$. Therefore we have built a ranking, namely $M''$, which is compatible with $T \setminus r$ and with $r$, but not with $V$. This ranking witnesses that $T$ and $U$ are not equivalent.                                                              □

Theorems (11) and (14) together entail that there is exactly one normal form tableau per equivalence class. Thus a tableau as described in Definition (9) is a true normal form: a full-fledged representative, or a "name", of its equivalence class.

In practical terms, that means that in our proofs, we can capitalize on the many nice properties of normal forms, knowing that the results will generalize to arbitrary tableaux. In the next section, we illustrate that the use of the normal form results in several simple corollaries.

## 4    CAPITALIZING ON THE NORMAL FORM RESULTS

Theorems in (15), (16) and (18) serve two purposes. First, they have independent value, especially the proof that Brasoveanu and Prince's SKB bases are unique in their equivalence classes. Second, the proofs of these statements illustrate how one can use the normal form results in practice to handle equivalence classes of OT tableaux.

(15)    Operations (3)–(7) form a *functionally complete set*: any tableau can be transformed into any equivalent tableau by a sequence of such operations.

*Proof of (15)*. By Theorems (11) and (14), any pair of equivalent tableaux may be transformed into the same normal form tableau by a sequence of operations in Operations (3)–(7). To conclude the proof, we observe that an inverted sequence transforms the normal form back into the original tableau. By normalizing the first tableau, and then denormalizing it by applying the inverted sequence built for the second tableau, we transform the first tableau into the second.        □

(16)    Equivalence of finite OT tableaux is computable in polynomial time.

*Proof of (16)*. To test tableaux $T$ and $U$ for equivalence, it suffices to normalize both and check whether the resulting normal forms are the same. All operations are computable, for finite tableaux.

The complexity of this test is polynomial: by Theorem (13), the time complexity of normalization is polynomial in the number of rows $m$ and the number of constraints $n$, and we need two such normalizations, plus a comparison of two resulting normal form tableaux which is also polynomial in $m$ and $n$ for the original tableaux. This fairly moderate complexity may be compared with the enormous factorial complexity of the brute-force test for equivalence that involves testing every possible ranking for compatibility with each tableau, cf. Footnote 2.        □

Brasoveanu and Prince (2011) define a dense format of tableaux called the Skeletal Basis (SKB) and an algorithm turning an arbitrary tableau into an equivalent tableau in that format. An SKB of tableau $T$ is a tableau $T'$ such that 1) there is no OT-equivalent tableau with a smaller number of rows; and 2) no other equivalent tableau of the same cardinality has more *es*. Tableau (17) is the Skeletal Basis of the normal form tableau in Tableau (10):

(17)

| $C1$ | $C2$ | $C3$ | $C4$ | $C5$ |
|------|------|------|------|------|
| W | *e* | L | L | L |
| *e* | W | *e* | L | *e* |

Brasoveanu and Prince (2011) claim to have proven, in an unpublished manuscript, the fact that *for a single tableau*, the SKB basis is unique. (Prince (2006, page 6) derives from that the result that MPGs, corresponding to our normal forms, are also unique for a single tableau.) Using our uniqueness theorem for normal forms in Theorem (14), we prove a much stronger result for SKBs in Theorem (18): each *equivalence class of tableaux* has a unique SKB.

(18)    Each equivalence class of OT tableaux has exactly one tableau in the Skeletal Basis (SKB) form of Brasoveanu and Prince (2011).

*Proof of (18).* By showing that SKBs are in one-one correspondence with normal forms.

If we apply all possible row mergers to a normal form tableau, we get an SKB: the original normal form tableau did not have superfluous rows, so the quantity of the rows in the resulting tableau will be minimal; furthermore, as the normal form tableau does not contain any false Ws, the resulting tableau will have the maximal number of *es*.

In the other direction, if we split all rows of an SKB into one-L rows, there can be no superfluous rows in the result (otherwise the L corresponding to a superfluous row could have been replaced with an *e*, contrary to the definition of an SKB which must have as many *es* as possible); as for false Ws, there can be none in the SKB tableau itself, and after all row splittings are applied, no new false Ws can arise (if a false W could arise in one of the resulting one-L rows, then the same W would have been false even before splitting).

What remains is to show that there can be no two SKBs in the same equivalence class. Suppose towards contradiction there are two SKBs $S_1$ and $S_2$. They both normalize to the same normal form tableau by the procedure above. From the definition of SKB, only row splittings are required. Pick an arbitrary set of rows $r_1, \ldots r_n$ with Ws in the same constraints from the resulting normal form tableau. If $S_1$ and $S_2$ each have only one row splitting into this same set, that must be the same row. If $S_1$ and $S_2$ have more than one row splitting into this set, we can actually merge those rows into just one, resulting in a smaller equivalent tableau $S_3$, contrary to the assumption of $S_1$ and $S_2$'s minimality. Thus either $S_1 = S_2$, or they are not minimal possible size in their equivalence class. Therefore there is only one SKB per class.                    □

Theorem (18) essentially means that all useful results about normal forms may be transferred to SKBs. For instance, the equivalence test in Theorem (16) may be replaced by an equivalence test comparing SKBs derived using Brasoveanu and Prince's Fusional Reduction algorithm. With 18 in hand, we may employ Brasoveanu and Prince's SKBs as representatives of their equivalence classes instead of our normal forms. Normal forms are often more convenient in complex proofs, because the relations between constraints in them are maximally untangled; but SKBs are more useful when it becomes convenient to have smaller-sized representatives.

## 5                CONCLUSION

We defined a normal form for OT tableaux, and showed that there is exactly one normal form in each equivalence class of OT tableaux. Moreover, we have demonstrated that each OT tableau can be computably normalized by a sequence of five pairs of previously known equivalence-preserving transformations in Operations (3)–(7). The computational cost of normalization is only polynomial in the number of rows $m$ and constraints $n$, thanks to the use of the efficient RCD-based algorithm for entailment checking proposed by Prince (2002, Section 5).

Those results provide us with a handle on equivalence classes of OT tableaux: using them, we may reason about tableaux without any loss of generality while only considering normal forms. The examples in Section 4, including Theorem (18) stating that Brasoveanu and Prince's Skeletal Bases are unique in their equivalence classes, illustrate how to capitalize on the presented OT normal form theorems.

## REFERENCES

Adrian BRASOVEANU and Alan PRINCE (2005), Ranking and Necessity, Part I, Rutgers Optimality Archive 794.

Adrian BRASOVEANU and Alan PRINCE (2011), Ranking and Necessity: the Fusional Reduction Algorithm, *Natural Language and Linguistic Theory*, 29(1):3–70, *revised version of Brasoveanu and Prince (2005)*.
Bruce HAYES (1997), Four Rules of Inference for Ranking Argumentation, ms., UCLA. http:
//www.linguistics.ucla.edu/people/hayes/otsoft/argument.pdf.

Renè KAGER (1999), *Optimality Theory*, Cambridge University Press, Cambridge.

Giorgio MAGRI (2009), *A Theory of Individual-Level Predicates Based on Blind Mandatory Implicatures. Constraint Promotion for Optimality Theory*, Ph.D. thesis, MIT. http://dspace.mit.edu/handle/1721.1/55182.

Alan PRINCE (2000), Comparative tableaux, Rutgers Optimality Archive 376.

Alan PRINCE (2002), Entailed Ranking Arguments, Rutgers Optimality Archive 500. http://roa.rutgers.edu/article/view/510.

Alan PRINCE (2006), No more than Necessary: beyond the Four Rules, and a bug report, Rutgers Optimality Archive 882. http://roa.rutgers.edu/article/view/905.

Alan PRINCE and Paul SMOLENSKY (1993), Optimality Theory: Constraint Interaction in Generative Grammar, Rutgers Optimality Archive 537. http://roa.rutgers.edu/article/view/547.

Alan PRINCE and Paul SMOLENSKY (2004), *Optimality Theory: Constraint Interaction in Generative Grammar*, Blackwell, Oxford.

Igor YANOVICH (2011), On sets of OT rankings, Rutgers Optimality Archive 1149. http://roa.rutgers.edu/article/view/1203.

# 2

# Erotetic Reasoning Corpus: A data set for research on natural question processing

*Paweł Łupkowski[1,2]\*, Mariusz Urbański[1,2], Andrzej Wiśniewski[1],*
*Wojciech Błądek[2], Agata Juska[2], Anna Kostrzewa[2], Dominika*
*Pankow[2], Katarzyna Paluszkiewicz[1,2], Oliwia Ignaszak[2], Joanna*
*Urbańska[1], Natalia Żyluk[1,2], Andrzej Gajda[1,2], and Bartosz Marciniak*

[1] Institute of Psychology, Adam Mickiewicz University, Poznań
[2] Reasoning Research Group, Adam Mickiewicz University, Poznań

*Keywords: questions, logic of questions, question processing, erotetic reasoning, corpus annotation*

## ABSTRACT

The aim of this paper is to present the Erotetic Reasoning Corpus (ERC) which constitutes a data set for research on natural question processing. We describe the theoretical background, linguistic data and tags used for the annotation process. We also discuss the potential areas in which the ERC can be exploited.

## 1    INTRODUCTION

The aim of this paper is to present a data set for research on natural question processing named the Erotetic Reasoning Corpus (hereafter ERC).[1] In discourse, interlocutors must deal with question processing in instances when questions are not followed by answers but by new questions or strategies of reducing said questions into auxiliary ques-

---

[\*]P. Łupkowski, M. Urbański and A. Wiśniewski designed the ERC and data-collection process, super-annotated the corpus and wrote the paper. W. Błądek, A. Juska, A. Kostrzewa and D. Pankow annotated the ERC. K. Paluszkiewicz, O. Ignaszak, N. Żyluk and J. Urbańska contributed to the linguistic data collection. A. Gajda and B. Marciniak implemented parts of the ERC interface.

[1]The term 'erotetic' stems from Greek 'erotema' meaning 'question'. The logic of question is sometimes called erotetic logic. For an overview of logically oriented approaches to questions and questioning see, e.g., Harrah (2002), or Wiśniewski (2015).

tions[2]. Usually, such a situation takes place when an agent wants to solve a certain problem (expressed in the form of an initial question) but is not able to reach the solution using his/her own information resources. Thus, new data, collected via questioning are necessary. This phenomenon is studied within such theoretical frameworks as Inferential Erotetic Logic (see Wiśniewski 1995, 2013, Łupkowski 2016), inquisitive semantics (see Groenendijk and Roelofsen 2011), or KoS (see Ginzburg 2012, Łupkowski and Ginzburg 2013, 2016). Natural question processing also constitutes an interesting subject for empirical research. In order to facilitate research concerning question processing in natural language dialogues, we have decided to construct the ERC. The corpus consists of the linguistic data collected in our previous studies on the question processing phenomenon. The data are annotated with a tagset, making them easy to browse for reasoning structure, pragmatic features used, and the presence of normative erotetic concepts (see Section 2).

The paper is structured as follows. We start by presenting the basic concepts of natural question processing as modelled in Inferential Erotetic Logic. We use these concepts as a normative yardstick for our design choices for the ERC tag set. Afterwards, we describe the architecture of the ERC and the linguistic data used for the corpus. Then, we introduce the tagging schema designed and used for the ERC, describe the tagging process, and discuss selected issues concerning annotation reliability. We conclude with a summary of the current stage of the project and discussion of potential future developments and applications of the ERC.

## 2    MODELLING QUESTION PROCESSING IN INFERENTIAL EROTETIC LOGIC

In this section, we present the underlying erotetic logic concepts used for the ERC. Our logical framework of choice is that of the Inferential Erotetic Logic (IEL; see Wiśniewski 1995, 2013). This logic focuses on inferences whose premises and/or conclusions are questions (erotetic inferences). This choice was motivated by several factors. Here, we

---

[2]For more details see https://intquestpro.wordpress.com/.

only mention some of them – for a detailed discussion see Urbański *et al.* (2016a). Firstly, IEL is flexible: it is not tied up to any specific logic of declaratives. Secondly, the formal representation of questions employed in IEL is friendly to the user. In general, these representations fall under the schema $?\Theta$, where $\Theta$ is an object-language expression that is equiform to a metalanguage expression which denotes the set of direct answers to a question. For example, $?\{A_1,...,A_n\}$ represents a question whose set of direct answers is the finite set of declarative formulas: $\{A_1,...,A_n\}$.[3] Yet, questions are object-language expressions of a strictly defined form and have meanings on their own; the approach is still a non-reductionistic one (see Belnap 1986; Wiśniewski 1995, pp. 37–42). On the other hand, this approach inherits the advantages of the so-called *set-of-answers methodology* (Harrah 2002; see Peliš 2016, for a comprehensive introduction, and Wiśniewski 2013, pp. 16–17 for a discussion of the semi-reductionistic approach sketched above), whose idea stems from Hamblin's (1958, p. 162) postulate: "Knowing what counts as an answer is equivalent to knowing the question." Thirdly, IEL offers some straightforward tools for modelling erotetic inferences. What is especially important from our perspective is that IEL proposes some criteria for the validity of erotetic inferences. In the case of erotetic inferences which lead from an initial question and a (possibly empty) set of declarative premises to a question, the following criteria of validity are proposed:

1. *transmission of truth/soundness into soundness*: if the initial question is sound (i.e., there exists a true direct answer to this question) and all the declarative premises, if there are any, are true, then the question which is the conclusion must be sound;

2. *cognitive usefulness*: each direct answer to a question which is the conclusion is useful in answering the initial question by narrowing down the "space of possibilities" offered by the initial question (more precisely: for each direct answer $B$ to the question which is the conclusion there exists a non-empty proper subset $Y$ of the set of direct answers to the initial question such that $Y$ must contain a true direct answer to the initial question if $B$ is true and the declarative premises, if there are any, are true).

---

[3]Thus $A_1,...,A_n$ are pairwise syntactically distinct formulas.

Valid erotetic inferences (of the above kind) can be defined as those in which *erotetic implication* (e-implication for short) holds between the initial question, the declarative premises, and the question which is the conclusion. As a matter of fact, the formal definition of e-implication offers precise explications for conditions of transmission of truth/soundness into soundness and of cognitive usefulness (Definition 1; see Wiśniewski 2013, p. 68). For the sake of simplicity, we consider here only questions with finite sets of direct answers, and assume that the underlying logic of declaratives is Classical Logic. Given this, erotetic implication can be defined as follows.

**Definition 1** (Erotetic implication). *A question $Q$ e-implies a question $Q_1$ on the basis of a set $X$ of declaratives ($Im(Q,X,Q_1)$) iff:*

1. *for each direct answer $A$ to the question $Q$: $X \cup \{A\}$ entails a disjunction of all the direct answers to the question $Q_1$, and*

2. *for each direct answer $B$ to the question $Q_1$ there exists a non-empty proper subset $Y$ of the set of direct answers to the question $Q$ such that $X \cup \{B\}$ entails a disjunction of all the elements of $Y$.*

It is easily seen that clauses (1) and (2) of Definition 1 mirror the criteria of validity discussed above.

Applying erotetic implication for modelling certain real-life linguistic phenomena resulted in identifying two other versions of this kind of relation, weaker than the one just defined (which we shall further on call the canonical erotetic implication). These are the weak erotetic implication (Urbański *et al.* 2016a) and the falsificationist erotetic implication (Grobler 2012; Wiśniewski 2013), both of which modify the second condition of the original definition.

**Definition 2** (Weak erotetic implication). *A question $Q$ weakly e-implies a question $Q_1$ on the basis of a set $X$ of declaratives ($Im_w(Q,X,Q_1)$) iff:*

1. *for each direct answer $A$ to the question $Q$: $X \cup \{A\}$ entails a disjunction of all the direct answers to the implied question $Q_1$, and*

2. *for some direct answer $B$ to the question $Q_1$ there exists a non-empty proper subset $Y$ of the set of direct answers to the question $Q$ such that $X \cup \{B\}$ entails a disjunction of all the elements of $Y$.*

**Definition 3** (Falsificationist erotetic implication). *A question Q f-implies a question $Q_1$ on the basis of a set X of declaratives ($Im_f(Q,X,Q_1)$) iff:*

1. *for each direct answer A to the question Q: $X \cup \{A\}$ entails a disjunction of all the direct answers to the question $Q_1$, and*

2. *for some direct answer B to the question $Q_1$, $X \cup \{B\}$ eliminates at least one direct answer to Q.*

The concept of elimination used in Definition 3 is construed as follows: a formula *A eliminates* a formula *B* just in case *B* must be false if *A* is true, given the underlying semantics (for a precise definition see Wiśniewski 2013, p. 34).

The properties described in the second clauses of definitions 1, 2, and 3 will be referred to below as 'usefulness', 'w-usefulness', and 'f-usefulness', respectively.

Table 1 presents examples of erotetic implication of the three presented types.

Table 1: Examples of canonical ($Im$), weak ($Im_w$) and falsificationist ($Im_f$) erotetic implication

| $Q, X, Q_1$ | e-implication |
|---|---|
| $?\{p, q \lor r\}, \emptyset, ?\{p, q, r\}$ | $Im$ |
| $?p, p \leftrightarrow q, ?q$ | $Im$ |
| $?\{\neg p, r, s\}, \emptyset, ?\{p, q, \neg q\}$ | $Im_f$ |
| $?\{p, q, v\}, s \rightarrow p, ?\{s, \neg s\}$ | $Im_w$ |
| $?\{\neg p, r, s\}, \neg p \lor r \lor s, ?\{p, q, \neg q\}$ | $Im_w, Im_f$ |
| $?\{p, q, w\}, p \lor q \rightarrow r, p \lor q \lor w, ?\{r, \neg r\}$ | $Im_w, Im_f$ |
| $?\{p, q, v\}, p \lor q, r \leftrightarrow q, ?\{r, \neg r\}$ | $Im, Im_w, Im_f$ |

Notions introduced in this section will be reflected by the tagset used to annotate the ERC, described in detail in Section 4 of the present paper.

Using e-implication as a tool allows for modelling many aspects of natural question processing, i.e. a situation in which an initial question is internally processed by an agent, and where the outcome is either a new question concerning the subject matter or a strategy of reducing the initial question into auxiliary questions. In both cases, e-implication allows for the description and assessment of the inferences which lead from questions to questions.

The basic areas of applicability of the analysis of the described phenomena include: the search for information in distributed resources, question answering (in particular, cooperative answering), problem solving (in particular, problem solving by interrogation), proof theory and automated deduction (proof search, complexity issues).

## 3              LINGUISTIC DATA

The linguistic data used for the ERC were gathered for research on question processing. The outcomes of three research projects are employed here. These are: the Erotetic Reasoning Test, QuestGen and Mind Maze.

*The Erotetic Reasoning Test* (in Polish: Test Rozumowań Erotetycznych, TRE) is a tool used in the research described in detail in (Urbański *et al.* 2016a). The test contains 3 items (with an imposed time limit of 30 min). Each item consists of a detective-like story in which the initial problem and evidence gained are indicated. The task is to pick a question (one out of four), each answer to which will lead to some solution to the initial problem. The subjects are asked to justify their choices.

Let us present here an exemplary tasks from TRE (translated into English). The task is entitled "The Bomb":

> In the capital of a certain country someone planted a bomb in the palace of the king. The best royal engineer, who arrived immediately, established the following facts:
> 1. There are three wires in the bomb: green, red and orange;
> 2. To disarm the bomb either the green or the red wire must be cut. Cutting the wrong wire will cause an explosion;
> 3. If the bomb has been planted by Steve, cutting the green wire will disarm it;
> 4. If the bomb has been planted by John, cutting the red wire will disarm it. Moreover, no one but John would have used the red wire;
> 5. If the bomb has not been planted on an even day of the month, the culprit is Steve;
> 6. The bomb has been planted either by Steve, or by John, or by someone else.

Each of the following questions below can be answered either 'yes' or 'no'. Mark the question to which the answer (regardless of it being 'yes' or 'no') will allow you to establish, in the shortest time possible, which wire should be cut in order to disarm the bomb:

> Was the bomb planted on an even day of the month?
>
> Was the bomb planted by Steve?
>
> Was the bomb planted by John?
>
> Was the bomb planted by someone else than Steve or John?

Justify your choice.

TRE-entries of the ERC have a well-established structure: there is a story, a question chosen by the subject and then a justification of the choice. An exemplary justification (translated into English) provided by a subject for the "Bomb" story is presented below (see Urbański *et al.* 2016a, p. 41).

> If we'll get an affirmative answer to this question, then we'll know that the green wire needs to be cut. If a negative one, then there will be only one possibility left – the red wire, and additionally we'll know that the culprit is John.

*QuestGen* is an online game the aim of which is to engage players in generating a large collection of questions for a certain piece of story written in a natural language (as such it might be perceived as an example of a game with a purpose – see Von Ahn and Dabbish 2008). The idea of the game was presented in (Łupkowski 2011), while its implementation is described in (Łupkowski and Wietrzycka 2015) and (Łupkowski and Ignaszak 2017). In the game, two randomly chosen players are engaged in solving a detective puzzle. One of them plays as the Detective, the other as the Informer. The Detective's objective is to solve the presented puzzle by questioning the Informer. Each story in the game has two versions (one for the Detective and one for the Informer), containing all the additional data necessary to solve the puzzle. The Detective is allowed to use only yes/no questions and cannot ask straightforwardly for the solution. The Detective may ask as many questions as s/he wants/needs (as long as they are simple yes-no questions). The Informer is obliged to answer the Detective's questions in accordance with the information presented in the Informer's part of the story. Each story is played within a time limit. The game is played in cooperative mode, i.e. the Detective and the Informer play together constrained by the time limit and obtain points for each puzzle solved.

As an example of the task from the QuestGen game, we present the Detective's part of a story entitled "Arsen L.":

> Imagine that you are a detective who is following the well-known international villain Arsen L. You are trying to establish if Arsen L. went to Paris, London, Kiev, or Moscow. You look through your notes and this is the information you have managed to gather so far:
> 1. Arsen L. left for Paris or London if and only if he departed in the morning;
> 2. Arsen L. left for Kiev or Moscow if and only if he departed in the evening;
> 3. If Arsen L. took a train, then he did not leave for London or Moscow;
> 4. If Arsen L. left for Paris or Kiev, then he took a train.
>
> So, where did Arsen L. go?
> Before you answer this question you may ask several auxiliary questions of the railway station employee. Remember: your time is limited. Ask only yes/no questions. It is pointless to ask the employee directly about where Arsen L. went because he does not have a clue.

Solutions gathered within the QuestGen project have a well-established structure, very much like the ones from TRE. A QG-entry of the ERC consists of the story which is followed by the main question (expressing the problem to be solved by the player). Afterwards, we observe the sequence of the Detective's questions and the Informer's answers which is ended by the proposed solution to the main question and the feedback given by the Informer. This gives us more interaction than in the TRE case. We observe short dialogues between players. An example (translated into English) of such a dialogue for the "Bomb" story is presented below (see Łupkowski and Ignaszak 2017, p. 239):

DETECTIVE:  Is it the case that Anthony has something to do with de bomb?

INFORMER:  No.

DETECTIVE:  So it is the case that Roger is guilty?!

INFORMER:  Yes.

DETECTIVE:  Orange, isn't it?

INFORMER:  Yes.

DETECTIVE:  Orange.

*Mind Maze* (in Polish "Takie życie") is a card game published by Igrology. In the game, one of the players plays the role of the game master (GM) and the other one tries to solve a puzzle presented by the game master. the GM tells a short story (inspired by true events) and the objective of the player is to figure out how the story happened by asking questions to the GM. Only yes/no questions are allowed here (with two additional admissible answers: "It is not important/relevant" and "It is not known"). *Mind Maze* was used as the core element for the semi-structured study of question processing (see Urbański and Żyluk 2016 and Urbański *et al.* 2016a). The researcher played the role of the GM and subjects were players. Game sessions were recorded and then transcribed.

To give an example (translated into English) of the types of problems to solve in the Mind Maze game, let us consider the one entitled "The Traveller":

> A man without a single visa visited eight different countries in a single day. None of the authorities of these countries tried to remove him. What was his profession and how did he manage to do this?

Solutions gathered in the described study are the most complex ones in the ERC data set. They have no clear structure as they are more or less free dialogue leading to the solution of the initial problem. The shortest conversation included in the ERC has 760 words, while

Table 2: Characteristics of the linguistic data set of ERC

| Source | Files | Words |
|--------|-------|---------|
| TRE | 270 | 81.169 |
| QG | 116 | 21.944 |
| TZ | 16 | 30.619 |
| Sum | 402 | 133.732 |

the longest one is 3.367.[4] An example *Mind Maze* interaction between the player and the game master (translated into English) is presented below:

PLAYER: Is this building a cultural one?

GM: Cultural one... in what sense it is a cultural building?

PLAYER: Related to culture, history, art? Related to culture?

GM: But, how would you define this „related"?

PLAYER: Related... it is used for cultural purposes, developement related issues, for people. To some extent educational ones?

To differentiate the aforementioned sources, we will refer to them as the ERC sub-corpora, the TRE, QG, and TZ, respectively. The whole ERC consists of 402 files (solutions). Table 2 presents a summary of the gathered data. Note that all of the data are in Polish; however, the tagset used for the annotation allows for the data to be analyzed by English-speaking researchers.

## 4                     TAGGING

The tagging schema for the ERC consists of three layers:

1. The structural layer – representing the structure of the tasks used for the studies described in Section 3. Here, we distinguish between elements such as: instructions, justifications, different types of questions, and declaratives.

2. The inferential layer – which allows for normative elements described in Section 2 to be identified.

3. The pragmatic layer – representing various events that may occur in the dialogue, like e.g. long pauses. It also contains tags that

---

[4]For comparison, the longest files for the TRE and the QG have 387 and 230 words respectively.

enable the expression of certain events related to the types of tasks used (like e.g. when a forbidden question – that is, question of the form which is not allowed in a certain entry – is used).

Let us now present, and explain in detail, the tags used in the ERC. Each task in the ERC is tagged with the KORPUS tag which has two obligatory attributes:

- first one specifying the sub-corpus of ERC (namely whether the task comes from Erotetic Reasoning Test: TRE, QuestGen: QG or Mind Maze: TZ),
- second one specifying the name of the task and the number of the subject/player who solved it.

4.1                     *Structural layer*

The structural layer of annotation consists of the following tags: INSTRUCTION; JUSTIFICATION; DECLARATIVE; QUESTION.

- The INSTRUCTION: the tag indicates instruction for a given task.
- The JUSTIFICATION: a justification given by a subject is indicated with this tag.
- The DECLARATIVE: tag marking declaratives.
- The QUESTION: tag for indicating questions.

The DECLARATIVE and QUESTION tags enable certain attributes to specify further details. These attributes are presented in Figure 1 and 2. Pointing out one of the attributes marked with a solid line is obligatory. The ones marked with a dashed line are non-obligatory.

The QUESTION tag is associated with the following attributes:

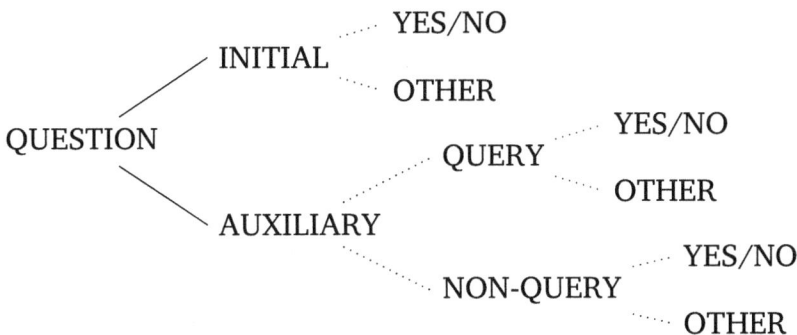

Figure 1: The QUESTION tag and its attributes

IQ-ANSW
- YES
- NO
- DON'T KNOW

AQ-ANSW
- YES
- NO
- DON'T KNOW
- IRRELEVANT

PREMISE
- NEGATION
- IMPLICATION
  - SIMPLE
  - REVERSED
- EQUIVALENCE
- CONJUNCTION
- DISJUNCTION
- EXCLUSIVE-DISJUNCTION

PREMISE-EX
- NEGATION
- IMPLICATION
  - SIMPLE
  - REVERSED
- EQUIVALENCE
- CONJUNCTION
- DISJUNCTION
- EXCLUSIVE-DISJUNCTION

DECLARATIVE

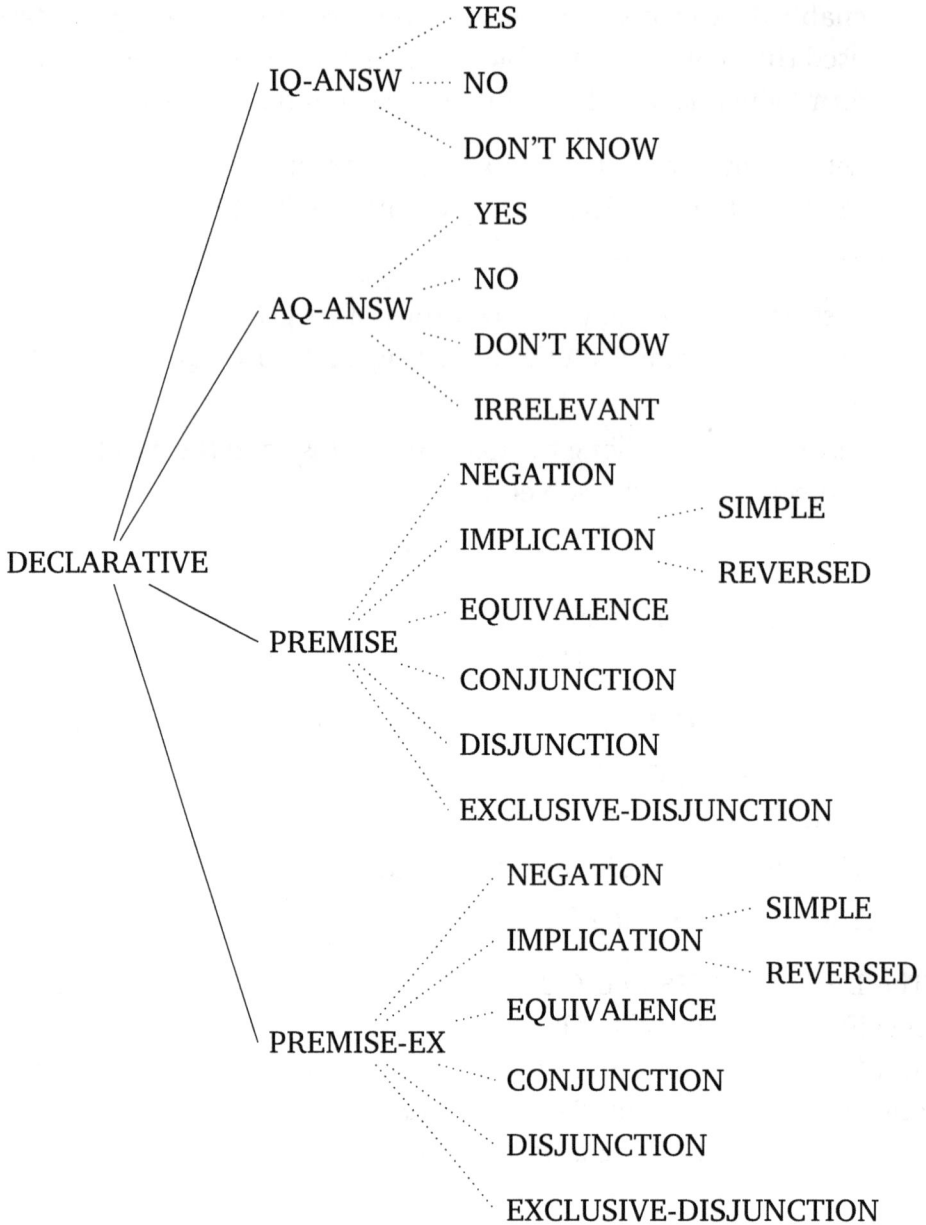

Figure 2: The DECLARATIVE tag and its attributes

1. INITIAL: points out the initial question. Additional attributes allow for specifying whether the initial question is of the yes/no or other type.

2. AUXILIARY: marks questions recognized as auxiliary ones. Attributes associated with the tag indicate whether the auxiliary question is a query and point to its type (yes/no or other type of question).

The DECLARATIVE tag is associated with the following attributes:

- IQ-ANSW: indicates an answer to the initial question. The type of answer given might be specified by: YES, NO, DON'T KNOW.

- AQ-ANSW: indicates an answer to the auxiliary question. Similarly to the IQ-ANSW case, the type of answer given might be further specified by: YES, NO, DON'T KNOW, IRRELEVANT.

- PREMISE: used for premises (declarative ones). Additional attributes may be used to specify a logical structure of the recognized premise. For the premises with the implication as the main connective a more detailed characteristics may be provided with the tags: SIMPLE or REVERSED.

- PREMISE-EX: used for a declarative premise which allows for exceptions. To exemplify such a premise, consider the following (from "The Party" task of TRE): "The King of Hearts stays till the end of only those parties at which the March Hare doesn't tell jokes (although even then the King sometimes leaves earlier)."

Additional attributes for these tags are the same as those for the PREMISE tag.

4.2                              *Inferential layer*

The inferential layer consists of nine tags: SOLUTION; TRANSMISSION; USEFULNESS; W-USEFULNESS; F-USEFULNESS; E-OTHER; ENTAILMENT; D-OTHER; IMP-ERROR. This layer plays an important role in the ERC making our data set unique. The tags used here stem from the IEL's ideas and concepts presented in Section 2. This layer makes it possible to track and study how these concepts are applied and used in the context of reasonings enforced by the tasks used for our sub-corpora.

SOLUTION: this tag indicates the solution given by a subject. Additional attributes allow for specifying whether the solution is correct (note that each task in the ERC has a predefined normative solution) and how this solution has been reached (i.e. whether it is in line with the assumed normative way of obtaining the solution – e.g. erotetic search scenario in the case of QG tasks). Attributes of the SOLUTION tag are presented in Figure 3.

```
                                    ⋯⋯ NORMATIVE
                    ⟋ CORRECT
    SOLUTION                      ⋯⋯ OTHER
                    ⟍ INCORRECT
```

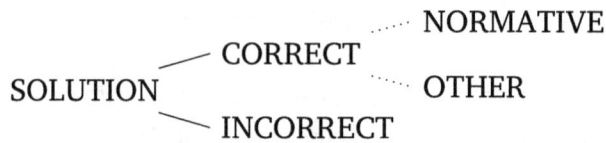

Figure 3: The SOLUTION tag and its attributes

TRANSMISSION: this tag is used for such justifications that cover the first condition of the definition of erotetic implication, i.e. transmission of truth/soundness (including the canonical one as well as the weak one and the falsificationist one – see Definitions 2 and 3 in Section 2).

USEFULNESS: this tag is used for such justifications that cover the second condition of the definition of (canonical) erotetic implication, i.e. cognitive usefulness.

W-USEFULNESS: this tag is used for such justifications that cover the second condition of the definition of the weak erotetic implication.

F-USEFULNESS: this tag is used for such justifications that cover the second condition of the definition of the falsificationist erotetic implication

E-OTHER: marks such justifications that are not modelled by Inferential Erotetic Logic.

ENTAILMENT: this tag is used for such justifications that correctly refer to logical entailment.

D-OTHER: this tag is used for such justifications that incorrectly refer to logical entailment or to a different type of relation between declaratives.

IMP-ERROR: denotes justifications in which a subject interpreted the material implication in the incorrect way (according to Classical Logic).

4.3                              *Pragmatic layer*

The pragmatic level consists of the five tags. It should be noted that certain pragmatic layer tags are used only within selected sub-corpora as described below.

Q-FORBIDDEN: allows one to point out when a forbidden question appears in the solution of tasks in the QG and TZ subcorpora. This refers to the rules provided for a given task. For example, this tag is used in the case of a QuestGen task when the Detective will ask directly about the solution. In the Mind Maze tasks, this tag appears when a player uses a question other than that of a yes/no type.

WRONGINFO: this tag is used in the QG sub-corpus. It denotes a situation wherein the Informer provides a wrong piece of information to the Detective in the game. "Wrong", in this case, means different than the one given in the Informer's part of the story. This tag will also be used in situations in which the Detective asks a question marked as Q-FORBIDDEN and the Informer answers with something different than the desired "I don't know" answer.

KEY-INFO: is used for the TZ sub-corpus. It indicates additional information provided by the game master (the information provided is not an answer to a question in the game).

TOPIC: is also a tag used in the TZ sub-corpus for marking topics (as defined by van Kuppevelt (1995)) as they appear in a dialogue.

LONG-PAUSE: the tag is used in the QG and TZ sub-corpora for indicating long pauses in the game.


An example annotated ERC file is presented in Figure 4. The figure presents the file from the TRE sub-corpus of the ERC, the task name is "Bomb" and the file number is 31 – this is visible in the first line containing the tag <KORPUS A1 = "TRE" A2 = "Bomba31">. The structure of the file is clearly visible owing to the structural layer of the tags used. We can identify the instruction part as well as the premises and the initial question, solution, and justification provided by the subject in this case. Tags used to annotate premises provide information about their structure (visible as the A2 attribute), e.g. in the last premise, an exclusive disjunction is used. The initial question is identified by a <QUESTION> tag with the A1 attribute stating "INITIAL". The A2 attribute informs us that this is not a simple yes/no question. Let us now take a closer look at the solution, which is indicated by the following tag: <SOLUTION A1 = "CORRECT" A2 = "NORMATIVE">. Attributes of this tag inform us that the solution provided by the subject is the correct one, what is more, it is also normative. This leads us to the justification part of this file. There we find two tags: <TRANSMISSION /> and <USEFULNESS />, which provide information about the normativity of the provided correct solution – this

```
<KORPUS A1="TRE" A2="Bomba31">

<INSTRUCTION>
 Wprowadzenie: W stolicy pewnego kraju ktoś podłożył bombę w pałacu króla. Najlepszy saper
    królewski, który przybył na miejsce, ustalił sobie jedynie znanymi sposobami kilka faktów:

(a) <DECLARATIVE A1="PREMISE" A2="CONJUNCTION" A4="1">W bombie znajdują się trzy kabelki:
    zielony, czerwony i pomarańczowy.</DECLARATIVE>
(b) <DECLARATIVE A1="PREMISE" A2="EXCLUSIVE-DISJUNCTION" A4="2">Żeby unieszkodliwić bombę trzeba
    przeciąć albo zielony, albo czerwony kabelek. Przecięcie niewłaściwego kabelka spowoduje
    wybuch.</DECLARATIVE>
(c) <DECLARATIVE A1="PREMISE" A2="IMPLICATION" A3="SIMPLE" A4="3">Jeżeli bombę podłożył Stefan,
    to unieszkodliwia ją przecięcie zielonego kabelka.</DECLARATIVE>
(d) <DECLARATIVE A1="PREMISE" A2="EQUIVALENCE" A4="4">Jeżeli bombę podłożył Ignacy, to
    unieszkodliwia ją przecięcie czerwonego kabelka. Co więcej, nikt inny do tego celu nie
    wykorzystałby czerwonego kabelka.</DECLARATIVE>
(e) <DECLARATIVE A1="PREMISE" A2="IMPLICATION" A3="SIMPLE" A4="5">Jeśli bomby nie podłożono w
    dzień parzysty, to zrobił to Stefan.</DECLARATIVE>
(f) <DECLARATIVE A1="PREMISE" A2="EXCLUSIVE-DISJUNCTION" A4="6">Bombę podłożył albo Stefan, albo
    Ignacy, albo jeszcze ktoś inny.</DECLARATIVE>

Instrukcja: Na każde z poniższych pytań można uzyskać jedną z dwóch odpowiedzi:
'tak' albo 'nie'. Zaznacz symbolem 'x' tylko jedno pytanie, na które dowolna
odpowiedź (niezależnie od tego, czy będzie to 'tak' czy 'nie') pozwoli jak najszybciej
ustalić, <QUESTION A1="INITIAL" A2="OTHER">który kabelek należy przeciąć, żeby unieszkodliwić
    bombę.</QUESTION>

[ ] <QUESTION A1="AUXILIARY" A2="QUERY" A3="YES/NO" A4="1">Czy bombę podłożono w dzień parzysty
    </QUESTION>
[ ] <QUESTION A1="AUXILIARY" A2="QUERY" A3="YES/NO" A4="2">Czy bombę podłożył Stefan?</QUESTION>
[x] <SOLUTION A1="CORRECT" A2="NORMATIVE"><QUESTION A1="AUXILIARY" A2="QUERY" A3="YES/NO"
    A4="3">Czy bombę podłożył Ignacy?</QUESTION></SOLUTION>
[ ] <QUESTION A1="AUXILIARY" A2="QUERY" A3="YES/NO" A4="4">Czy bombę podłożył ktoś inny niż
    Stefan lub Ignacy?</QUESTION>

Uzasadnij, dlaczego wybrałaś/wybrałeś to właśnie pytanie.
</INSTRUCTION>

<JUSTIFICATION>
<TRANSMISSION />
<USEFULNESS />
Bomba Stefana może mieć zielony Bomba Ignacego – kabel czerwony i zielony Bomba kogoś innego –
    kabel zielony Jeśli dowiemy się, że to Ignacy to trzeba będzie przeciąć czerwony, gdy okaże
    się, że to nie on, to w każdym innym przypadku będzie to kabel zielony niezależnie czy to
    Stefan cze ktoś inny podłożył bombę.
</JUSTIFICATION>
</KORPUS>
```

Figure 4: An exemplary annotated ERC file

warrants the conclusion that the solution provided can be modelled in terms of canonical erotetic implication (see Definition 1).

4.4          *Descriptive statistics of the annotation*

Let us now take a closer look at the descriptive statistics of the ERC annotation.

   We will start with the *structural layer* of the annotation. The number of INSTRUCTION tags is the same as the number of ERC files, as each task comes with its own instruction. We have 402 INSTRUCTION

tags (270 for TRE, 116 for QG and 16 for TZ). As for the JUSTIFICA-
TION tag, it is present only in the TRE sub-corpus and the number
of these tags is equivalent to the number of TRE files in the ERC, i.e.
270. The reason for this is that each TRE solution consists of an auxiliary question indicated a subject and a justification provided for this
choice (as described in Section 3). The ERC has 2.234 QUESTION tags,
1.350 in TRE sub-corpus, 375 in the QG and 527 in the TZ. Details are
presented in Table 3. As for DECLARATIVE tags, there are 2.855 (TRE:
1.530, QG: 777, TZ: 548) – details are presented in Table 4.

Table 3: Descriptive statistics for the QUESTION tag

|  | TRE | QG | TZ | Sum |
|---|---|---|---|---|
| QUESTION | 1.335 | 357 | 527 | 2.234 |
| INITIAL | 270 | 116 | 16 | 402 |
| INITIAL YES/NO | 0 | 19 | 0 | 19 |
| INITIAL OTHER | 270 | 97 | 16 | 383 |
| AUXILIARY | 1.080 | 241 | 511 | 1.832 |
| QUERY | 1.080 | 238 | 452 | 1.770 |
| QUERY YES/NO | 1.080 | 238 | 442 | 1.760 |
| QUERY OTHER | 0 | 0 | 10 | 10 |
| NON-QUERY | 0 | 3 | 59 | 62 |
| NON-QUERY YES/NO | 0 | 3 | 13 | 16 |
| NON-QUERY OTHER | 0 | 0 | 46 | 46 |

For the *inferential layer* we will first discuss the SOLUTION tag.
The detailed numbers for this tag are presented in Table 5. The total
number of occurances of the SOLUTION tag for the TZ sub-corpus is
larger than the number of files. This is because the solution is divided
into two parts for each file, corresponding to the dialogue structure. It
should be noted that the vast majority of solutions for the ERC tasks
were correct ones. (For the TZ sub-corpus NORMATIVE and OTHER
attributes were not used).

For the TRE sub-corpus, additional inferential tags were also used.
This is due to the structure of the solutions provided by the subjects,
i.e. answers to initial questions and their corresponding justifications.
There are 205 TRANSMISSION and 160 USEFULNESS tags used. For
149 cases the TRANSMISSION and USEFULNESS tags are both present,
which constitutes the number of correct and normative solutions for
the sub-corpus.

Table 4: Descriptive statistics for the DECLARATIVE tag

|  | TRE | QG | TZ | Sum |
|---|---|---|---|---|
| DECLARATIVE | 1.530 | 777 | 548 | 2.855 |
| IQ-ANSWER | 0 | 109 | 11 | 120 |
| YES | 0 | 5 | 0 | 5 |
| NO | 0 | 10 | 0 | 10 |
| DON'T KNOW | 0 | 1 | 0 | 1 |
| AQ-ANSWER | 0 | 241 | 500 | 741 |
| YES | 0 | 109 | 191 | 300 |
| NO | 0 | 120 | 216 | 336 |
| DON'T KNOW | 0 | 12 | 21 | 33 |
| IRRELEVANT | 0 | 0 | 25 | 25 |
| PREMISE | 1.350 | 427 | 36 | 1.813 |
| IMPLICATION | 720 | 271 | 0 | 991 |
| EQUIVALENCE | 180 | 96 | 0 | 276 |
| CONJUNCTION | 90 | 0 | 0 | 90 |
| EXCLUSIVE-DISJ | 270 | 20 | 0 | 290 |

Table 5: Descriptive statistics for the SOLUTION tag

|  | TRE | QG | TZ | Sum |
|---|---|---|---|---|
| SOLUTION | 268 | 109 | 17 | 394 |
| CORRECT | 190 | 91 | 17 | 298 |
| CORRECT NORMATIVE | 149 | 44 | – | 192 |
| CORRECT OTHER | 41 | 47 | – | 88 |
| INCORRECT | 78 | 18 | 0 | 94 |

Let us now discuss the *pragmatic layer* of annotation. As can be expected, there are no pragmatic tags in the ERC sub-corpus, due to the nature of the task involved. The numbers for this layer will get bigger for sub-corpora with more interaction involved. And we have 8 Q-FORBIDDEN and 29 WRONGINFO tags for the QG sub-corpus. As it was described above, the WRONGINFO tag is specific to the QG sub-corpus. The reason why this is the case for these tasks is that a randomly chosen player has to play the role of the informer in the game. S/he has to process additional information related to the puzzle and provide answers to the Detective within the specified time limit. As a result, we sometimes observe that the Informer provides wrong information. It is important to mark these utterances in the ERC, as this makes solving the puzzle harder or sometimes impossible for the Detective. In the TZ sub-corpus, we observe more pragmatic tags, as here we are dealing with (almost) free dialogue. There are 16 Q-FORBIDDEN, 61 KEY-INFO, 438 TOPIC and 100 LONG-PAUSE tags used for these tasks. In the TZ context, especially, KEY-INFO and TOPIC are interesting as they were designed especially for this sub-corpus. TOPIC allows one to track how new topics related to the solution of a given story are introduced and resolved. As for the KEY-INFO tag, it is crucial for understanding how the solution to the initial question is reached as this tag indicates situations in which a game-master provides addition information, which facilitates the solving process.

To sum up, we observe 24 Q-FORBIDDEN, 29 WRONGINFO, 61 KEY-INFO, 438 TOPIC, and 100 LONG-PAUSE pragmatic layer tags in the ERC data. As we have mentioned, due to the nature of the tasks, these tags are present only in the QG and TZ sub-corpora of the ERC.

4.5          *Annotation and its reliability*

The tagging process was performed by 5 volunteers with solid background in erotetic logic. Each file was tagged by one annotator. What is more, each annotator tagged files only from one sub-corpus of the ERC. Thanks to this, s/he dealt with a consistent file structure and consistent subset of the tagset.

Annotation quality was ensured via a variety of measures. First of all, the structural tags layer is very intuitive and standardised for the TRE and QG sub-corpora (see description in Section 3). For these files, an experienced super-annotator (with expert knowledge in IEL) prepared and controlled the annotation schemas used. Each controversial case was discussed by the annotators.

Secondly, the output consists of XML files, thus RELAX NG XML schema was defined with the purpose of facilitating the annotation process. The schema specifies a pattern for the structure and the content of XML files and prevents incorrect use of tags by annotators. All of the ERC files were validated by the annotators themselves and afterwards by a super-annotator. The validation was performed in two steps: first general XML validity was checked and in the second step ERC XML schema were used to control the use of the ERC tagset. Structural validity was also checked within the ERC tools described below.

Thirdly, all of the ERC files were thoroughly controlled by the super-annotator. Every issue has been discussed between the annotators; and this is how final tagging was established.

In order to check the reliability of the annotation process, inter- and intra-annotator tests were performed.

For the inter-annotator test, a sample of 100 randomly chosen text units (retrieved from all three sub-corpora of ERC) was used. The units were chosen in such a way that they could be annotated with at least one ERC tag. The structure of the sample was the same as the whole ERC, i.e. 67% of units were retrieved from the TRE sub-corpus; 29% from the QG and 16% from the TZ. All of the units were supplemented with a necessary context.

The guideline for annotators contained explanations of all the ERC tags and examples of annotated text units. The control sample was annotated by two annotators (two logicians, one of whom had a solid background in the logic of question).

The reliability of the annotation was evaluated using $\kappa$ (Carletta 1996), established by using the R statistical software (R Core Team 2013; version 3.3.1) with the *irr* package (Gamer *et al.* 2012). The interpretation of the kappa values is based on that of Viera and Garrett (2005).

The Fleiss $\kappa$ for all three annotators was 0.8 (i.e. substantial) with 75% agreement over 100 cases. The agreements between the main annotation and others were high, as presented below:

- main and first annotator: $\kappa = 0.85$, with 86% agreement (almost perfect agreement);
- main and second annotator: $\kappa = 0.78$, with 80% agreement (substantial).

As can be expected, when it comes to a detailed analysis of the annotation, the most unproblematic cases were the ones annotated with tags from the structural and pragmatic layers of the ERC tagset. Annotation with the use of the inferential layer was more problematic. Cases where we observe disagreement between annotators concern the use of <TRANSMISSION /> and <USEFULNESS /> tags for the TRE sub-corpus samples. The reason for this may be that the use of these tags involves the interpretation of the justification provided by a subject in the light of an answer given for a particular task. As it was explained above, we have paid special attention to this layer of annotation of the ERC. All of the tags used were checked by the super-annotator and each controversial case was discussed by the main ERC annotators.

We have also performed intra-annotator agreement rating test. For this test, another control sample of 100 examples was randomly chosen from the data (with the same structure as the sample for the inter-annotation study). In this case, two ERC annotators were employed to annotate the sample. The agreement between the main annotation and the two annotators was almost perfect – Fleiss $\kappa = 0.86$ with 82% agreement over 100 cases. The detailed results for annotators are presented below:

- main and first annotator: $\kappa = 0.87$, with 88% agreement;
- main and second annotator: $\kappa = 0.85$, with 86% agreement;
- first and second annotator: $\kappa = 0.86$, with 87% agreement.

## 5                                ERC ON-LINE

The corpus is available via its web-site[5]. ERC is distributed under the Creative Commons Attribution-NonCommercial-NoDerivatives 4.0 International License.

Several tools that allow one to to work with the corpus are provided on the ERC web-site.[6] The central tool is *ERC Search & Browse Tool*. This application allows one to display and browse ERC files, both with and without tags. It also allows one to search through corpus files. Keyword and tag search options have likewise been made available to users. In order to use a certain fragment of the ERC in one's paper, presentation, or poster one may take advantage of the ERC XML/LaTeX Parser (Gajda and Łupkowski 2016). The parser transforms original XML-annotated ERC files into appropriate LaTeX files. The parser is responsible for formatting and displaying the data form the corpus – it will be especially useful for preparing papers and presentations based on the ERC data. Hence the choice of using LaTeX as the output format for our tool. Obtained files may be simply pasted into an article,

---

[5]See https://ercorpus.wordpress.com/
[6]See https://ercorpus.wordpress.com/tools/.

presentation, or poster.[7] The last tool provided is *ERC XML Schema*. The ERC XML Schema describes the structure of corpus XML files. It allows for quick syntactic validation of corpus files and is very useful in the annotation process.

## 6           SUMMARY

In this paper, we have presented the Erotetic Reasoning Corpus. So far, the ERC data have been mainly analysed in the light of the normative yardstick provided by IEL. Urbański *et al.* (2016a) present research on correlations between the level of fluid intelligence and fluencies in two kinds of deductions: simple (syllogistic reasoning) and difficult ones (erotetic reasoning). The tool used to investigate erotetic reasoning is the Erotetic Reasoning Test. The paper presents the detailed analysis of the justifications provided by subjects. Urbański *et al.* (2016b) contains analyses of solutions to Mind Maze games. Łupkowski and Ignaszak (2017) model and discuss selected solutions of QuestGen tasks with focusing on normative vs. non-normative solutions.

In our opinion, however the ERC's potential scope of use is broad and reaches far beyond studies of the normative logical concepts vs. instances of real erotetic reasoning. The ERC consists of a significant amount of natural language data (see Table 2). The potential applications may cover the following example areas of interests:

- linguistic studies of the way questions are formulated in different contexts;
- research on dialogue management (this applies in particular to the TZ sub-corpus of the TRE, which consists of long natural language dialogues);
- problem solving studies concerning strategies of handling question decomposition, especially those with imposed time limits (such as the tasks in the QG sub-corpus of the ERC);
- studies focusing on the way a question should be asked (or an initial problem/task should be formulated) in order to make the solution easier to reach.

---

[7]For an overview of LᴬTᴇX in academic use see e.g. (de Souza e Silva Filho and Pinheiro 2010), (Flom 2005), (Hofert and Kohm 2010), (Łupkowski 2015), (Łupkowski and Urbański 2013).

# ACKNOWLEDGEMENTS

Work on the Erotetic Reasoning Corpus was supported by the National Science Centre, Poland (DEC-2013/10/E/HS1/00172 and DEC-2012/04/A/HS1/00715).

# REFERENCES

Nuel BELNAP (1986), Approaches to the semantics of questions in natural language: part 1, in *From models to modules*, pp. 257–284, Ablex Publishing Corp.

Jean CARLETTA (1996), Assessing Agreement on Classification Tasks: The Kappa Statistic, *Computational Linguistics*, 22(2):249–254.

Paulo Rogério DE SOUZA E SILVA FILHO and Rian Gabriel Santos PINHEIRO (2010), Design and Preparation of Effective Scientific Posters using LaTeX, *The PracTeX Journal*, 2010(2),
`http://tug.org/pracjourn/2010-2/rogerio.html`.

Peter FLOM (2005), LaTeX for academics and researchers who (think they) don't need it, *The PracTeX Journal*, 2005(4),
`http://tug.org/pracjourn/2005-4/flom/flom.pdf`.

Andrzej GAJDA and Paweł ŁUPKOWSKI (2016), Using LaTeX as an element of the Erotetic Reasoning Corpus interface, in Tomasz PRZECHLEWSKI, Karl BERRY, and Jerzy LUDWICHOWSKI, editors, *BachoTeX 2016: Convergence*, pp. 47–52, Polish TeX Users Group GUST, Bachotek.

M. GAMER, J. LEMON, and I.F.P. SINGH (2012), irr: Various Coefficients of Interrater Reliability and Agreement. R package version 0.84,
http://CRAN.R-project.org/package=irr.

Jonathan GINZBURG (2012), *The Interactive Stance: Meaning for Conversation*, Oxford University Press, Oxford.

Adam GROBLER (2012), Fifth part of the definition of knowledge, *Philosophica*, 86:33–50.

Jeroen GROENENDIJK and Floris ROELOFSEN (2011), Compliance, in Alain LECOMTE and Samuel TRONÇON, editors, *Ludics, Dialogue and Interaction*, pp. 161–173, Springer-Verlag, Berlin Heidelberg.

C. L. HAMBLIN (1958), Questions, *The Australasian Journal of Philosophy*, 36:159–168.

David HARRAH (2002), The Logic of Questions, in D. M. GABBAY and F. GUENTHNER, editors, *Handbook of Philosophical Logic, Second Edition*, pp. 1–60, Kluwer, Dordrecht/Boston/London.

Marius HOFERT and Markus KOHM (2010), Scientific Presentations with LaTeX, *The PracTeX Journal*, 2010(2),
`http://tug.org/pracjourn/2010-2/hofert.html`.

Paweł ŁUPKOWSKI (2011), Human computation—how people solve difficult AI problems (having fun doing it), *Homo Ludens*, 3(1):81–94, ISSN 2080–4555.

Paweł ŁUPKOWSKI (2015), Making your researcher's life easier. How to prepare transparent and dynamic research reports with LaTeX, in Tomasz PRZECHLEWSKI, Karl BERRY, Bogusław JACKOWSKI, and Jerzy LUDWICHOWSKI, editors, *BachoTeX 2015: various faces of typography*, pp. 42–48, Polish TeX Users Group GUST, Bachotek.

Paweł ŁUPKOWSKI (2016), *Logic of Questions in the Wild. Inferential Erotetic Logic in Information Seeking Dialogue Modelling*, College Publications, London.

Paweł ŁUPKOWSKI and Jonathan GINZBURG (2013), A corpus-based taxonomy of question responses, in *Proceedings of the 10th International Conference on Computational Semantics (IWCS 2013)*, pp. 354–361, Association for Computational Linguistics, Potsdam, Germany, http://www.aclweb.org/anthology/W13-0209.

Paweł ŁUPKOWSKI and Jonathan GINZBURG (2016), Query Responses, *Journal of Language Modelling*, 4(2):245–293.

Paweł ŁUPKOWSKI and Olivia IGNASZAK (2017), Inferential Erotetic Logic in Modelling of Cooperative Problem Solving Involving Questions in the QuestGen Game, *Organon F*, 24(2):214–244, http://www.klemens.sav.sk/fiusav/doc/organon/2017/2/214-244.pdf.

Paweł ŁUPKOWSKI and Mariusz URBAŃSKI (2013), Preparing for scientific conferences with LaTeX: A short practical how-to, *TUGboat*, 34(2):184–189.

Paweł ŁUPKOWSKI and Patrycja WIETRZYCKA (2015), Gamification for Question Processing Research—the QuestGen Game, *Homo Ludens*, 7(1):161–171.

Michal PELIŠ (2016), *Inferences with Ignorance: Logics of Questions (Inferential Erotetic Logic & Erotetic Epistemic Logic)*, Acta Universtitatis Carolinae – Philosophica et Historica, Karolinum, Praha.

R CORE TEAM (2013), *R: A language and environment for statistical computing*, R Foundation for Statistical Computing, Vienna, Austria, http://www.R-project.org/, acess 20.03.2017.

Mariusz URBAŃSKI, Katarzyna PALUSZKIEWICZ, and Joanna URBAŃSKA (2016a), Erotetic Problem Solving: From Real Data to Formal Models. An Analysis of Solutions to Erotetic Reasoning Test Task, in Fabio PAGLIERI, Laura BONETTI, and Silvia FELLETT, editors, *The Psychology of Argument: Cognitive Approaches to Argumentation and Persuasion*, pp. 33–46, College Publications, London.

Mariusz URBAŃSKI and Natalia ŻYLUK (2016), Sets of situations, topics, and question relevance, Technical report, AMU Institute of Psychology.

Mariusz URBAŃSKI, Natalia ŻYLUK, Katarzyna PALUSZKIEWICZ, and Joanna URBAŃSKA (2016b), A Formal Model of Erotetic Reasoning in Solving Some what Ill-Defined Problems, in D. MOHAMMED and M. LEWIŃSKI, editors, *Argumentation and Reasoned Action Proceedings of the 1st European Conference on Argumentation*, pp. 973–983, College Publications, London.

Jan VAN KUPPEVELT (1995), Discourse structure, topicality and questioning, *Journal of Linguistics*, 31:109–147.

Anthony J. VIERA and Joanne M. GARRETT (2005), Understanding Interobserver Agreement: The Kappa Statistic, *Family Medicine*, 37(5):360–363.

Luis VON AHN and Laura DABBISH (2008), Designing games with a purpose, *Communications of the ACM*, 51(8):58–67.

Andrzej WIŚNIEWSKI (1995), *The Posing of Questions: Logical Foundations of Erotetic Inferences*, Kluwer AP, Dordrecht, Boston, London.

Andrzej WIŚNIEWSKI (2013), *Questions, Inferences and Scenarios*, College Publications, London.

Andrzej WIŚNIEWSKI (2015), Semantics of Questions, in S. LAPPIN and Ch. FOX, editors, *The Handbook of Contemporary Semantic Theory, 2nd Edition*, pp. 273–313, Wiley-Blackwell, Oxford.

# 3

# Graded hyponymy for compositional distributional semantics

*Dea Bankova*[1]*, Bob Coecke*[1]*, Martha Lewis*[2]*, and Dan Marsden*[1]

[1] Quantum Group, University of Oxford

[2] ILLC, University of Amsterdam

*Keywords: categorical compositional distributional semantics, computational linguistics, entailment, density operator*

## ABSTRACT

The categorical compositional distributional model of natural language provides a conceptually motivated procedure to compute the meaning of a sentence, given its grammatical structure and the meanings of its words. This approach has outperformed other models in mainstream empirical language processing tasks, but lacks an effective model of lexical entailment. We address this shortcoming by exploiting the freedom in our abstract categorical framework to change our choice of semantic model. This allows us to describe hyponymy as a graded order on meanings, using models of partial information used in quantum computation. Quantum logic embeds in this graded order.

## 1        INTRODUCTION

Finding a formalization of language in which the meaning of a sentence can be computed from the meaning of its parts has been a long-standing goal in formal and computational linguistics.

Distributional semantics represents individual word meanings as vectors in finite dimensional real vector spaces. On the other hand, symbolic accounts of meaning combine words via compositional rules to form phrases and sentences. These two approaches are in some sense orthogonal. Distributional schemes have no obvious compositional structure, whereas compositional models lack a canonical way of determining the meaning of individual words. In Coecke *et al.* (2010), the authors develop the categorical compositional distributional model of natural language semantics. This model exploits the shared categorical structure of pregroup grammars and vector spaces to provide a compositional structure for distributional semantics. It has produced state-of-the-art results in measuring sentence similarity (Kartsaklis *et al.* 2012; Grefenstette and Sadrzadeh 2011), effectively describing aspects of the human understanding of sentences.

A satisfactory account of natural language should incorporate a suitable notion of lexical entailment. Until recently, categorical compositional distributional models of meaning have lacked this crucial feature. In order to address the entailment problem, we exploit the freedom inherent in our abstract categorical framework to change models. We move from a pure state setting to a category used to describe mixed states and partial knowledge in the semantics of categorical quantum mechanics. Meanings are now represented by density matrices rather than simple vectors. We use this extra flexibility to capture the concept of hyponymy, where one word may be seen as an instance of another. For example, *red* is a hyponym of *colour*. The hyponymy relation can be associated with a notion of logical entailment. Some entailment is crisp, for example: *dog* entails *animal*. However, we may also wish to permit entailments of differing strengths. For example, the concept *dog* gives high support to the concept *pet*, but does not completely entail it: some dogs are working dogs. The hyponymy relation we describe here can account for these phenomena. Some crisp entailment can be seen as encoding linguistic knowledge. The kind of entailment we are interested in here is, in general, about the properties that objects have in the world, rather than grammatically based entailment. In particular, we explicitly avoid downward-monotone contexts such as negation. We do, however, examine the hyponymy between an adjective-noun compound and the head noun. We should also be able to measure entailment strengths at the sentence level. For example, we require that *Cujo is a dog* crisply entails *Cujo is an animal*, but that the statement *Cujo is a dog* does not completely entail *Cujo is a pet*. Again, the relation we describe here will successfully describe this behaviour at the sentence level. Closely related to the current work are the ideas in Balkır (2014), Balkır *et al.* (2016), and Sadrzadeh *et al.* (2018). In this work, the authors develop a graded form of entailment based on von Neumann entropy and with links to the distributional inclusion hypotheses developed by Geffet and Dagan (2005). The authors show how entailment at the word level carries through to entailment at the sentence level. However, this is done without taking account of the grading. In contrast, the measure that we develop here provides a lower bound for the entailment strength between sentences, based on the entailment strength between words. Some of the work presented here was developed in the first author's MSc thesis (Bankova 2015).

An obvious choice for a logic built upon vector spaces is quantum logic (Birkhoff and von Neumann 1936). Briefly, this logic represents propositions about quantum systems as projection operators on an appropriate Hilbert space. These projections form an orthomodular lattice where the distributive law fails in general. The logical structure is then inherited from the lattice structure in the usual way. In the current work, we propose an order that embeds the orthomodular lattice of projections, and so contains quantum logic. This order is based on the Löwner ordering with propositions represented by density matrices. When this ordering is applied to density matrices with the standard trace normalization, no propositions compare, and therefore the Löwner ordering is useless as applied to density operators. The trick we use is to develop an approximate entailment relationship which arises naturally from any commutative monoid. We introduce this in general terms and describe conditions under which this gives a graded measure of entailment. This grading becomes continuous with respect to noise. Our framework is flexible enough to subsume the Bayesian partial ordering of Coecke and Martin (2011) and provides it with a grading. A procedure is given for determining the hyponymy strength between *any* pair of phrases of the same overall grammatical type. The pair of phrases can have differing lengths. So, for example, we can compare 'blond men' to 'men', as these are both noun phrases. This is possible because within categorical compositional semantics, phrases of each type are reduced to one common space according to their type, and can be compared within that space. Furthermore, this notion is consistent with hyponymy at the word level, giving a lower bound on phrase hyponymy.

Density matrices have also been used in other areas of distributional semantics such as Kartsaklis (2015), Piedeleu (2014),

Piedeleu *et al.* (2015), and Blacoe *et al.* (2013). Quantum logic is used in (Widdows and Peters 2003) and Rijsbergen (2004).

Entailment is an important and thriving area of research within distributional semantics. The PASCAL Recognising Textual Entailment Challenge (Dagan *et al.* 2006) has attracted a large number of researchers in the area and generated a number of approaches. Previous lines of research on entailment for distributional semantics investigate the development of directed similarity measures which can characterize entailment (Weeds *et al.* 2004; Kotlerman *et al.* 2010; Lenci and Benotto 2012). Geffet and Dagan (2005) introduce a pair of *distributional inclusion hypotheses*, where if a word $v$ entails another word $w$, then all the typical features of the word $v$ will also occur with the word $w$. Conversely, if all the typical features of $v$ also occur with $w$, $v$ is expected to entail $w$. Clarke (2009) defines a vector lattice for word vectors, and a notion of graded entailment with the properties of a conditional probability. Rimell (2014) explores the limitations of the distributional inclusion hypothesis by examining the properties of those features that are not shared between words. An interesting approach in Kiela *et al.* (2015) is to incorporate other modes of input into the representation of a word. Measures of entailment are based on the dispersion of a word representation, together with a similarity measure. All of these look at entailment at the word level.

Attempts have also been made to incorporate entailment measures with elements of compositionality. Baroni *et al.* (2012) exploit the entailment relations between adjective-noun and noun pairs to train a classifier that can detect similar relations. They further develop a theory of entailment for quantifiers. The approach that we propose here has the characteristic that it can be applied to more types of phrases and sentences than just adjective-noun and noun-noun type phrases.

Another approach to compositional vector-based entailment is the use of deep neural networks to represent logical semantics, as in Bowman *et al.* (2015), for example. The drawback with the use of this sort of method is that the transparency of the compositional method is lost: the networks may indeed learn how to represent logical semantics but it is not clear how they do so. In contrast, the method we propose has a clear basis in formal semantics and links to quantum logic.

## 2    CATEGORICAL COMPOSITIONAL DISTRIBUTIONAL MEANING

Compositional and distributional accounts of meaning are unified in Coecke *et al.* (2010), constructing the meaning of sentences from the meanings of their component parts using their syntactic structure.

### 2.1                          *Pregroup grammars*

In order to describe syntactic structure, we use Lambek's pregroup grammars (Lambek 1997). Within the standard categorical compositional distributional model, it is possible to move to other forms of categorial grammar, as argued in Coecke *et al.* (2013). This is due to the fact that the category of finite-dimensional vector spaces is particularly well-behaved, and so grammars with greater or lesser structure may be used. A pregroup $(P, \leq, \cdot, 1, (-)^l, (-)^r)$ is a partially ordered monoid $(P, \leq, \cdot, 1)$ where each element $p \in P$ has a left adjoint $p^l$ and a right adjoint $p^r$, such that the following inequalities hold:

$$(1) \qquad p^l \cdot p \leq 1 \leq p \cdot p^l \quad \text{and} \quad p \cdot p^r \leq 1 \leq p^r \cdot p$$

Intuitively, we think of the elements of a pregroup as linguistic types. The monoidal structure allows us to form composite types, and the partial order encodes type reduction. The important right and left adjoints then enable the introduction of types requiring further elements on either their left or right respectively.

The pregroup grammar $\text{Preg}_{\mathscr{B}}$ over an alphabet $\mathscr{B}$ is freely constructed from the atomic types in $\mathscr{B}$. In what follows we use an alphabet $\mathscr{B} = \{n, s\}$. We use the type $s$ to denote a declarative sentence and $n$ to denote a noun. A transitive verb can then be denoted $n^r s n^l$. If a string of words and their types reduces to the type $s$, the sentence is judged grammatical. The sentence *John kicks cats* is typed $n \, (n^r s n^l) \, n$, and can be reduced to $s$ as follows:

$$n \, (n^r s n^l) \, n \leq 1 \cdot s n^l n \leq 1 \cdot s \cdot 1 \leq s$$

This symbolic reduction can also be expressed graphically, as shown in Figure 1. In this diagrammatic notation, the elimination of types by means of the inequalities $n \cdot n^r \leq 1$ and $n^l \cdot n \leq 1$ is denoted by a 'cup'. The fact that the type $s$ is retained is represented by a straight wire.

$$\text{John} \qquad \text{kicks} \qquad \text{cats}$$

$$n \qquad n^r \; s \; n^l \qquad n$$

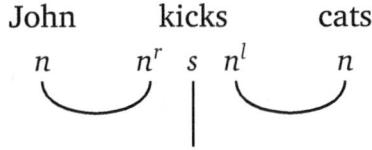

Figure 1: A transitive sentence in the graphical calculus

## 2.2 *Compositional distributional models*

The symbolic account and distributional approaches are linked by the fact that they are both compact closed categories. This compatibility allows the compositional rules of the grammar to be applied in the vector space model. In this way, we can map syntactically well-formed strings of words into one shared meaning space.

A *compact closed category* is a monoidal category in which for each object $A$ there are left and right dual objects $A^l$ and $A^r$, and corresponding unit and counit morphisms $\eta^l : I \to A \otimes A^l$, $\eta^r : I \to A^r \otimes A$, $\epsilon^l : A^l \otimes A \to I$, $\epsilon^r : A \otimes A^r \to I$ such that the *snake equations* hold:

$$(1_A \otimes \epsilon^l) \circ (\eta^l \otimes 1_A) = 1_A \qquad (\epsilon^r \otimes 1_A) \circ (1_A \otimes \eta^r) = 1_A$$

$$(\epsilon^l \otimes 1_{A^l}) \circ (1_{A^l} \otimes \eta^l) = 1_{A^l} \qquad (1_{A^r} \otimes \epsilon^r) \circ (\eta^r \otimes 1_{A^r}) = 1_{A^r}$$

The underlying poset of a pregroup can be viewed as a compact closed category with the monoidal structure given by the pregroup monoid, and $\epsilon^l, \eta^l, \eta^r, \epsilon^r$ the unique morphisms witnessing the inequalities of (1).

Distributional vector space models live in the category **FHilb** of finite dimensional real Hilbert spaces and linear maps. **FHilb** is compact closed. Each object $V$ is its own dual and the left and right unit and counit morphisms coincide. Given a fixed basis $\{|v_i\rangle\}_i$ of $V$, we define the unit by $\eta : \mathbb{R} \to V \otimes V :: 1 \mapsto \sum_i |v_i\rangle \otimes |v_i\rangle$ and counit by $\epsilon : V \otimes V \to \mathbb{R} :: \sum_{ij} c_{ij} |v_i\rangle \otimes |v_j\rangle \mapsto \sum_i c_{ii}$. Here, we use the physicists' bra-ket notation, for details see Nielsen and Chuang (2011).

## 2.3 *Graphical calculus*

The morphisms of compact closed categories can be expressed in a convenient graphical calculus (Kelly and Laplaza 1980) which we will exploit in the following sections. Objects are labelled wires, and morphisms are given as vertices with input and output wires. Composing morphisms consists of connecting input and output wires, and the tensor product is formed by juxtaposition, as shown in Figure 2.

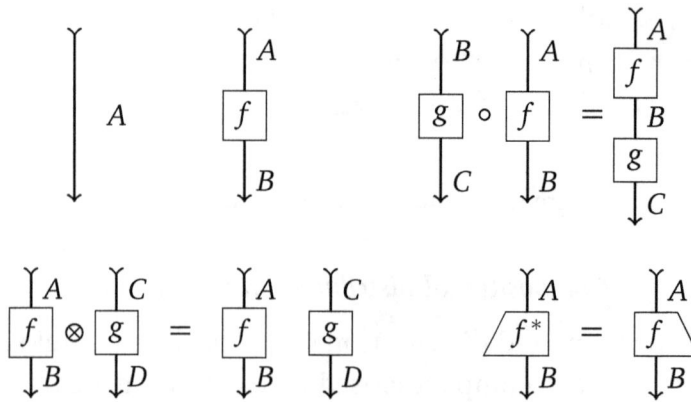

Figure 2: Monoidal graphical calculus

By convention the wire for the monoidal unit is omitted. The morphisms $\epsilon$ and $\eta$ can then be represented by 'cups' and 'caps' as shown in Figure 3. The snake equations can be seen as straightening wires, as shown in Figure 4.

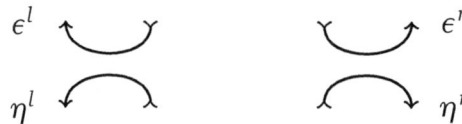

Figure 3: Compact structure graphically

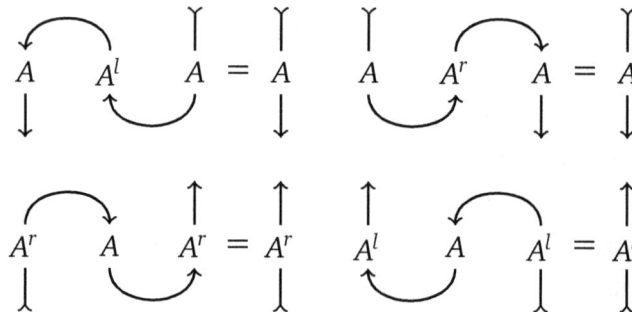

Figure 4: The snake equations

### 2.4　　　　　　　*Grammatical Reductions in Vector Spaces*

Following Preller and Sadrzadeh (2011), reductions of the pregroup grammar may be mapped onto the category **FHilb** of finite dimensional Hilbert spaces and linear maps using an appropriate strong monoidal functor Q:

$$Q : \textbf{Preg} \rightarrow \textbf{FHilb}$$

Strong monoidal functors automatically preserve the compact closed structure. For our example $\textbf{Preg}_{\{n,s\}}$, we must map the noun and sentence types to appropriate finite dimensional vector spaces:

$$Q(n) = N \qquad Q(s) = S$$

Composite types are then constructed functorially using the corresponding structure in **FHilb**. Each morphism $\alpha$ in the pregroup is mapped to a linear map interpreting sentences of that grammatical type. Then, given word vectors $|w_i\rangle$ with types $p_i$, and a type reduction $\alpha : p_1, p_2, \ldots, p_n \to s$, the meaning of the sentence $w_1 w_2 \ldots w_n$ is given by:

$$|w_1 w_2 \ldots w_n\rangle = Q(\alpha)(|w_1\rangle \otimes |w_2\rangle \otimes \ldots \otimes |w_n\rangle)$$

For example, as described in Section 2.1, transitive verbs have type $n^r s n^l$, and can, therefore, be represented in **FHilb** as a rank 3 space $N \otimes S \otimes N$. The transitive sentence *John kicks cats* has type $n(n^r s n^l)n$, which reduces to the sentence type via $\epsilon^r \otimes 1_s \otimes \epsilon^l$. So representing $|kicks\rangle$ by:

$$|kicks\rangle = \sum_{ijk} c_{ijk} |e_i\rangle \otimes |s_j\rangle \otimes |e_k\rangle$$

using the definitions of the counits in **FHilb** we then have:

$$|John\ kicks\ cats\rangle = \epsilon_N \otimes 1_S \otimes \epsilon_N(|John\rangle \otimes |kicks\rangle \otimes |cats\rangle)$$

$$= \sum_{ijk} c_{ijk} \langle John|e_i\rangle \otimes |s_j\rangle \otimes \langle e_k|cats\rangle$$

$$= \sum_{j} \sum_{ik} c_{ijk} \langle John|e_i\rangle \langle e_k|cats\rangle |s_j\rangle$$

Diagrammatically,

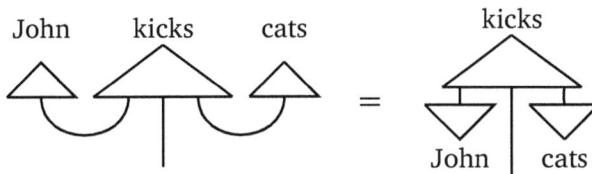

The category **FHilb** is actually a †-compact closed category. A †-compact closed category is a compact closed category with an additional *dagger functor* that is an identity-on-objects involution, satisfying natural coherence conditions. In the graphical calculus, the dagger operation "flips diagrams upside-down". In the case of **FHilb**

the dagger sends a linear map to its adjoint, and this allows us to reason about inner products in a general categorical setting, so that meanings of sentences may be compared using the inner product to calculate the cosine distance between vector representations.

The abstract categorical framework we have introduced allows meanings to be interpreted not just in **FHilb**, but in any †-compact closed category. We will exploit this freedom when we move to density matrices. Detailed presentations of the ideas in this section are given in Coecke *et al.* (2010) and Preller and Sadrzadeh (2011) and an introduction to relevant category theory in Coecke and Paquette (2011).

# 3     DENSITY MATRICES IN CATEGORICAL COMPOSITIONAL DISTRIBUTIONAL SEMANTICS

## 3.1          *Positive operators and density matrices*

The methods outlined in Section 2 can be applied to the richer setting of density matrices. Density matrices are used in quantum mechanics to express uncertainty about the state of a system. For unit vector $|v\rangle$, the projection operator $|v\rangle\langle v|$ onto the subspace spanned by $|v\rangle$ is called a *pure state*. Pure states can be thought of as giving sharp, unambiguous information. In general, density matrices are given by a convex sum of pure states, describing a probabilistic mixture. States that are not pure are referred to as *mixed states*. Necessary and sufficient conditions for an operator $\rho$ to encode such a mixture are:

- $\forall v \in V. \langle v|\rho|v\rangle \geq 0,$
- $\rho$ is self-adjoint,[1]
- $\rho$ has trace 1.

Operators satisfying the first two axioms are called *positive operators*. The third axiom ensures that the operator represents a convex mixture of pure states. Relaxing this condition gives us different choices for normalization.

---

[1] As we are dealing with real-valued positive operators, this condition is necessary.

## 3.2 *Representing words as positive matrices*

Within standard distributional semantics, words are represented as vectors, where the values on specific dimensions correspond to some function of the frequency with which they co-occur with the words represented by the basis vectors. The vector space induced can be modified or reduced using singular value decomposition or other techniques, where the basis vectors no longer have specific meanings. In order to represent words as density matrices, we first observe that each word vector has a corresponding pure matrix:

$$|cat\rangle \mapsto |cat\rangle \langle cat|$$

Words which are more general can be built up by taking sums over pure matrices. We can think of the meaning of the word *pet* as represented by:

$$[\![pet]\!] = p_d \, |dog\rangle \langle dog| + p_c \, |cat\rangle \langle cat| + p_t \, |tarantula\rangle \langle tarantula| + \ldots$$
$$\text{where} \quad \forall i.p_i \geq 0 \quad \text{and} \quad \sum_i p_i = 1$$

In general, we consider the meaning of a word $w$ to be given by a collection of unit vectors $\{|w_i\rangle\}_i$, where each $|w_i\rangle$ represents an instance of the concept expressed by the word. Each $|w_i\rangle$ is weighted by $p_i \in [0,1]$, such that $\sum_i p_i = 1$. These describe the meaning of $w$ as a weighted combination of exemplars. Then the density operator:

$$[\![w]\!] = \sum_i p_i \, |w_i\rangle \langle w_i|$$

represents the word $w$.

This is an extension of the distributional hypothesis. The coefficients $p_i$ may be determined as a function of the frequency with which each word represented by a pure matrix co-occurs with the word represented by $[\![w]\!]$, for example.

## 3.3 *The CPM construction*

Applying Selinger's CPM construction (Selinger 2007) to FHilb produces a new †-compact closed category in which the states are positive operators. This construction has previously been exploited in a linguistic setting in Kartsaklis (2015), Piedeleu *et al.* (2015), and Balkır *et al.* (2016).

Throughout this section $\mathscr{C}$ denotes an arbitrary †-compact closed category.

**Definition 1** (Completely positive morphism). *A $\mathscr{C}$-morphism $\varphi$ : $A^* \otimes A \to B^* \otimes B$ is said to be completely positive (Selinger 2007) if there exists $C \in \mathrm{Ob}(\mathscr{C})$ and $k \in \mathscr{C}(C \otimes A, B)$, such that $\varphi$ can be written in the form:*

$$(k_* \otimes k) \circ (1_{A^*} \otimes \eta_C \otimes 1_A)$$

Identity morphisms are completely positive, and completely positive morphisms are closed under composition in $\mathscr{C}$, leading to the following:

**Definition 2.** *If $\mathscr{C}$ is a †-compact closed category then CPM($\mathscr{C}$) is a category with the same objects as $\mathscr{C}$ and its morphisms are the completely positive morphisms.*

The †-compact structure required for interpreting language in our setting lifts to **CPM**($\mathscr{C}$):

**Theorem 1.** *CPM($\mathscr{C}$) is also a †-compact closed category. There is a functor:*

$$\mathsf{E} : \mathscr{C} \to \mathbf{CPM}(\mathscr{C})$$
$$k \mapsto k_* \otimes k$$

*This functor preserves the †-compact closed structure, and is faithful "up to a global phase" (Selinger 2007).*

3.4                    *Diagrammatic calculus for* **CPM**($\mathscr{C}$)

As **CPM**($\mathscr{C}$) is also a †-compact closed category, we can use the graphical calculus described in Section 2.3. By convention, the diagrammatic calculus for **CPM**($\mathscr{C}$) is drawn using thick wires. The corresponding diagrams in $\mathscr{C}$ are given in Table 1.

In the vector space model of meaning the transition between syntax and semantics was achieved by using a strong monoidal functor $Q : \mathbf{Preg} \to \mathbf{FHilb}$. Language can be assigned semantics in **CPM(FHilb)** in an entirely analogous way via a strong monoidal functor:

$$\mathsf{S} : \mathbf{Preg} \to \mathbf{CPM(FHilb)}$$

$$\epsilon : |e_i\rangle \otimes |e_j\rangle \otimes |e_k\rangle \otimes |e_l\rangle \mapsto \langle e_i|e_k\rangle \langle e_j|e_l\rangle$$

$$\eta : 1 \mapsto \sum_{ij} |e_i\rangle \otimes |e_j\rangle \otimes |e_i\rangle \otimes |e_j\rangle$$

$$f_1 \otimes f_2 : A^* \otimes C^* \otimes C \otimes A \to B^* \otimes D^* \otimes D \otimes B$$

Table 1: Table of diagrams in **CPM**($\mathscr{C}$) and $\mathscr{C}$

**Definition 3.** *Let* $w_1, w_2 \ldots w_n$ *be a string of words with corresponding grammatical types* $t_i$ *in* **Preg**$_{\mathscr{B}}$. *Suppose that the type reduction is given by* $t_1, \ldots t_n \xrightarrow{r} x$ *for some* $x \in \mathrm{Ob}(\mathbf{Preg}_{\mathscr{B}})$. *Let* $[\![w_i]\!]$ *be the meaning of word* $w_i$ *in* **CPM(FHilb)**, *i.e. a state of the form* $I \to S(t_i)$. *Then the meaning of* $w_1 w_2 \ldots w_n$ *is given by:*

$$[\![w_1 w_2 \ldots w_n]\!] = S(r)([\![w_1]\!] \otimes \ldots \otimes [\![w_n]\!])$$

We now have all the ingredients to derive sentence meanings in **CPM(FHilb)**.

**Example 1.** *We firstly show that the results from* **FHilb** *lift to* **CPM(FHilb)**. *Let the noun space* $N$ *be a real Hilbert space with basis vectors given by* $\{|n_i\rangle\}_i$, *where for some* $i$, $|n_i\rangle = |Clara\rangle$ *and for some* $j$, $|n_j\rangle = |beer\rangle$. *Let the sentence space be another space* $S$ *with basis* $\{|s_i\rangle\}_i$. *The verb* $|likes\rangle$ *is given by:*

$$|likes\rangle = \sum_{pqr} C_{pqr} |n_p\rangle \otimes |s_q\rangle \otimes |n_r\rangle$$

*The density matrices for the nouns Clara and beer are in fact pure states given by:*

$$[\![Clara]\!] = |n_i\rangle \langle n_i| \qquad and \qquad [\![beer]\!] = |n_j\rangle \langle n_j|$$

*and similarly, $[\![likes]\!]$ in* **CPM(FHilb)** *is:*

$$[\![likes]\!] = \sum_{pqrtuv} C_{pqr} C_{tuv} |n_p\rangle \langle n_t| \otimes |s_q\rangle \langle s_u| \otimes |n_r\rangle \langle n_v|$$

*The meaning of the composite sentence is simply $(\varepsilon_N \otimes 1_S \otimes \varepsilon_N)$ applied to $([\![Clara]\!] \otimes [\![likes]\!] \otimes [\![beer]\!])$ as shown in Figure 5, with interpretation in* **FHilb** *shown in Figure 6.*

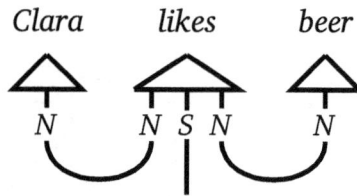

Figure 5: A transitive sentence in **CPM($\mathscr{C}$)**

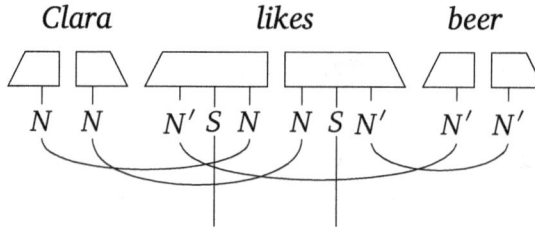

Figure 6: A transitive sentence in $\mathscr{C}$ with pure states

*In terms of linear algebra, this corresponds to:*

$$[\![Clara\ likes\ beer]\!] = \varphi([\![Clara]\!] \otimes [\![likes]\!] \otimes [\![beer]\!])$$
$$= \sum_{qu} C_{iqj} C_{iuj} |s_q\rangle \langle s_u|$$

*This is a pure state corresponding to the vector $\sum_q C_{iqj} |s_q\rangle$.*

However, in **CPM(FHilb)** we can work with more than the pure states.

**Example 2.** *Let the noun space N be a real Hilbert space with basis vectors given by $\{|n_i\rangle\}_i$. Let:*

$$|Annie\rangle = \sum_i a_i |n_i\rangle, \quad |Betty\rangle = \sum_i b_i |n_i\rangle, \quad |Clara\rangle = \sum_i c_i |n_i\rangle$$

Figure 7: *The sisters* *enjoy* *drinks*

A transitive sentence in $\mathscr{C}$ with impure states

$$|beer\rangle = \sum_i d_i \, |n_i\rangle, \quad |wine\rangle = \sum_i e_i \, |n_i\rangle$$

*and with the sentence space S, we define:*

$$|likes\rangle = \sum_{pqr} C_{pqr} \, |n_p\rangle \otimes |s_q\rangle \otimes |n_r\rangle$$

$$|appreciates\rangle = \sum_{pqr} D_{pqr} \, |n_p\rangle \otimes |s_q\rangle \otimes |n_r\rangle$$

*Then, we can set:*

$$[\![\,the\ sisters\,]\!] = \frac{1}{3}(|Annie\rangle \langle Annie| + |Betty\rangle \langle Betty| + |Clara\rangle \langle Clara|)$$

$$[\![\,drinks\,]\!] = \frac{1}{2}(|beer\rangle \langle beer| + |wine\rangle \langle wine|)$$

$$[\![\,enjoy\,]\!] = \frac{1}{2}(|like\rangle \langle like| + |appreciate\rangle \langle appreciate|)$$

*Then, the meaning of the sentence:*

$$s = \textit{The sisters enjoy drinks}$$

*is given by:*

$$[\![s]\!] = (\varepsilon_N \otimes 1_S \otimes \varepsilon_N)([\![\,the\ sisters\,]\!] \otimes [\![\,enjoy\,]\!] \otimes [\![\,drinks\,]\!])$$

*Diagrammatically, this is shown in Figure 7.*

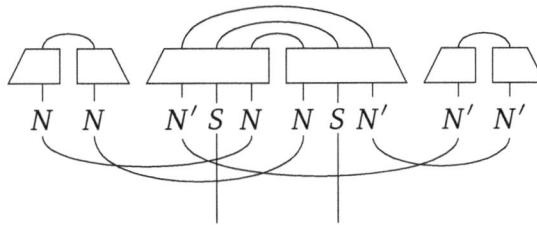

The impurity is indicated by the fact that the pairs of states are connected by wires (Selinger 2007).

## 4 PREDICATES AND ENTAILMENT

If we consider a model of (non-deterministic) classical computation, a state of a set $X$ is just a subset $\rho \subseteq X$. Similarly, a predicate is a subset $A \subseteq X$. We say that $\rho$ satisfies $A$ if:

$$\rho \subseteq A$$

which we write as $\rho \Vdash A$. Predicate $A$ entails predicate $B$, written $A \models B$, if for every state $\rho$:

$$\rho \Vdash A \quad \Rightarrow \quad \rho \Vdash B$$

Clearly this is equivalent to requiring $A \subseteq B$.

### 4.1                              *The Löwner order*

As our linguistic models derive from a quantum mechanical formalism, positive operators form a natural analogue for subsets as our predicates. This follows ideas in D'Hondt and Panangaden (2006) and earlier work in a probabilistic setting in Kozen (1983). Crucially, we can order positive operators (Löwner 1934).

**Definition 4** (Löwner order). *For positive operators $A$ and $B$, we define:*

$$A \sqsubseteq B \iff B - A \text{ is positive}$$

If we consider this as an entailment relationship, we can follow our intuitions from the non-deterministic setting. Firstly, we introduce a suitable notion of satisfaction. For positive operator $A$ and density matrix $\rho$, we define $\rho \Vdash A$ as the positive real number $\mathrm{tr}(\rho A)$.

This generalizes satisfaction from a binary relation to a binary function into the positive reals. We then find that the Löwner order can equivalently be phrased in terms of satisfaction as follows:

**Lemma 1** (D'Hondt and Panangaden 2006). *Let $A$ and $B$ be positive operators. $A \sqsubseteq B$ if and only if for all density operators $\rho$:*

$$\rho \Vdash A \quad \leq \quad \rho \Vdash B$$

Linguistically, we can interpret this condition as saying that every noun, for example, satisfies predicate $B$ at least as strongly as it satisfies predicate $A$.

### 4.2                              *Quantum logic*

Quantum logic (Birkhoff and von Neumann 1936) views the projection operators on a Hilbert space as propositions about a quantum system. As the Löwner order restricts to the usual ordering on projection operators, we can embed quantum logic within the poset of projection operators, providing a direct link to existing theory.

## 4.3 *A general setting for approximate entailment*

We can build an entailment preorder on any commutative monoid, viewing the underlying set as a collection of propositions. We then write $A \models B$ and say $A$ entails $B$ if there exists a proposition $D$ such that $A + D = B$. If our commutative monoid is the powerset of some set $X$, with union the binary operation and unit the empty set, then we recover our non-deterministic computation example from the previous section. If, on the other hand, we take our commutative monoid to be the positive operators on some Hilbert space, with addition of operators and the zero operator as the monoid structure, we recover the Löwner ordering.

In linguistics, we may ask ourselves: does *dog* entail *pet*? Naïvely, the answer is clearly no, not every dog is a pet. This seems too crude for realistic applications though, most dogs are pets, and so we might say *dog* entails *pet* to some extent. This motivates our need for an approximate notion of entailment.

For proposition $E$, we say that $A$ entails $B$ to the extent $E$ if:

$$A \models B + E$$

We think of $E$ as a error term, for instance in our dogs and pets example, $E$ adds back in dogs that are not pets. Expanding definitions, we find $A$ entails $B$ to extent $E$ if there exists $D$ such that:

(2) $$A + D = B + E$$

From this more symmetrical formulation it is easy to see that for arbitrary propositions $A$, $B$, proposition $A$ trivially entails $B$ to extent $A$, as by commutativity:

$$A + B = B + A$$

It is therefore clear that the mere existence of a suitable error term is not sufficient for a weakened notion of entailment. If we restrict our attention to errors in a complete meet semilattice $\mathscr{E}_{A,B}$, we can take the lower bound on the $E$ satisfying equation (2) as our canonical choice. Finally, if we wish to be able to compare entailment strengths globally, this can be achieved by choosing a partial order $\mathscr{K}$ of "error sizes" and monotone functions:

$$\mathscr{E}_{A,B} \xrightarrow{\kappa_{A,B}} \mathscr{K}$$

sending errors to their corresponding size.

For example, if $A$ and $B$ are positive operators, we take our complete lattice of error terms $\mathscr{E}_{A,B}$ to be all operators of the form $(1-k)A$ for $k \in [0,1]$, ordered by the size of $1-k$. We then take $k$ as the strength of the entailment, and refer to it as *k-hyponymy*.

In the case of finite sets $A$, $B$, we take $\mathscr{E}_{A,B} = \mathscr{P}(A)$, and take the size of the error terms as:

$$\frac{\text{cardinality of } E}{\text{cardinality of } A}$$

measuring "how much" of $A$ we have to supplement $B$ with, as indicated in the shaded region below:

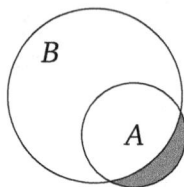

In terms of conditional probability, the error size is then:

$$P(A \mid \neg B)$$

These general error terms are strictly more general than the $k$-hyponymy.

## 5   HYPONYMY IN CATEGORICAL COMPOSITIONAL DISTRIBUTIONAL SEMANTICS

Modelling hyponymy in the categorical compositional distributional semantics framework was first considered in Balkır (2014). She introduced an asymmetric similarity measure called *representativeness* on density matrices based on quantum relative entropy. This can be used to translate hyponym-hypernym relations to the level of positive transitive sentences. Our aim here will be to provide an alternative measure which relies only on the properties of density matrices and the fact that they are the states in **CPM(FHilb)**. This will enable us to quantify the *strength* of the hyponymy relationship, described as $k$-hyponymy. The measure of hyponymy that we use has an advantage over the representativeness measure. Due to the way it combines with linear maps, we can give a quantitative measure to sentence-level entailment based on the entailment strengths between words, whereas representativeness is not shown to combine in this way.

## 5.1          *Properties of hyponymy*

Before proceeding with defining the concept of *k-hyponymy*, we give two properties of hyponymy that can be captured by our new measure.

- **Asymmetry.** If A is a hyponym of B, then usually, B is not a hyponym of A.
- **Pseudo-transitivity.** If X is a hyponym of Y and Y is a hyponym of Z, then X is a hyponym of Z. However, if the hyponymy is not perfect, then we get a weakened form of transitivity.

The measure of hyponymy that we described above and named *k-hyponymy* will be defined in terms of density matrices – the containers for word meanings. The idea is then to define a quantitative order on the density matrices, which is not a partial order, but does give us an indication of the asymmetric relationship between words.

## 5.2          *Ordering positive matrices*

A density matrix can be used to encode the precision that is needed when describing an action. In the sentence *I took my pet to the vet*, we do not know whether the pet is a dog, cat, tarantula, and so on. The sentence *I took my dog to the vet* is more specific. We then wish to develop an order on density matrices so that *dog*, as represented by $|dog\rangle \langle dog|$ is more specific than *pet* as represented by $[\![pet]\!]$. This ordering may then be viewed as an entailment relation, and entailment between words can lift to the level of sentences, so that the sentence *I took my dog to the vet* entails the sentence *I took my pet to the vet*. Note that we do not require that the sentences have exactly the same structure. For example, we would like *I took my brown dog to the vet* to entail *I took my dog to the vet*, and we would expect this to happen because *brown dog* should entail *dog*.

We now define our notion of approximate entailment, following the discussions of Section 4.3:

**Definition 5** (*k*-hyponym). *We say that A is a k-hyponym of B for a given value of k in the range* $(0, 1]$ *and write* $A \preccurlyeq_k B$ *if:*

$$0 \sqsubseteq B - kA$$

Note that such a $k$ need not be unique or even exist at all.

**Definition 6** ($k_{max}$ hyponym). *$k_{max}$ is the maximum value of $k \in (0, 1]$ for which we have $A \preccurlyeq_{k_{max}} B$.*

In general, we are interested in the maximal value $k_{max}$ for which $k$-hyponymy holds between two positive operators. This $k_{max}$ value quantifies the strength of the entailment between the two operators.

In what follows, for operator $A$ we write $A^+$ for the corresponding Moore-Penrose pseudo-inverse and $supp(A)$ for the support of $A$.

**Lemma 2** (Balkır 2014). *Let $A, B$ be positive operators.*

$$supp(A) \subseteq supp(B) \iff \exists k. k > 0 \text{ and } B - kA \geq 0$$

**Lemma 3.** *For positive self-adjoint matrices $A$, $B$ such that:*

$$supp(A) \subseteq supp(B)$$

*$B^+A$ has non-negative eigenvalues.*

We now develop an expression for the optimal $k$ in terms of the matrices $A$ and $B$.

**Theorem 2.** *For positive self-adjoint matrices $A$, $B$ such that:*

$$supp(A) \subseteq supp(B)$$

*the maximum $k$ such that $B - kA \geq 0$ is given by $1/\lambda$ where $\lambda$ is the maximum eigenvalue of $B^+A$.*

*Proof.* We wish to find the maximum $k$ for which

$$\forall |x\rangle \in \mathbb{R}^n. \langle x| (B - pA) |x\rangle \geq 0$$

Since $supp(A) \subseteq supp(B)$, such a $k$ exists. We assume that for $k = 1$, there is at least one $|x\rangle$ such that $\langle x| (B - kA) |x\rangle \leq 0$, since otherwise we're done. For all $|x\rangle \in \mathbb{R}^n$, $\langle x| (B - kA) |x\rangle$ increases continuously as $k$ decreases. We therefore decrease $k$ until $\langle x| (B - kA) |x\rangle \geq 0$, and there will be at least one $|x_0\rangle$ at which $\langle x_0| (B - kA) |x_0\rangle = 0$. These points are minima so that the vector of partial derivatives $\nabla \langle x_0| (B - k_0A) |x_0\rangle = 2(B - k_0A) |x_0\rangle = \vec{0}$ (requires $B, A$ self-adjoint).

Therefore $B |x_0\rangle = k_0 A |x_0\rangle$, and so $1/k_0 B^+B |x_0\rangle = B^+A |x_0\rangle$. Since $B^+B$ is a projector onto the support of $B$ and $supp(A) \subseteq supp(B)$, we have:

$$1/k_0 |v_0\rangle = B^+A |v_0\rangle$$

where $|v_0\rangle = B^+B |x_0\rangle$, i.e., $1/k_0$ is an eigenvalue of $B^+A$.

Now, $B^+A$ has only non-negative eigenvalues, and in fact any pair of eigenvalue $1/k$ and eigenvector $|v\rangle$ will satisfy the condition $B|v\rangle = kA|v\rangle$. We now claim that to satisfy $\forall |x\rangle \in \mathbb{R}^n. \langle x|(B-kA)|x\rangle \geq 0$, we must choose $k_0$ equal to the reciprocal of the maximum eigenvalue $\lambda_0$ of $B^+A$. For a contradiction, take $\lambda_1 < \lambda_0$, so $1/\lambda_1 = k_1 > k_0 = 1/\lambda_0$. Then we require that $\forall |x\rangle \in \mathbb{R}^n. \langle x|(B-k_1A)|x\rangle \geq 0$, and in particular for $|v_0\rangle$. However:

$$\langle v_0|(B-k_1A)|v_0\rangle \geq 0 \iff \langle v_0|B|v_0\rangle \geq k_1 \langle v_0|A|v_0\rangle$$
$$\iff k_0 \langle v_0|A|v_0\rangle \geq k_1 \langle v_0|A|v_0\rangle$$
$$\text{contradiction, since } k_0 < k_1$$

We therefore choose $k_0$ equal to $1/\lambda_0$ where $\lambda_0$ is the maximum eigenvalue of $B^+A$, and $\langle x|(B-k_0A)|x\rangle \geq 0$ is satisfied for all $|x\rangle \in \mathbb{R}^n$. $\square$

5.3                    *Properties of k-hyponymy*

- Reflexivity: $k$-hyponymy is reflexive for $k = 1$.
- Symmetry: $k$-hyponymy is neither symmetric nor anti-symmetric.
- Transitivity: $k$-hyponymy satisfies a version of transitivity. Suppose $A \preccurlyeq_k B$ and $B \preccurlyeq_l C$. Then $A \preccurlyeq_{kl} C$, since:

$$B \sqsubseteq kA \text{ and } C \sqsubseteq lB \implies C \sqsubseteq klA$$

  by transitivity of the Löwner order.
  For the maximal values $k_{max}, l_{max}, m_{max}$ such that $A \preccurlyeq_{k_{max}} B$, $B \preccurlyeq_{l_{max}} C$ and $A \preccurlyeq_{m_{max}} C$, we have the inequality $m_{max} \geq k_{max}l_{max}$.
- Continuity: For $A \preccurlyeq_k B$, when there is a small perturbation to $A$, there is a correspondingly small decrease in the value of $k$. The perturbation must lie in the support of $B$, but can introduce off-diagonal elements.

**Theorem 3.** *Given $A \preccurlyeq_k B$ and density operator $\rho$ such that $supp(\rho) \subseteq supp(B)$, then for any $\varepsilon > 0$ we can choose a $\delta > 0$ such that:*

$$A' = A + \delta\rho \implies A' \preccurlyeq_{k'} B \text{ and } |k-k'| < \varepsilon$$

*Proof of Theorem 3.* We wish to show that we can choose $\delta$ such that $|k - k'| < \varepsilon$. We use the notation $\lambda_{max}(A)$ for the maximum eigenvalue of $A$. $A' = A + \delta\rho$ satisfies the condition of Theorem 2, that

$supp(A') \subseteq supp(B)$, since suppose $|x\rangle \notin supp(B)$. $supp(A) \subseteq supp(B)$, so $|x\rangle \notin supp(A)$ and $A|x\rangle = 0$. Similarly, $\rho|x\rangle = 0$. Therefore $(A+\rho)|x\rangle = A'|x\rangle = 0$, so $|x\rangle \notin supp(A')$.

By Theorem 2 we have:

$$k = \frac{1}{\lambda_{max}(B^+A)}, \quad \text{and} \quad k' = \frac{1}{\lambda_{max}(B^+A')}$$

(3)
$$k - k' = \frac{\lambda_{max}(B^+A') - \lambda_{max}(B^+A)}{\lambda_{max}(B^+A')\lambda_{max}(B^+A)}$$

We may treat the denominator of (3) as a constant. We expand the numerator and apply Weyl's inequalities (Weyl 1912). These inequalities apply only to Hermitian matrices, whereas we need to apply these to products of Hermitian matrices. Since $B^+$, $A$, and $\rho$ are all real-valued positive semidefinite, the products $B^+A$ and $B^+\rho$ have the same eigenvalues as the Hermitian matrices $A^{\frac{1}{2}}B^+A^{\frac{1}{2}}$ and $\rho^{\frac{1}{2}}B^+\rho^{\frac{1}{2}}$. Now:

$$\lambda_{max}(B^+A') - \lambda_{max}(B^+A) = \lambda_{max}(B^+A + \delta B^+\rho) - \lambda_{max}(B^+A)$$
$$\leq \lambda_{max}(B^+A) + \delta\lambda_{max}(B^+\rho) - \lambda_{max}(B^+A)$$
$$= \delta\lambda_{max}(B^+\rho) \leq \delta\lambda_{max}(B^+)\lambda_{max}(\rho) \leq \delta\lambda_{max}(B^+)$$

Therefore:

(4)
$$k - k' \leq \delta\frac{\lambda_{max}(B^+)}{\lambda_{max}(B^+A')\lambda_{max}(B^+A)}$$

so that given $\varepsilon$, $A$, $B$, we can always choose a $\delta$ to make $k - k' \leq \varepsilon$.  $\square$

5.4                                     *Scaling*

When comparing positive operators, in order to standardize the magnitudes resulting from calculations, it is natural to consider normalizing their trace so that we work with density operators. Unfortunately, this is a poor choice when working with the Löwner order as distinct pairs of density operators are never ordered with respect to each other, i.e., for density operators $\sigma$, $\tau$, $\sigma \sqsubseteq \tau \Rightarrow \sigma = \tau$. Another option is to bound operators as having maximum eigenvalue 1, as suggested in D'Hondt and Panangaden (2006). With this ordering, the projection operators regain their usual ordering and we recover quantum logic as a suborder of our setting.

Our framework is flexible enough to support other normalization strategies. The optimal choice for linguistic applications is left to future empirical work. Other ideas are also possible. For example we can embed the Bayesian order (Coecke and Martin 2011) within our setting via a suitable transformation on positive operators as follows:

1. Diagonalize the operator, choosing a permutation of the basis vectors such that the diagonal elements are in descending order.

2. Let $d_i$ denote the $i^{th}$ diagonal element. We define the diagonal of a new diagonal matrix inductively as follows:

$$d_0' = d_0 \qquad\qquad d_{i+1}' = d_i' * d_{i+1}$$

3. Transform the new operator back to the original basis.

Further theoretical investigations of this type are left to future work.

5.5          *Representing the order in the 'Bloch disc'*

The Bloch sphere, Bloch (1946), is a geometrical representation of quantum states. Very briefly, points on the sphere correspond to pure states, and states within the sphere to impure states. Since we consider matrices only over $\mathbb{R}^2$, we disregard the complex phase which allows us to represent the pure states on a circle. A pure state $\cos(\theta/2)|0\rangle + \sin(\theta/2)|1\rangle$ is represented by the vector $(\sin(\theta), \cos(\theta))$ on the circle.

We can calculate the entailment factor $k$ between any two points on the disc. Figure 8 shows contour maps of the entailment strengths for the state with Bloch vector $v = (\frac{3}{4}\sin(\pi/5), \frac{3}{4}\cos(\pi/5))$, using the maximum eigenvalue normalization.

6          RESULTS ON COMPOSITIONALITY

This section provides results and examples on how the notion of hyponymy we have proposed interacts with the compositionality outlined in Section 2. We firstly give an example showing that phrases of different lengths can be compared. We then give a theorem and example to show that our notion of hyponymy 'lifts' to the sentence level, and that the $k$-values are preserved in a very intuitive fashion.

6.1          *k-hyponymy in phrases of varying length*

We can calculate the extent to which any pair of sentences or phrases are hyponyms of each other. We go back to the simple example in

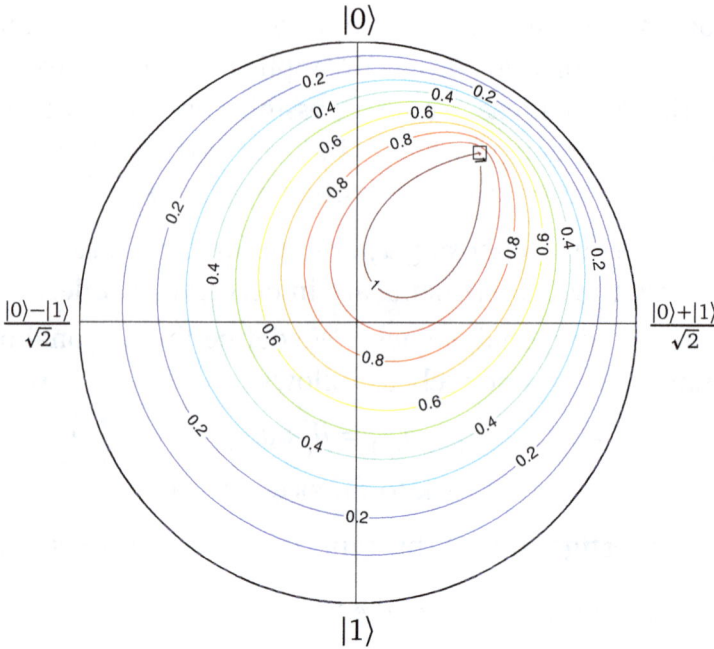

Figure 8: Entailment strengths in the Bloch disc for the state with Bloch vector $v$

the introduction, comparing 'blond men' to 'men'. Suppose our vector space has basis vectors $|blond\rangle$, $|brunette\rangle$, $|male\rangle$, $|female\rangle$. Then the word 'men' can be given by:

$$[\![men]\!] = \frac{1}{3}(|blond\rangle \langle blond| + |brunette\rangle \langle brunette| + |male\rangle \langle male|)$$

signifying that we are agnostic over all vectors with dimensions $|blond\rangle$, $|brunette\rangle$, $|male\rangle$.

The adjective 'blond' is viewed as an operator which takes nouns to blond nouns. This is given by the following:

$$[\![blond_{adj}]\!] = (|blond\rangle \otimes |blond\rangle)(\langle blond| \otimes \langle blond|)$$
$$+ (|blond\rangle \otimes |brunette\rangle)(\langle brunette| \otimes \langle blond|)$$
$$+ \sum_{i,j \notin \{blond,brunette\}} (|i\rangle \otimes |i\rangle)(\langle j| \otimes \langle j|)$$

Then

$$[\![blond\ men]\!] = (1_{N \otimes N} \otimes \epsilon_{N \otimes N})([\![blond_{adj}]\!] \otimes [\![men]\!])$$
$$= \frac{2}{3}|blond\rangle \langle blond| + \frac{1}{3}|male\rangle \langle male|$$

Then if Carlos is described by the pure state

$$|Carlos\rangle = \frac{1}{\sqrt{2}}(|blond\rangle + |male\rangle)$$

we have

$$\llbracket Carlos \rrbracket = |Carlos\rangle \langle Carlos| \preccurlyeq_k \llbracket blond\ men \rrbracket$$

for $k = \frac{4}{9}$ by Theorem 2. For Janette described by the pure state $|Janette\rangle = \frac{1}{\sqrt{2}}(|blond\rangle + |female\rangle)$, we have

$$\llbracket Janette \rrbracket = |Janette\rangle \langle Janette| \preccurlyeq_k \llbracket blond\ men \rrbracket$$

for $k = 0$, since $supp(\llbracket Janette \rrbracket) \nsubseteq supp(\llbracket blond\ men \rrbracket)$.

An obvious line of enquiry here is to consider how to build this type of adjective operator computationally. One strategy might be to extend the linear regression approach from Baroni and Zamparelli (2010) and Grefenstette *et al.* (2013), having built representations of 'noun' and the noun phrase '*blond noun*'. Techniques for building density matrix representations of nouns are described in Sadrzadeh *et al.* (2018).

6.2 *Sentence k-hyponymy*

We can show that the application of $k$-hyponymy to various phrase types holds in the same way. In this section we provide a general proof for varying phrase types. We adopt the following conventions:

- A *positive phrase* is assumed to be a phrase in which individual words are upwardly monotone in the sense described by (Barwise and Cooper 1981; MacCartney and Manning 2007). This means that, for example, the phrase does not contain any negations, including words like *not*.

- The *length* of a phrase is the number of words in it, not counting definite and indefinite articles.

**Theorem 4** (Sentence $k$-hyponymy). *Let $\Phi$ and $\Psi$ be two positive phrases of the same length and grammatical structure, expressed in the same noun spaces $N$ and sentence spaces $S$. Denote the words of $\Phi$, in the order in which they appear, by $A_1, \ldots, A_n$. Similarly, denote these in $\Psi$ by $B_1, \ldots, B_n$. Let their corresponding density matrices be denoted by $\llbracket A_1 \rrbracket, \ldots, \llbracket A_n \rrbracket$ and $\llbracket B_1 \rrbracket, \ldots, \llbracket B_n \rrbracket$ respectively. Suppose that $\llbracket A_i \rrbracket \preccurlyeq_{k_i} \llbracket B_i \rrbracket$ for $i \in \{1, \ldots, n\}$ and some $k_i \in (0, 1]$. Finally, let $\varphi$ be the sentence meaning map for both $\Phi$ and $\Psi$, such that $\varphi(\Phi)$ is the meaning of $\Phi$ and $\varphi(\Psi)$ is the meaning of $\Psi$. Then:*

$$\varphi(\Phi) \preccurlyeq_{k_1 \cdots k_n} \varphi(\Psi)$$

so $k_1 \cdots k_n$ *provides a lower bound on the extent to which* $\varphi(\Phi)$ *entails* $\varphi(\Psi)$.

*Proof of Theorem 4.* First of all, we have $[\![A_i]\!] \preccurlyeq_{k_i} [\![B_i]\!]$ for $i \in \{1, \ldots, n\}$. This means that for each $i$, we have positive matrices $\rho_i$ and nonnegative reals $k_i$ such that $[\![B_i]\!] = k_i [\![A_i]\!] + \rho_i$. Now consider the meanings of the two sentences. We have:

$$\varphi(\Phi) = \phi([\![A_1]\!] \otimes \ldots \otimes [\![A_n]\!])$$
$$\varphi(\Psi) = \varphi([\![B_1]\!] \otimes \ldots \otimes [\![B_n]\!])$$
$$= \varphi((k_1 [\![A_1]\!] + \rho_1) \otimes \ldots \otimes (k_n [\![A_n]\!] + \rho_n))$$
$$= (k_1 \cdots k_n)\varphi([\![A_1]\!] \otimes \ldots \otimes [\![A_n]\!]) + \varphi(P)$$

where $P$ consists of a sum of tensor products of positive matrices, namely:

$$P = \sum_{S \subset \{1, \ldots, n\}} \bigotimes_{i=1}^{n} \sigma_i$$

where:

(5)
$$\sigma_i = \begin{cases} k_i [\![A_i]\!] & \text{if } i \in S \\ \rho_i & \text{if } i \notin S \end{cases}$$

Then we have:

$$\varphi(\Psi) - (k_1 \ldots k_n)\varphi(\Phi) = \varphi(P) \geq 0$$

since $P$ is a sum of tensor products of positive matrices, and $\varphi$ is a completely positive map. Therefore:

$$\varphi(\Phi) \preccurlyeq_{k_1 \cdots k_n} \varphi(\Psi)$$

as required.                                                              □

Intuitively, this means that if (some of) the words of a sentence $\Phi$ are $k$-hyponyms of (some of) the words of sentence $\Psi$, then this hyponymy is translated into sentence hyponymy. Upward-monotonicity is important here, in particular as introduced by some implicit quantifiers. It might be objected that *dogs bark* should not imply *pets bark*. If the implicit quantification is universal, then this is true, however the universal quantifier is downward monotone in the first argument, and therefore does not conform to the convention concerning positive phrases. If the implicit quantification is existential, then *some dogs bark* does entail *some pets bark*, and the problem is averted. Discussion of the behaviour of quantifiers and other word types is given in, for example, Barwise and Cooper (1981) or MacCartney and Manning (2007).

The quantity $k_1 \cdots k_n$ is not necessarily maximal, and indeed usually is not. As we only have a lower bound, zero entailment strength between a pair of components does not imply zero entailment strength between entire sentences.

**Corollary 1.** *Consider two sentences:*

$$\Phi = \bigotimes_i [\![A_i]\!] \qquad \Psi = \bigotimes_i [\![B_i]\!]$$

*such that for each $i \in \{1,\dots,n\}$ we have $[\![A_i]\!] \sqsubseteq [\![B_i]\!]$, i.e. there is strict entailment in each component. Then there is strict entailment between the sentences $\varphi(\Phi)$ and $\varphi(\Psi)$.*

*Proof of Corollary 1.* Since $k_i = 1$ for each $i = \{1,\dots,n\}$,

$$\varphi(\Phi) \preccurlyeq_{k_1 \cdots k_n} \varphi(\Psi) \implies \varphi(\Phi) \preccurlyeq_1 \varphi(\Psi)$$
$$\implies \varphi(\Phi) \leq \varphi(\Psi) \qquad\qquad \square$$

We consider a concrete example. Suppose we have a noun space $N$ with basis $\{|e_i\rangle\}_i$, and sentence space $S$ with basis $\{|x_j\rangle\}_j$ We consider the verbs *nibble, scoff* and the nouns *cake, chocolate*:

where these nouns and verbs are pure states. The more general *eat* and *sweets* are given by:

sweets $= \frac{1}{2} \Big($ cake $+$ chocolate $\Big)$

Then

scoff $\preccurlyeq_{1/2}$ eat   and   cake $\preccurlyeq_{1/2}$ sweets

We consider the sentences:

$s_1 =$ John scoffs cake ,    $s_2 =$ John eats sweets

and as per Theorem 4, we will show that $[\![s_1]\!] \preccurlyeq_{kl} [\![s_2]\!]$ where $kl = \frac{1}{2} \times \frac{1}{2} = \frac{1}{4}$. Expanding $[\![s_2]\!]$ we obtain:

$$s_2 = \frac{1}{4} \Big( \text{John scoffs cake} + \text{John scoffs choc}$$
$$+ \text{John nibbles cake} + \text{John nibbles choc} \Big)$$

Therefore:

$$s_2 - \frac{1}{4} s_1 = \frac{1}{4} \Big( \text{John scoffs choc} + \text{John nibbles cake}$$
$$+ \text{John nibbles choc} \Big)$$

We can see that $[\![s_2]\!] - \frac{1}{4}[\![s_1]\!]$ is positive by positivity of the individual elements and the fact that positivity is preserved under addition and tensor product. Therefore $[\![s_1]\!] \preccurlyeq_{kl} [\![s_2]\!]$ as required.

## 7  A TOY EXPERIMENT

To investigate the effectiveness of the model we perform a toy experiment using a simplified version of the model. We use the dataset introduced in Balkır *et al.* (2016). This dataset consists of pairs of simple sentences annotated by humans as to whether the first sentence entails the second. Example pairs are:

> recommend development $\models$ suggest improvement
> progress reduce $\models$ development replace

The first sentence is rated highly by humans for entailment, whereas the second has lower ratings. The sentences are either noun-verb or verb-noun, and they are of the same type within the pairs.

We use simplified models of composition which we detail as follows. The first model is a baseline, where we use only the verb to predict the entailment between the two sentences. For the second and third models, we use the notion of a Frobenius algebra. As described in Kartsaklis *et al.* (2012), we can 'lift' lower-order vectors and tensors to higher-order ones. This means that we can obtain a representation for the verb by lifting a density matrix representation. This has the important aspect that the dimensionality needed to represent the word is greatly reduced. In the category **CPM(FHilb)**, there are two Frobenius algebras we can use. The first equates to a pointwise multiplication of the noun and the verb, and the second is expressed by

$$\rho(s) = \rho(n)^{1/2}\rho(v)\rho(n)^{1/2}$$

where $\rho(s)$, $\rho(n)$, and $\rho(v)$ indicate density matrices for the sentence, noun, and verb respectively.

The last model we examine is an additive model. In general, addition of two positive operators will not be a morphism in **CPM(FHilb)**. However, in the particular case where the operators are density matrices, we can design a morphism that will implement addition. We give this morphism diagrammatically in Figure 9.

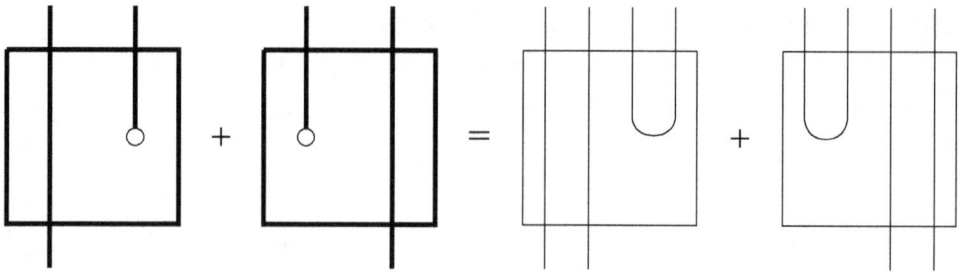

Figure 9: Morphism implementing addition of density matrices

To build density matrices for the nouns and verbs, we firstly collect a set of hyponyms for each word. To do this, we use Word-Net (Miller 1995) via the Natural Language ToolKit (nltk) package in Python (Bird *et al.* 2009). We traverse the WordNet graph below each word to a depth of 8, and collect lemma names of every hyponym encountered. We then use GloVe vectors (Pennington *et al.* 2014) to build representations of each word as follows. Firstly, note that in fact the majority of the hyponyms encountered in WordNet were not present in the off-the-shelf GloVe dataset. Approximately 47,000 hyponyms were found across all words in the sentence pairs, of which approximately 10,000 were in the GloVe dataset. To build the density matrix representations for each word, we simply summed the density matrices corresponding to each GloVe vector for each hyponym of the word, and normalised. We added in some small random values along the diagonal, uniformly distributed over $[0, 10^{-3})$ and renormalised. This step is used to ensure that there is some minimal amount of entailment between every word. After creating sentence vectors from the composition of noun and verb vectors, we calculated the entailment using the result from Theorem 2. We ran the experiments over 50, 100, 200, and 300 dimension vectors. We judged the results by computing Spearman's $\rho$ between the generated results and the mean of the human judgements. The best results were obtained with 50 dimensional vectors which we report in Table 2.

Table 2: Results in the sentence entailment task

| Model | $\rho$ | $p$ |
|---|---|---|
| Verb-only | 0.268 | $> 0.25$ |
| Frobenius mult. | 0.508 | $> 0.05$ |
| Frobenius n.c. | 0.436 | $> 0.05$ |
| Additive | 0.643 | $> 0.001$ |
| Inter-annotator | 0.66 | – |

All the compositional models beat the verb-only baseline. The highest scoring model was the additive model, achieving close to inter-annotator agreement. Note that the sentences were extremely simple, and so it would be good to see how the commutative additive model fares when presented with more complex sentences. The best results from Balkır *et al.* (2016) were $\rho = 0.66$ for a vector-based model using the Spearman's $\rho$ metric and our results are comparable. These vectors were built using part-of-speech information which our model did not use, so there is scope for improvement in that direction.

## 8                        CONCLUSION

Integrating a logical framework with compositional distributional semantics is an important step in improving this model of language. By moving to the setting of density matrices, we have described a graded measure of hyponymy that may be used to describe the extent of hyponymy between two words represented within this enriched framework. This approach extends uniformly to provide hyponymy strengths between two phrases of the same type. That type can be any part of speech for which entailment makes sense, such as a noun phrase, verb phrase, or sentence. This includes pairs of phrases with differing numbers of words. We have also shown how a lower bound on hyponymy strength of phrases of the same structure can be calculated from their components.

Whilst we have given a means for modelling hyponymy in a compositional manner, and provided results on how hyponymy strengths compose, the task of integrating logical and distributional semantics is extremely wide-ranging. We mention here a number of areas to which we can start to contribute.

As mentioned in the introduction, some forms of crisp entailment are based in grammatical structure. So, for example, some adjectives interact with nouns to narrow down concepts, as in our example of 'blond men', and we therefore have that 'blond men' is a hyponym of 'men'. Other adjectives should not operate in this way, such as *former* in *former president*. This phenomenon is related to the notion of downward monotone contexts and the inclusion of negative words like *not*, or negative prefixes. At present, our model cannot effectively account for downward-monotone phenomena. In order to do so, additional structure, such as some form of involution, must be added to begin to model these phenomena.

The area of grammatical kinds of entailment also includes phenomena such as verb-phrase ellipsis. The framework developed here is all within the category of pregroups, and in order to be able to model more complex grammatical phenomena, we may need to move to other grammar categories. This has started to be developed in Kartsaklis *et al.* (2016) and we may therefore be able to use these methods within our current model.

The area of quantification is an important one. Hedges and Sadrzadeh (2016) have started to develop a theory of quantification within this framework, and so this is an area is which extension could be possible.

Another line of inquiry is to examine transitivity behaves. In some cases entailment can strengthen. We had that *dog* entails *pet* to a certain extent, and that *pet* entails *mammal* to a certain extent, but that *dog* completely entails *mammal*.

Our framework supports different methods of scaling the positive operators representing propositions. Empirical work will be required to establish the most appropriate method in linguistic applications.

## ACKNOWLEDGEMENTS

Bob Coecke, Martha Lewis, and Dan Marsden gratefully acknowledge funding from AFOSR grant Algorithmic and Logical Aspects when Composing Meanings. Martha Lewis gratefully acknowledges funding from NWO Veni grant Metaphorical Meanings for Artificial Agents.

## REFERENCES

Esma BALKIR (2014), *Using Density Matrices in a Compositional Distributional Model of Meaning*, Master's thesis, University of Oxford, http://www.cs.ox.ac.uk/people/bob.coecke/Esma.pdf.

Esma BALKIR, Mehrnoosh SADRZADEH, and Bob COECKE (2016), Distributional Sentence Entailment Using Density Matrices, in Mohammad T. HAJIAGHAYI and Mohammad R. MOUSAVI, editors, *Topics in Theoretical Computer Science*, volume 9541 of *Lecture Notes in Computer Science*, pp. 1–22, Springer, Cham, https://doi.org/10.1007/978-3-319-28678-5_1.

Dea BANKOVA (2015), *Comparing Meaning in Language and Cognition: P-Hyponymy, Concept Combination, Asymmetric Similarity*, Master's thesis, University of Oxford,
http://www.cs.ox.ac.uk/people/bob.coecke/Dea.pdf.

Marco BARONI, Raffaella BERNARDI, Ngoc-Quynh DO, and Chung-chieh SHAN (2012), Entailment above the word level in distributional semantics, in *Proceedings of the 13th Conference of the European Chapter of the Association for Computational Linguistics*, pp. 23–32, Association for Computational Linguistics, http://aclweb.org/anthology/E12-1004.

Marco BARONI and Roberto ZAMPARELLI (2010), Nouns are Vectors, Adjectives are Matrices: Representing Adjective-Noun Constructions in Semantic Space, in *Proceedings of the 2010 Conference on Empirical Methods in Natural Language Processing*, pp. 1183–1193, Association for Computational Linguistics, http://aclweb.org/anthology/D10-1115.

Jon BARWISE and Robin COOPER (1981), Generalized Quantifiers and Natural Language, *Linguistics and Philosophy*, 4:159–219.

Steven BIRD, Ewan KLEIN, and Edward LOPER (2009), *Natural Language Processing with Python: Analyzing Text with the Natural Language Toolkit*, O'Reilly Media, Inc.

Garrett BIRKHOFF and John VON NEUMANN (1936), The Logic of Quantum Mechanics, *Annals of Mathematics*, 37(4):823–843, ISSN 0003486X, http://www.jstor.org/stable/1968621.

William BLACOE, Elham KASHEFI, and Mirella LAPATA (2013), A Quantum-Theoretic Approach to Distributional Semantics, in *Proceedings of the 2013 Conference of the North American Chapter of the Association for Computational Linguistics: Human Language Technologies*, pp. 847–857, Association for Computational Linguistics, http://aclweb.org/anthology/N13-1105.

Felix BLOCH (1946), Nuclear Induction, *Phys. Rev.*, 70:460–474, doi:10.1103/PhysRev.70.460, https://link.aps.org/doi/10.1103/PhysRev.70.460.

Samuel R. BOWMAN, Christopher POTTS, and Christopher D. MANNING (2015), Recursive Neural Networks Can Learn Logical Semantics, in *Proceedings of the 3rd Workshop on Continuous Vector Space Models and their Compositionality*, pp. 12–21, Association for Computational Linguistics, doi:10.18653/v1/W15-4002, http://aclweb.org/anthology/W15-4002.

Daoud CLARKE (2009), Context-theoretic Semantics for Natural Language: An Overview, in *Proceedings of the Workshop on Geometrical Models of Natural Language Semantics*, GEMS '09, pp. 112–119, Association for Computational Linguistics, Stroudsburg, PA, USA, http://dl.acm.org/citation.cfm?id=1705415.1705430.

Bob COECKE, Edward GREFENSTETTE, and Mehrnoosh SADRZADEH (2013), Lambek vs. Lambek: Functorial vector space semantics and string diagrams for Lambek calculus, *Annals of Pure and Applied Logic*, 164(11):1079 – 1100, ISSN 0168-0072, https://doi.org/10.1016/j.apal.2013.05.009, special issue on Seventh Workshop on Games for Logic and Programming Languages (GaLoP VII).

Bob COECKE and Keye MARTIN (2011), A partial order on classical and quantum states, in *New Structures for Physics*, pp. 593–683, Springer.

Bob COECKE and Éric Oliver PAQUETTE (2011), Categories for the practising physicist, in *New Structures for Physics*, pp. 173–286, Springer, https://doi.org/10.1007/978-3-642-12821-9_3.

Bob COECKE, Mehrnoosh SADRZADEH, and Stephen J CLARK (2010), Mathematical Foundations for a Compositional Distributional Model of Meaning, *Linguistic Analysis*, 36(1):345–384.

Ido DAGAN, Oren GLICKMAN, and Bernardo MAGNINI (2006), The PASCAL Recognising Textual Entailment Challenge, in Joaquin QUIÑONERO-CANDELA, Ido DAGAN, Bernardo MAGNINI, and Florence D'ALCHÉ BUC, editors, *Machine Learning Challenges. Evaluating Predictive Uncertainty, Visual Object Classification, and Recognising Textual Entailment*, volume 3944 of *Lecture Notes in Computer Science*, pp. 177–190, Springer, Berlin, Heidelberg, https://doi.org/10.1007/11736790_9.

Ellie D'HONDT and Prakash PANANGADEN (2006), Quantum Weakest Preconditions, *Mathematical Structures in Computer Science*, 16(3):429–451, https://doi.org/10.1017/S0960129506005251.

Maayan GEFFET and Ido DAGAN (2005), The Distributional Inclusion Hypotheses and Lexical Entailment, in *Proceedings of the 43rd Annual Meeting of the Association for Computational Linguistics (ACL'05)*, pp. 107–114, Association for Computational Linguistics, http://aclweb.org/anthology/P05-1014.

Edward GREFENSTETTE, Georgiana DINU, Yi ZHANG, Mehrnoosh SADRZADEH, and Marco BARONI (2013), Multi-Step Regression Learning for Compositional Distributional Semantics, in *Proceedings of the 10th International Conference on Computational Semantics (IWCS 2013) – Long Papers*, pp. 131–142, Association for Computational Linguistics, http://aclweb.org/anthology/W13-0112.

Edward GREFENSTETTE and Mehrnoosh SADRZADEH (2011), Experimental Support for a Categorical Compositional Distributional Model of Meaning, in *Proceedings of the 2011 Conference on Empirical Methods in Natural Language Processing*, pp. 1394–1404, Association for Computational Linguistics, http://aclweb.org/anthology/D11-1129.

Jules HEDGES and Mehrnoosh SADRZADEH (2016), A Generalised Quantifier Theory of Natural Language in Categorical Compositional Distributional

Semantics with Bialgebras, *CoRR*, abs/1602.01635,
http://arxiv.org/abs/1602.01635.

Dimitri KARTSAKLIS (2015), *Compositional Distributional Semantics with Compact Closed Categories and Frobenius Algebras*, Ph.D. thesis, University of Oxford,
https://arxiv.org/abs/1505.00138.

Dimitri KARTSAKLIS, Matthew PURVER, and Mehrnoosh SADRZADEH (2016),
Verb Phrase Ellipsis using Frobenius Algebras in Categorical Compositional Distributional Semantics, in *DSALT Workshop, European Summer School on Logic, Language and Information*, https://www.eecs.qmul.ac.uk/~mpurver/
papers/kartsaklis-et-al16dsalt.pdf.

Dimitri KARTSAKLIS, Mehrnoosh SADRZADEH, and Stephen PULMAN (2012), A Unified Sentence Space for Categorical Distributional-Compositional Semantics: Theory and Experiments, in *Proceedings of COLING 2012: Posters*, pp. 549–558,
The COLING 2012 Organizing Committee,
http://aclweb.org/anthology/C12-2054.

Graham M. KELLY and Miguel L. LAPLAZA (1980), Coherence for compact closed categories, *Journal of Pure and Applied Algebra*, 19:193 – 213, ISSN 0022-4049, https://doi.org/10.1016/0022-4049(80)90101-2.

Douwe KIELA, Laura RIMELL, Ivan VULIĆ, and Stephen CLARK (2015),
Exploiting Image Generality for Lexical Entailment Detection, in *Proceedings of the 53rd Annual Meeting of the Association for Computational Linguistics and the 7th International Joint Conference on Natural Language Processing (Volume 2: Short Papers)*, pp. 119–124, Association for Computational Linguistics,
doi:10.3115/v1/P15-2020, http://aclweb.org/anthology/P15-2020.

Lili KOTLERMAN, Ido DAGAN, Idan SZPEKTOR, and Maayan ZHITOMIRSKY-GEFFET (2010), Directional distributional similarity for lexical inference, *Natural Language Engineering*, 16(4):359—389,
https://doi.org/10.1017/S1351324910000124.

Dexter KOZEN (1983), A Probabilistic PDL, in David S. JOHNSON, Ronald FAGIN, Michael L. FREDMAN, David HAREL, Richard M. KARP, Nancy A. LYNCH, Christos H. PAPADIMITRIOU, Ronald L. RIVEST, Walter L. RUZZO, and Joel I. SEIFERAS, editors, *Proceedings of the 15th Annual ACM Symposium on Theory of Computing, 25-27 April, 1983, Boston, Massachusetts, USA*,
pp. 291–297, ACM, https://doi.org/10.1145/800061.808758.

Joachim LAMBEK (1997), Type Grammar Revisited, in Alain LECOMTE,
François LAMARCHE, and Guy PERRIER, editors, *Logical Aspects of Computational Linguistics, Second International Conference, LACL '97, Nancy, France, September 22-24, 1997, Selected Papers*, volume 1582 of *Lecture Notes in Computer Science*, pp. 1–27, Springer, ISBN 3-540-65751-7,
https://doi.org/10.1007/3-540-48975-4_1.

Alessandro LENCI and Giulia BENOTTO (2012), Identifying hypernyms in distributional semantic spaces, in *SEM 2012: The First Joint Conference on Lexical and Computational Semantics – Volume 1: Proceedings of the main conference and the shared task, and Volume 2: Proceedings of the Sixth International Workshop on Semantic Evaluation (SemEval 2012)*, pp. 75–79, Association for Computational Linguistics, http://aclweb.org/anthology/S12-1012.

Karl LÖWNER (1934), Über monotone Matrixfunktionen, *Mathematische Zeitschrift*, 38(1):177–216.

Bill MACCARTNEY and Christopher D. MANNING (2007), Natural Logic for Textual Inference, in *Proceedings of the ACL-PASCAL Workshop on Textual Entailment and Paraphrasing*, RTE '07, pp. 193–200, Association for Computational Linguistics, Stroudsburg, PA, USA, http://dl.acm.org/citation.cfm?id=1654536.1654575.

George A. MILLER (1995), WordNet: A Lexical Database for English, *Communinications of the ACM*, 38(11):39–41, ISSN 0001-0782, doi:10.1145/219717.219748, http://doi.acm.org/10.1145/219717.219748.

Michael A. NIELSEN and Isaac L. CHUANG (2011), *Quantum Computation and Quantum Information: 10th Anniversary Edition*, Cambridge University Press, New York, NY, USA, 10th edition, ISBN 1107002176, 9781107002173.

Jeffrey PENNINGTON, Richard SOCHER, and Christopher MANNING (2014), Glove: Global Vectors for Word Representation, in *Proceedings of the 2014 Conference on Empirical Methods in Natural Language Processing (EMNLP)*, pp. 1532–1543, Association for Computational Linguistics, doi:10.3115/v1/D14-1162, http://aclweb.org/anthology/D14-1162.

Robin PIEDELEU (2014), *Ambiguity in Categorical Models of Meaning*, Master's thesis, University of Oxford, http://www.cs.ox.ac.uk/people/bob.coecke/Robin.pdf.

Robin PIEDELEU, Dimitri KARTSAKLIS, Bob COECKE, and Mehrnoosh SADRZADEH (2015), Open System Categorical Quantum Semantics in Natural Language Processing, in Lawrence S. MOSS and Pawel SOBOCI'NSKI, editors, *6th Conference on Algebra and Coalgebra in Computer Science, CALCO 2015, June 24-26, 2015, Nijmegen, The Netherlands*, volume 35 of *LIPIcs*, pp. 270–289, Schloss Dagstuhl - Leibniz-Zentrum fuer Informatik, ISBN 978-3-939897-84-2, https://doi.org/10.4230/LIPIcs.CALCO.2015.270.

Anne PRELLER and Mehrnoosh SADRZADEH (2011), Bell States and Negative Sentences in the Distributed Model of Meaning, *Electronic Notes in Theoretical Computer Science*, 270(2):141 – 153, ISSN 1571-0661, https://doi.org/10.1016/j.entcs.2011.01.028, proceedings of the 6th International Workshop on Quantum Physics and Logic (QPL 2009).

C. J. van RIJSBERGEN (2004), *The Geometry of Information Retrieval*, Cambridge University Press, New York, NY, USA, ISBN 0521838053.

Laura RIMELL (2014), Distributional Lexical Entailment by Topic Coherence, in *Proceedings of the 14th Conference of the European Chapter of the Association for Computational Linguistics*, pp. 511–519, Association for Computational Linguistics, doi:10.3115/v1/E14-1054, http://aclweb.org/anthology/E14-1054.

Mehrnoosh SADRZADEH, Dimitri KARTSAKLIS, and Esma BALKIR (2018), Sentence entailment in compositional distributional semantics, *Annals of Mathematics and Artificial Intelligence*, 82(4):189–218, https://doi.org/10.1007/s10472-017-9570-x.

Peter SELINGER (2007), Dagger Compact Closed Categories and Completely Positive Maps: (Extended Abstract), *Electronic Notes in Theoretical Computer Science*, 170:139 – 163, ISSN 1571-0661, https://doi.org/10.1016/j.entcs.2006.12.018, proceedings of the 3rd International Workshop on Quantum Programming Languages (QPL 2005).

Julie WEEDS, David WEIR, and Diana MCCARTHY (2004), Characterising Measures of Lexical Distributional Similarity, in *COLING 2004: Proceedings of the 20th International Conference on Computational Linguistics*, http://aclweb.org/anthology/C04-1146.

Hermann WEYL (1912), Das asymptotische Verteilungsgesetz der Eigenwerte linearer partieller Differentialgleichungen (mit einer Anwendung auf die Theorie der Hohlraumstrahlung), *Mathematische Annalen*, 71(4):441–479.

Dominic WIDDOWS and Stanley PETERS (2003), Word vectors and quantum logic: Experiments with negation and disjunction, in *Proceedings of Mathematics of Language 8*, pp. 141–154.

# 4

# Aligning speech and co-speech gesture in a constraint-based grammar

*Katya Alahverdzhieva*[1]*, Alex Lascarides*[1]*, and Dan Flickinger*[2]
[1] School of Informatics, University of Edinburgh, UK
[2] Center for the Study of Language and Information,
Stanford University, USA

*Keywords: co-speech gesture, constraint-based grammar, compositional semantics, underspeci ication*

## ABSTRACT

This paper concerns the form-meaning mapping of communicative actions consisting of speech and improvised co-speech gestures. Based on the findings of previous cognitive and computational approaches, we advance a new theory in which this form-meaning mapping is analysed in a constraint-based grammar. Motivated by observations in naturally occurring examples, we propose several construction rules, which use linguistic form, gesture form and their relative timing to constrain the derivation of a single speech-gesture syntax tree, from which a meaning representation can be composed via standard methods for semantic composition. The paper further reports on implementing these speech-gesture construction rules within the English Resource Grammar (Flickinger 2000). Since gestural form often underspecifies its meaning, the logical formulae that are composed via syntax are underspecified so that current models of the semantics/pragmatics interface support the range of possible interpretations of the speech-gesture act in its context of use.

## 1     INTRODUCTION

In face to face conversation, people exchange information via a range of meaningful and visibly accessible communication channels (Goffman 1963); in particular they use "visible bodily actions"

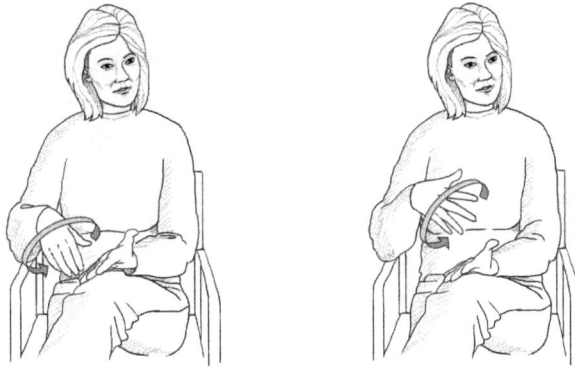

Figure 1: Gesture depicting mixing mud, example (1)

(Kendon 2004). For instance, in utterance (1),[1] extracted from a conversation where the speaker is describing installing drywall. (Loehr 2004),[2] the speaker performs a circular movement with the right hand over the left palm (see Figure 1) along with the spoken utterance. Both the speech and the hand movement are relevant for the conveyed meaning of mixing mud, and both are produced and perceived as a coherent idea unit (McNeill 1992).

(1)  So he mixes [$_N$mud] ...

In this article, we analyse signals like (1), in which the hand is spontaneously used to convey meaning in tandem with speech. In the literature, these hand signals are known as *co-speech gesture, co-verbal gesture* or *gesticulation* (e.g., Kendon 1972). In *depicting/referential* gestures, the form of the hands visually characterises a salient feature of the referent. The depiction could be *iconic* (McNeill 1992) (e.g., in (1) the hands perform a rotating movement to depict the mud being mixed), or *metaphoric* (McNeill 1992) (e.g., a rotating hand while saying "This was a long, boring process" can designate an iterative process). In *deixis/pointing* gestures, the hand points to a region in space

---

[1] We adopt the following conventions in utterance transcriptions: the part of the speech signal that is simultaneous with the expressive phase of the gesture, the so-called stroke, is underlined. We include words that start or end at midpoint in relation to the gesture phase boundaries. The pitch accented words are shown in square brackets with the accent type in the left corner: PN (pre-nuclear), NN (non-nuclear) and N (nuclear).

[2] For this and for all subsequent examples that are cited as Loehr (2004), we are grateful to Daniel Loehr who kindly provided us with an annotated corpus of speech and co-speech gesture. We used this corpus to study depicting gestures.

so as to identify the referent's location in Euclidean space. The pointing can be *concrete* (McNeill 1992), as when pointing to something that's physically present in the communicative situation. It can also be *abstract* (McNeill 1992): the referent is a virtually created object in the gesture space just in front of the speaker, and its location in the gesture space constrains its physical location; e.g., a speaker, while describing her apartment that's on the other side of town, extends her right hand to the right periphery while saying "The bedroom is on the right". Formless flicks of the hand, beating the time along with the rhythm of the speech are known as *beats*. The current analysis focusses on depicting and pointing co-speech gestures.

We adhere to current theories of gesture (Cassell *et al.* 1999; Lascarides and Stone 2009a; Pfeiffer *et al.* 2013), in that we assume that co-speech gesture can affect the truth-conditional content of the speech-and-gesture action. Both deictic gestures and iconic representations say something about the world and as such they have propositional content; this extends to pictorial representations as well (Abusch 2014; Grzankowski 2015).

Our paper contributes to the existing approaches to integrating the contents of speech of co-speech gesture in a single semantic unit (McNeill 1992; Kendon 2004; Bavelas and Chovil 2006; Engle 2000; Giorgolo 2012) in that we explore the coordination patterns of the two modalities, we formalise them within an integrated grammar, and we spell out the gesture's semantic contributions to the proposition that is conveyed by the speech-gesture action. The main challenges are two-fold: on the one hand, the gesture signal is massively ambiguous (Lascarides and Stone 2009a); on the other, the speech-gesture integration is not a free-for-all, in that the *form* of the speech-gesture action rules out certain interpretations of it, whatever its context of use. To illustrate gesture's ambiguity, consider again the hand movement in (1). Taken out of its speech context, this gesture could be a depiction of a circular movement (e.g., the turning of a wheel), or it could refer to the object being rotated (e.g., the wheel itself), or it could refer to an iterative process. It is only via context that gesture receives a specific meaning: the content conveyed by the rotating movement while saying "He mixes mud" is distinct from that while saying "It's a huge, long boring process".

The form of a deictic gesture is also imprecise on the region pointed out by the hand and what is being designated (Kühnlein *et al.* 2002): when pointing in the direction of a book with an extended index finger, does the deictic gesture identify the physical object book, the book's content, or the location of the book – e.g., the table?

This ambiguity notwithstanding, the form of the gesture, abstracted away from its context of use, conveys some meaning, no matter how incomplete it might be. A depicting gesture, by the definition of iconicity, must support a perceptual resemblance between the gesture's form and its denotation (Kendon 2004; Kopp *et al.* 2007): i.e., the gesture's movement, hand shape etc. visualise qualitative characteristics of the referent. Deixis, on the other hand, indexes spatial reference in Euclidean space by projecting the hand to a region that is proximal or distal in relation to the speaker's location (e.g., Levinson 1983). Through deictic gestures, people anchor the referents in their utterances to the physical context (Kaplan 1989). This difference between depicting gestures and deictic gestures is accounted for in how we model the form-meaning mapping, and we also support the analysis of gestures that are *both* deictic and depictive simultaneously (and so inherit the characteristics of both gestural types).

## *Outline*

This article is structured as follows: in Section 2, we discuss the ambiguous form-meaning mappings of the speech-and-gesture signal, assuming a coherence-based pragmatic theory. In Section 3, we introduce examples to motivate a grammar-based approach to co-speech gesture. We then proceed with a discussion of related work and our distinct contribution (Section 4). In Section 5, we discuss how to formally represent gesture form and map this form to (underspecified) meaning. In Section 6, we propose domain-independent grammar rules which are based on the empirically extracted generalisations. Section 7 reports on the grammar implementation and evaluation.

## 2        AMBIGUOUS FORM–MEANING MAPPING

There is a balance to be struck between constraining the mapping from form to meaning, while ensuring that existing pragmatic theories will support inferring the context-specific interpretations from the under-specified meanings derived only from form. The aim of this section is to use examples of speech-gesture actions to motivate one way of striking that balance. We first introduce an existing coherence-based model of pragmatics, which we assume underlies the inferences from the meaning that is derived from form alone to a preferred pragmatic interpretation in context. We then use this to motivate speech-gesture attachment ambiguities by illustrating how each syntax tree supports a different interpretation of the speech-and-gesture action, given the assumed pragmatics model. We also argue that licensed attachments are constrained, despite the multiple ways co-speech gestures can relate to speech.

2.1                    *Pragmatic theory background*

In this paper, we assume a coherence-based model of the semantics/pragmatics interface as discussed in the literature of discourse interpretation (e.g., Hobbs 1985, Kehler 2002). The main principle of a coherence-based pragmatic theory is that discourse content is dependent on *coherence relations* – e.g., Elaboration, Explanation, Contrast, Contiguity – which link the meaning of its segments together. Identifying coherence relations is a defeasible process, informed by the compositional and lexical semantics of the units and contextual information such as real-world knowledge.

For instance, the pragmatic interpretation of the discourse in (2) involves the following contents: Max fell, John pushed Max, and the latter explains the former (so the pushing caused the falling and hence preceded it).

(2)  Max fell. John pushed him.

Using the notation of Segmented Discourse Representation Theory (SDRT, Asher and Lascarides 2003), as shown in (3), this is represented as a rooted hierarchical set of labels – each label corresponds to a discourse segment – with each label associated with some content: $\pi_1$ is associated with the content that the event $e_1$ of Max $m$ falling happened before now; segment $\pi_2$ with the content that the event $e_2$ of John $j$ pushing $x$, where $x$ is identical to $m$, happened before now; and the (root) segment $\pi_0$ stipulates that $\pi_2$ explains $\pi_1$ (in other words, the content of $\pi_2$ explains why the content of $\pi_1$ is true).

(3) $\pi_0 : Explanation(\pi_1, \pi_2)$
$\quad \pi_1 : fall(e_1, m) \wedge e_1 < now$
$\quad \pi_2 : push(e_2, j, x) \wedge x = m \wedge e_2 < now$

The linguistic grammar doesn't identify the antecedent $m$ to the pronoun $x$. Rather, "him" introduces an *underspecified* equality condition between the newly introduced referent $x$ and some antecedent – written $x =?$. Generally, (disambiguated) linguistic form yields an Underspecified Logical Form (ULF), because syntax on its own does not fully resolve all semantic and anaphoric ambiguities. Similarly, the grammar does not introduce the Explanation relation between the segments. Rather, identifying this coherence relation and the antecedent $m$ to $x$ (thereby replacing $x = ?$ with $x = m$ in the logical form of the discourse) is achieved via commonsense reasoning, using the ULFs of the clauses as premises. Moreover, the assumption that $\pi_2$ is coherently related to $\pi_1$ is what makes $m$ an available antecedent for $x$.

Following Lascarides and Stone (2009a), we assume that gestures are elementary discourse units (that is, segments at the leaves of the hierarchical discourse structure); so interpreting gesture involves inferring coherence relation(s) between it and other speech units and gesture units. Furthermore, Lascarides and Stone (2009a) stipulate that co-speech gesture *must* be coherently related to its synchronous speech, and it *can* be related to other units as well. The main aim of this paper is to model this *necessary* connection between co-speech gesture and its synchronous speech. In line with theories of dynamic semantics and discourse interpretation (Hobbs 1985; Kehler 2002; Asher and Lascarides 2003), we further assume that there are constraints on which antecedents are available for resolving the anaphoric elements of the current discourse unit. In speech-only discourse, antecedents to anaphora in the discourse unit $\pi$ must be introduced in $\pi$ itself or in a unit $\pi'$ that $\pi$ is coherently related to. Following Lascarides and Stone (2009a), we carry over these constraints to gesture: i.e., *all* individuals that are a part of the pragmatic interpretation of a gesture behave like anaphoric expressions – they must bind via a bridging relation to an available antecedent (Asher and Lascarides 1998). Thus inferring a pragmatic interpretation of gesture is dependent on inferring how it coherently connects to available speech unit(s).

The meaning representations that we derive from the form of a sentence with co-speech gesture must respect the above constraints on interpretation. To achieve this, we make the choices of speech and gesture integration – which we formally express by attachments in the syntax tree – determine the speech phrase that the gesture is coherently related to. This in turn affects which referents, introduced in speech, are available antecedents for resolving the underspecified gesture meaning (given just its form).

Lascarides and Stone (2009a) observe additional constraints on antecedents for resolving gesture interpretation; constraints that we assume here. Specifically, they claim that the antecedent for resolving gesture can be introduced by a gesture or a linguistic discourse unit, but antecedents for resolving linguistic anaphora cannot be introduced by depicting gestures. This doesn't apply to deixis: a linguistic anaphor can co-refer with a referent that's pointed at. For instance, when a person points at a knife and says "It's sharp", it is perfectly acceptable for "it" to refer to the knife introduced by the deictic gesture. In contrast, when a person says "He cut the cake" and makes a 'cutting' gesture with a vertically flat palm to depict the instrument used for cutting, it is rather unnatural to continue this discourse with "It was sharp" where "it" refers to the knife introduced by the iconic gesture.

By drawing on standard methods from formal linguistics, our goal is to make the analysis of a discourse featuring co-speech gestures compatible with the analysis of purely linguistic discourse. Given the fact that we are adopting a coherence-based theory, the pragmatic interpretation of co-speech gesture is dependent on the content of the linguistic signal it is coherently related to. With this in mind, we introduce the notion of *speech-gesture alignment* to roughly designate: (i) that speech and gesture are coherently related; and (ii) that resolving the (underspecified) semantics of gesture to a specific interpretation and inferring a coherence relation are logically co-dependent tasks. We shall refine the notion of alignment in Section 3.3 after a discussion of how linguistic form and gestural form, including their relative timings, constrain the alignment configurations. In the next section, we illustrate the various ways in which a gesture can be interpreted in context.

## 2.2 *Ambiguous form-meaning mapping*

Syntactic attachment ambiguities and semantic scope ambiguities are ubiquitous in grammars. For instance there is the non-unique choice for attaching the PP in "John saw the man with the telescope". And there's the non-unique semantic scope of the quantifier in "every dog probably did not walk" – "probably" semantically outsopes the negation, which outscopes "walk", but the quantifier "every man" may outscope "probably", or have narrow scope to "probably" but outscope the negation, or have narrow scope to the negation. Most grammars have to handle semantic scope ambiguity in the absence of syntactic ambiguity.[3] So syntax derives a ULF that underspecifies semantic scope.

We will now argue that the range of plausible pragmatic interpretations of co-speech gesture can likewise be analysed via a non-unique choice of attachment of the co-speech gesture to speech and a non-unique way of resolving scope in the ULF that gets composed via such attachments. In essence, these sources of ambiguity familiar from linguistics can also capture ambiguities in co-speech gestures. In Section 3.1, we will then argue that not only *can* one model co-speech gesture ambiguity this way, but one *should*.

We use a slight modification of example (1), namely (4), to discuss the ambiguous form-meaning mapping of depicting gestures. Its plausible pragmatic interpretations are presented in SDRT notation, except that we ignore tense and presupposition, and (following the English Resource Grammar (ERG, Flickinger 2000)), events are not existentially bound.

(4)  <u>John mixes mud</u>
     *Same gesture as in* (1)

Intuitively, one of the possible denotations of the circular hand movement is paraphrasable as "the mud is going round in horizontal circles". This interpretation is regimented in the LF in (5), which features an Elaboration relation between the speech content $mud(x)$ (labelled $\pi_s$) and the gesture content labelled $\pi_g$ – a horizontal rotating event $e'$ over a substance $x'$ that is made equal to the 'mud'

---

[3] For instance, CCG (Steedman 2000) and Montague Grammar (Montague 1988).

referent $x$ introduced in $\pi_s$. The speech-gesture action conveys "John mixes mud, (specifically) the mud that is going round". Like (2), this LF consists of a hierarchical structure of coherently related segments.

(5)   $\pi_s : mud(x)$

     $\pi_g : \exists x'(substance(x') \wedge rotate(e',x') \wedge horizontal\_motion(e'',e')$

     $\wedge x = x')$

     $\pi_0 : \exists x(john(j) \wedge mix(e,j,x) \wedge Elaboration(\pi_s, \pi_g))$

The constraints on anaphoric reference imposed by the discourse structure in (5) license using $x$ as an antecedent for specifying the content of $\pi_g$ (Asher and Lascarides 2003; Lascarides and Stone 2009b): $x$ is available because it's 'introduced' by the predication $mud(x)$ – or more precisely, using HPSG terminology, $x$ is the semantic index of $mud(x)$ (its first argument which introduces a noun variable) – and $mud(x)$ is a part of $\pi_s$, to which $\pi_g$ is coherently related.

Further, this LF represents one way of resolving the underspecified semantic scope of the ULF that you would get by attaching the gesture to the NP "mud" in the syntax tree. Specifically, following the standard approach to semantic composition (Sag and Wasow 1999; Copestake *et al.* 2001), assume the semantic component of the construction rule that attaches gesture to a linguistic unit introduces an (underspecified) *coherence relation* – here resolved to Elaboration – between the gesture and the predications in that linguistic unit, but the ULF so derived underspecifies the relative scope of this (underspecified) coherence relation and the quantifiers in the linguistic unit. Then the ULF derived by attaching the gesture to the NP "mud" would force the coherence relation to outscope the predicate $mud(x)$ but it won't outscope the predicates $mixes(e,j,x)$ or $john(j)$. Proposition (5) is a fully specific logical form that is licensed by this ULF. Here, $\exists x$ *must* outscope the coherence relation because free occurrences of $x$ are forbidden (Copestake *et al.* 2005).

An alternative pragmatic interpretation of the co-speech gesture in (4) is that it depicts the event of mud going round as a *result* of the mixing. A formal rendition of this interpretation is given in (6).

(6)   $\pi_s : \exists x(mud(x) \wedge mix(e,j,x))$

     $\pi_g : \exists x'(substance(x') \wedge rotate(e',x') \wedge$

         $horizontal\_motion(e'',e') \wedge x = x' \wedge cause(e,e'))$

     $\pi_0 : john(j) \wedge Result(\pi_g, \pi_s)$

Unlike (5), the gesture qualifies the event $e$ of mixing – $e$ is available because it's the semantic index of $mix(e, j, x)$, which is a part of $\pi_s$. Here, the speech content $\pi_s$ and the gesture content $\pi_g$ are coherently related via Result (rather than Elaboration): a rough linguistic paraphrase would be "By making it go round, John was mixing mud". In essense, the gesture here functions roughly like a free adjunct.

This interpretation can be derived by attaching the gesture to a linguistic unit whose timing is (again) not *equal* to the timing of the gesture (though they temporally overlap), and then resolving the ULF that results from this attachment to a fully specific logical form. Here, (6) can be derived from the ULF you get by attaching the gesture to the VP "mixes mud": this attachment forces $\pi_s$ to include the predication $mix(e, j, x)$. Consequently, the quantifier $\exists x$ can now have narrower scope than the coherence relation, as shown. This contrasts with attachment to the NP "mud": this attachment ruled out $mix(e, j, x)$, and hence also $\exists x$, from being within the scope of the coherence relation. Further, since the predication $john(j)$ in (6) isn't a part of $\pi_s$, $j$ is not available for resolving the content of $\pi_g$.

The particular linguistic grammar that we use in this paper to analyse co-speech gesture – specifically the ERG (Flickinger 2000) – makes the ULF generated by VP attachment the same as that derived by S attachment. For example, the adverbial in *Probably John mixed mud* and *John probably mixed mud* attaches to the S and VP nodes respectively, but in both cases the ULF forces the modal introduced by *probably* to outscope $mixes(e, j, x)$ and it *underspecifies* whether it also outscopes $john(j)$ and/or $mud(x)$, or not. Thus (6) is also derivable from the ULF you get by attaching the gesture to the S node. An alternative fully scoped form of this ULF corresponds to a further plausible interpretation of the gesture:

(7) $\pi_s : \exists x(john(j) \wedge mud(x) \wedge mix(e,j,x))$
$\pi_g : \exists x'(agent(j') \wedge substance(x') \wedge rotate(e',j',x') \wedge$
$\quad\quad horizontal\_motion(e'',e') \wedge x = x' \wedge e = e' \wedge j = j')$
$\pi_0 : Depiction(\pi_s, \pi_g)$

Unlike (5) and (6), $john(j)$ is now outscoped by the coherence relation; so $j$ is available for resolving the content of $\pi_g$. As before, the choice of antecedents for specifying the content of $\pi_g$ interacts with the choice of coherence relation: here, the coherence relation is Depiction and the overall content is roughly paraphrasable as another free adjunct: "As he was making it go round, John was mixing mud".

The interpretations in (5), (6) and (7) all feature identity between a referent introduced by the co-speech gesture and a referent introduced by speech. However in (8) the gesture does not denote a salient property of the referents introduced in speech: instead, it qualifies the speech act of questioning (signalled by a rising intonation). A rough paraphrase of the meaning of the multimodal action in (8) would be "Are you telling me that John mixes mud?". Interpreting the gesture in this metaphorical way (see the LF in (9)), and inferring a Metatalk relation (Polanyi 1985) whose semantics is defined in terms of the *speech act* rather than the domain-level content, would be supported via an attachment of the co-speech gesture to the S node.

(8)  <u>John mixes mud?</u>
     *Speaker's right hand is vertically open with palm facing up. The speaker moves it forward to the frontal space.*

(9)  $\pi_s : question(\exists x(john(j) \land mud(x) \land mix(e,j,x)))$
     $\pi_g : question(tell(e',you,p) \land p = \pi_s)$
     $\pi_0 : Metatalk(\pi_s, \pi_g)$

While the attachments we've proposed deviate from McNeill's (1992) claim that co-speech gesture is semantically related to its *temporally simultaneous* speech phrase, we remain agnostic about his claims (and those of others) about the underlying production processes – e.g., McNeill's claim that decisions about which contents are expressed in which channel stem from a single (complex) thought.

3          SPEECH–GESTURE ALIGNMENT
              AS SHOWN IN DATA

This section introduces examples of speech-gesture actions that illustrate that despite their ambiguities, speech-gesture alignment is jointly constrained by prosody, linguistic syntax and relative timing of speech and co-speech gesture. This serves as qualitative evidence for: (a) encoding the constraints on speech-gesture alignment within a grammar (rather than entirely via pragmatics); and in particular (b) suitably constraining the application of construction rules of the kind we described in the prior section. The examples we use as evidence include both constructed examples (to illustrate our judgements about ill-formedness) and examples extracted from existing corpora.

### 3.1          *Speech-gesture alignment and prosody*

We begin with the constructed example (10), which reflects intuitions of native speakers about multimodal grammaticality.

(10)  * Your [$_N$mother] <u>called</u>.
      *The speaker puts his hand to the ear to imitate holding a receiver.*

Intuitively, it seems anomalous to perform the gesture along the unaccented "called", even though the gesturing hand is shaped as holding a receiver and can thus be associated with calling. This anomaly would not arise if the gesture was performed along the whole utterance (or a part of it) which, importantly, includes the prosodically prominent element "mother": e.g., "mother called" or "your mother called". As suggested by Mark Steedman (personal communication), gestures exhibit contrastive properties in analogy to those conveyed by pitch accents. If this is so, then it's not surprising if a co-speech gesture is well-formed only if, unlike (10), it temporally overlaps with a contrastive component that's signalled via prosodic prominence (this is not to say that gesture performance is *driven* by prosody, but rather that their performances are mutually constraining). Further, a pragmatic interpretation where the gesture depicts calling must be sourced in a syntactic derivation where the gesture is aligned with a linguistic unit that includes "called" – prosody constrains the gesture to be aligned with a phrase that includes "mother", but the event of calling is available to its interpretation only if it aligns with a phrase that includes "called" as well. Thus, just like with purely linguistic discourse, considerations about plausible pragmatic interpretations can serve to resolve syntactic ambiguities that are licensed by the construction rules in the grammar. Further, this strong relationship in (10) between the performance of the gesture and prosody is in line with the empirical findings of Giorgolo and Verstraten (2008), who isolated prosody as the parameter that influences the perception of multimodal well-formedness vs. multimodal ill-formedness.

Considering that form (here, prosody) constrains what part of the speech signal a co-speech gesture can align with, we define align-

Figure 2: Gesture depicting "greasy", example (11) (Kendon 2004)

ment as a constraint on grammaticality. Ungrammatical (and hence misaligned) speech and co-speech gestures comprise cases where the timing of co-speech gesture relative to the timing of speech does not validate *any* construction rule in the grammar by which speech and gesture may be combined; and our aim is to ensure that such constraints on the construction rules match native speakers' judgements about ill-formedness.

### 3.2          *Speech-gesture alignment and syntax*

To illustrate that linguistic syntax influences decisions about which phrase a co-speech gesture semantically aligns with, consider utterance (11), where the speaker is discussing new owners of a factory finding it filthy. Along with "greasy...", the speaker's hands spread out to the left and right periphery (Figure 2) so as to designate some spatial extent, some closed area being made greasy (Kendon 2004).

(11)  First of all they made [pause 0.1 sec] everything
      [$_N$* gre]asy in the whole room place.

Consider how moving the timing of this gesture affects its meaning. If the gesture onset was moved a few milliseconds earlier so that it happened along "made everything greasy" or if it was held further so as to span "made everything greasy in the whole room", this would not change the interpretation of it: it still designates an enclosed area that's greasy. This interpretation would also remain unchanged if the primary pitch accent were on "everything" rather than "greasy", and the gesture temporally coincided with "everything". However, the gesture cannot receive this interpretation if it temporally coincides only with the subject NP "they" (which in turn would need to be accented for the speech-gesture action to be well-formed): now it designates a spatial referent for "they" in the gestural space, and cannot qualify the spatial extent of greasiness. These variations suggest that a gesture that temporally coincides with "they" can only semantically align with "they", but a gesture temporally coinciding with any element in a VP can semantically align with the VP, sub-portions of the VP containing the temporally coinciding words, and with the whole clause.

A special class of deictic gestures behave differently with regards to the semantic effects of prosody and timing, however. In (12) from the annotated AMI corpus (Carletta 2007), the deictic gesture is performed along with the prominent "Thank you" but its denotation binds to that of the NP "the mouse". The alternative interpretation where the gesture signal and the speech signal are bound through a causal relationship – i.e., handing the mouse is the reason for thanking the addressee – is not possible, since it's clear in context that "Thank you" is related to what came in the *previous* discourse (i.e., projecting the presentation in slide show mode in response to the speaker's request).

(12) [$_N$ Thank] you. [$_{NN}$ I'll] take the [$_N$ mouse]
*Speaker's right hand is loosely open, index finger is loosely extended, pointing at the computer mouse.*

In (13) (again from the AMI corpus), the deixis happens along the nuclear accent "said", but it identifies the individual that resolves the pronoun "she" coming from speech.

(13) And a as she [$_N$ said], it's an environmentally friendly uh material
*The speaker extends her arm with a loosely open palm towards the participant seated diagonally from the speaker.*

In these examples, the gesture would fail to map to the intended meaning if the grammar were to license attaching a co-speech gesture only to its temporally simultaneous linguistic phrase.

Based on Lascarides and Stone (2009a), we formalise the location of the pointing hand with the constant $\vec{c}$; this marks the physical location of the tip of the index finger. This combines with the features of the pointing hand – the hand shape, the orientation of the palm and fingers, and the hand movement – to determine the spatial region $\vec{p}$ that's designated by the gesture – e.g., a stroke with an extended index finger will make $\vec{p}$ a line (or a cone) that starts at $\vec{c}$ and continues in the direction of the index finger. Abstract deixis identifies referents that are not physically salient in the communicative situation. To account for this inequality between the gestured space and actual denotation, Lascarides and Stone (2009a) use the function $v$ to map the physical space $\vec{p}$ designated by the gesture to the space $v(\vec{p})$ it denotes (and they claim that the value of $v$ is pragmatically determined). Essentially, $\vec{p}$ is not equal to $v(\vec{p})$ in cases where the referent introduced in the gesture space is not physically present. Conversely, $\vec{p}$ equals $v(\vec{p})$ when the referent introduced by the gesture is at the physical coordinates identified in the gesture space.

With this in mind, we observed in all the annotated corpora we examined[4] that the temporal/prosodic mismatch occurred only in cases where the visible space $\vec{p}$ designated by the gesture was *equal* to the space $v(\vec{p})$ it denoted, i.e., the function $v$ that maps the space identified by gesture to the actually denoted space resolves to equality. So we shall capture this finding in the grammar via a construction rule that allows gesture to align with a spoken word that is not prosodically marked and/or that doesn't temporally overlap with the gesture, but only if the deictic referent is physically located at the exact coordinates identified by the pointing hand.

Bearing in mind that we are restricting our study and analysis to only those gestures that temporally overlap with speech (i.e., co-speech gestures), these examples provide evidence that their semantic alignment depends on the syntax and prosody of the speech signal, as well as the relative timing of the gesture and speech. This motivates encoding the constraints on alignment *within a grammar*, for this is where information about syntactic constituency is expressed. The alternative approach would be to infer speech-gesture alignment at the pragmatic level, via the commonsense reasoning that resides there for inferring which discourse units are coherently connected to which other units. But this alternative is incompatible with existing and well-established assumptions about the interface between syn-

---

[4] To study depicting gestures, we used a 165-second collection of four recorded meetings, annotated for gesture events and intonation events in the ToBI framework (Loehr 2004). To study deictic gestures, we used two multimodal corpora: a 5.53 min recording from the Talkbank Data,[5] and observation IS1008c, speaker C from the AMI corpus (Carletta 2006).[6]

tax, semantics and pragmatics. For instance, our discussion of example (11) showed that the temporal relationship between subject NP/VP boundary and the gesture profoundly affect the possible interpretations. To capture this fact, pragmatics would need access to the *syntax* of the speech. However, there is no formal model of pragmatics that supports that kind of architecture, without pragmatics being fully integrated into the grammar itself along the lines of Dynamic Syntax (Kempson *et al.* 2000). In contrast to the non-modular approach of Dynamic Syntax, we aim to maintain a conservative, well-established and modularised interface between syntax, semantics and pragmatics, so that implementations of our grammar can be supported by standard methods for computing discourse meanings (e.g., statistical discourse parsers, Afantenos *et al.* 2015).

Accordingly, we will develop a speech-gesture grammar using standard techniques for syntactic derivation and semantic composition, where the constraints on attaching co-speech gesture to a linguistic constituent are defined in terms of relative timing, prosody and linguistic syntax.

The examples we've discussed so far motivate allowing attachments of gesture to linguistic constituents whose timing is *not* identical to the timing of the gesture; we saw in Section 2.2 that making alignment equivalent to temporal simultaneity would under-generate the range of plausible pragmatic interpretations. Rather, the choices of attachment, and hence ultimately the choices of what the gesture means, are determined by the prosodic properties and constituent boundaries of the speech signal as well as relative timing.

3.3                      *Speech-gesture alignment*

Given our assumptions about constrained inference in pragmatics, and also given our observations of how form affects the speech-gesture interaction, we now refine the notion of alignment as follows:

**Definition 1** (Speech-gesture alignment). *Our choice of which speech phrase a gesture (stroke) can align with is guided by the following factors:*

  i. *the final interpretation of the gesture in specific context of use;*

  ii. *the speech phrase whose content is semantically related to that of the gesture given the value of (i); and iii. the syntactic structure that, with standard semantic composition rules, would yield a ULF supporting (i) and hence also (ii).*

The derivation of the single speech-gesture syntactic structure, which is constrained by the prosody of the temporally overlapping speech signal, is achieved within the grammar. This definition encompasses both form (introduced in clause (iii)) and meaning (all three clauses). We capture semantic alignment of speech and gesture via attachment in a single syntax derivation tree, because – as shown – syntax (among other things) governs semantic alignment. If there is a choice as to which phrase a co-speech gesture can align to, then this is modelled via a combination of structural – i.e., attachment – ambiguity and semantic scope ambiguity that's licensed by the ULF so-derived. The semantic effects of alignment are thus captured using standard methods of semantic composition on the derivation tree. Given the theory of pragmatics we aim to support, the construction rules combining speech and a depicting gesture introduce an (under-specified) semantic relation $vis\_rel(s, g)$ (visualising relation) between the content $g$ of the depicting gesture and the content $s$ of the speech constituent to which the gesture attaches, which captures the fact that speech and gesture are coherently connected (Lascarides and Stone 2009a). The (underspecified) relation that's introduced by the construction rules that combine deixis and speech is $deictic\_rel(s, g)$ (Lascarides and Stone 2009a). The resolution of these underspecified relations to a pragmatically preferred and specific value happens externally to the grammar at the semantics/pragmatics interface.[7] In Section 6 we discuss the formal framework and in Section 7 the implementation in HPSG.

## 4      PREVIOUS WORK AND CONTRIBUTION

This paper aims to demonstrate that informal observations about the relationship between speech-gesture form and meaning can be regimented formally, using standard techniques from linguistics. In par-

---

[7] Resolving the underspecified relations is a matter of commonsense reasoning which includes the underspecified semantics produced by the grammar, as well as real-world knowledge. A relation such *vis_rel* is a supertype of the more specific Depiction and Result.

ticular, we use standard techniques for deriving logical form from a syntax tree within a grammar, while ensuring that the meaning representations so derived comply with the requirements imposed by existing formal models of pragmatics.

The idea of integrating speech and gesture within a grammar is by no means new, with several such proposals established over the past 20 years (see, *inter aliae*, Johnston 1998a,b, Kühnlein *et al.* 2002, Paggio and Navarretta 2009, Giorgolo and Asudeh 2011). Further, the "constituent structure" of gesture, as well as its syntactic function for the integration within the language, has also been a matter of research (see Fricke 2008, Müller *et al.* 2013). And the construction of meaning across speech and gesture has been the subject of analysis within construction grammars (Steen 2013).

But there are a few main differences between this prior work and our approach. First, we claim that the speech phrase that gesture aligns with is not determined uniquely by when the gesture was performed. Whilst the TIME feature matters, we also constrain alignment via prosody and syntactic notions such as headedness. Further, in contrast to these prior grammars, we aim for a *domain independent* analysis, and so we must fully capture all linguistically licensed semantic alignments between speech and co-speech gesture, rather than only those that are plausible in the chosen domain of application. The other main difference lies in the semantic component of the grammar. In particular, we draw on recent advances in deriving an Underspecified Logical Formula (ULF), which allows the grammar developer to capture semantic ambiguity in the absence of syntactic ambiguity. The above grammatical approaches all assume that every semantic ambiguity corresponds to a syntactic ambiguity.

There are previous semantic analyses of gesture (Lücking *et al.* 2006b; Lascarides and Stone 2009a) that assume a grammar produces an underspecified meaning representation: these theories focus on how contextual information contributes to mapping the underspecified meaning that's derived from form into a fully specific and pragmatically preferred interpretation. Our work contributes to this by providing a grammar framework that produces the form-meaning mappings they assume. In doing so, we not only capture informal observations about gestural ambiguity, but our formal model uses well-established methods from linguistics to produce a meaning representation that is compliant with current models for multimodal processing at the semantics/pragmatics interface.

To achieve that, we perform two dependent tasks: first, we extract generalisations from the existing literature and from our own observations in annotated multimodal corpora about the syntactic and semantic well-formedness of speech-gesture signals; second, we use the extracted generalisations to define a precise grammar that models the form of the speech, the form of the gesture and the form of their combination, producing ULFs of speech and gesture using standard methods of syntactic derivation and semantic composition from linguistics. We also demonstrate that the grammar can be implemented by extending an existing linguistic grammar.

## 5          MAPPING GESTURE FORM TO MEANING

### 5.1                    *Modelling gesture form*

One major difference between speech and gesture is how the meaning gets derived from the form of the signal. Gestures are 'global' and 'synthetic' (McNeill 1992), i.e., the meanings of the various features of a gesture's form – such as the direction of the movement, the hand shape, the location of the hands, etc. – determine the meaning of the gesture as a whole. This is unlike the semantic compositionality via natural language syntax. Following previous work (Kopp *et al.* 2004, Lascarides and Stone 2006, Hahn and Rieser 2010, among others), we regiment this difference by using Typed Feature Structures (TFS) since they support a *non-hierarchical* representation of the distinct aspects of the gesture's form. The gesture type designates its category: e.g., *depict-literal* for literally depicting gestures (Figure 3) and *deictic-abstract* for abstract deixis (Figure 4), of the kind exhibited in (14):

(14)  I [$_{PN}$enter] my [$_{N}$apartment]
      *Speaker's hands are in centre, palms are open vertically, finger tips*
      *point upward; along with "enter" they move briskly downwards,*
      *after the downward move, the palms are still vertically open but this*
      *time the finger tips point forward.*

The feature-value pairs of a depicting gesture capture every aspect of the form of the hand that (potentially) contributes to its meaning: the hand shape, the orientation of the palm and fingers, the location

$$
\begin{bmatrix}
\textit{depict-literal} & \\
\text{HAND-SHAPE} & \text{bent} \\
\text{PALM-ORIENT} & \text{towards-down} \\
\text{FINGER-ORIENT} & \text{towards-down} \\
\text{HAND-LOCATION} & \text{lower-periphery} \\
\text{HAND-MOVEMENT} & \text{circular}
\end{bmatrix}
$$

Figure 3: TFS representation of the form of the depicting gesture in (1)

$$
\begin{bmatrix}
\textit{deictic-abstract} & \\
\text{HAND-SHAPE} & \text{flat} \\
\text{PALM-ORIENT} & \text{towards-centre} \\
\text{FINGER-ORIENT} & \text{away-body} \\
\text{HAND-MOVEMENT} & \text{down} \\
\text{HAND-LOCATION} & \vec{c}
\end{bmatrix}
$$

Figure 4: TFS representation of the form of the deictic gesture in (14)

of the hand relative to the speaker's torso and the hand movement. With deictic gestures, the shape of the hand determines the region of space that is identified by the pointing hand: e.g., an extended index finger identifies a line or a cone that starts from the tip of the index finger; with a vertical open hand, the designated region is a plane. Recording the form of the pointing hand is essential, because prior work shows that it is significant for interpreting its meaning in context (Kendon 2004): e.g., an extended index finger typically singles out an individuated object while a vertical open hand typically denotes a *class* of objects rather than an individuated object, or it serves a pragmatic function such as offering the floor or citing someone else's contribution to the discourse. The hand location of a deictic gesture is represented via the constant $\vec{c}$. This, combined with the deixis form features, determines the region $\vec{p}$ actually marked by the gesture.

## 5.2                          *Modelling meaning*

As we've already highlighted, a well-established method for handling cases where form does not fully determine meaning is semantic underspecification. All frameworks for semantic underspecification – e.g., Quasi-Logical Form (Alshawi 1992), Underspecified Discourse Representation Theory (Reyle 1993), the Constraint Language for Lambda Structures (Egg *et al.* 2001), Hole Semantics (Bos 2004), Minimal Recursion Semantics (Copestake *et al.* 2005), Regular Tree Grammars (Koller *et al.* 2008) – construct from a fully disambiguated form an abstract representation of meaning that can resolve to several distinct specific messages in context, rather than deriving those specific representations from syntax directly, and assuming a syntactic ambiguity for every semantic ambiguity. Technically, the ULF derived by syntax *partially describes* the form of a fully specific logical form, which in turn represents a context-specific interpretation which can be evaluated against a model or the actual situation at hand.

To map the form of the gesture to an underspecified meaning representation, we use the underspecification formalism of Robust Minimal Recursion Semantics (RMRS, Copestake 2007) – a factorised version of ERG's semantic framework, Minimal Recursion Semantics (MRS, Copestake *et al.* 2005). RMRS was originally developed to support the integration of deep and shallow processing. Modelling gesture is somewhat akin to shallow processing in that one has to handle the large degree of underspecificity.

To illustrate it, consider the MRS for "every dog chased some cat" in (15). Here, the semantic scope ambiguities are captured by the so called *qeq* ($=_q$) contraints which allow for two alternative fully scoped formulas.

(15) $l_1 : every(x_0, h_3, h_1)$
$\quad l_{11} : dog(x_1)$
$\quad l_2 : some(y_0, h_4, h_2)$
$\quad l_{21} : cat(y_1)$
$\quad l_3 : chase(e_1, x_2, y_3), \qquad h_3 =_q l_{11}, \; h_4 =_q l_{21}$

While MRS underspecifies scope, it still requires a fully specified predicate-argument structure. However, neither shallow language processors nor gestural form on their own can fully determine a unique predicate argument structure. Refining MRS to RMRS solves this. One simply produces a highly factorised representation of each elementary predication: each one is equipped with its own unique *anchor (a)*, which serves as a locus for specifying the predicate's arguments; equations (e.g., $x_0 = x_1 = x_2$) are also added to express unifiability between variables. So (16) is a notational variant of (15).

(16) $l_1 : a_1 : every(x_0), l_1 : a_1 : RSTR(h_3), l_1 : a_1 : BODY(h_1)$
$\quad l_{11} : a_{11} : dog(x_1)$
$\quad l_2 : a_2 : some(y_0), l_2 : a_2 : RSTR(h_4), l_2 : a_2 : BODY(h_2)$
$\quad l_{21} : a_{21} : cat(y_1)$
$\quad l_3 : a_3 : chase(e_1), l_3 : a_3 : ARG1(x_2), l_3 : a_3 : ARG2(y_3)$
$\quad h_3 =_q l_{11}, \; h_4 =_q l_{21}$
$\quad x_0 = x_1 = x_2, \qquad y_0 = y_1 = y_3$

For instance, a POS tagger would yield (17) instead of the more specific (16). Proposition (17) captures the semantic insight that, for example, knowing that the word *chase* is tagged as a verb, one knows that its semantic index is an event, but one does not know how many arguments the predicate symbol introduced by *chase* takes because the POS tagger lacks information about lexical subcategorisation.

(17) $l_1 : a_1 : every(x_0)$
$\quad l_{11} : a_{11} : dog(x_1)$
$\quad l_2 : a_2 : some(y_0)$
$\quad l_{21} : a_{21} : cat(y_1)$
$\quad l_3 : a_3 : chase(e_1)$

Semantic composition with RMRS follows the semantic algebra of Copestake *et al.* (2001): the predications and *qeq* on the mother are accumulated from those in the daughters and the semantic head daughter has its 'hook' (roughly equivalent to a $\lambda$-term) replaced by the semantic index of the non-head.

5.3                          *Form-meaning mapping*

5.3.1                          Depicting gestures

Following Lascarides and Stone (2009a), mapping the form of a depicting gesture to its meaning involves mapping each feature value pair in the TFS representing its form to an RMRS-based underspecified predication: the ULF of the gesture from Figure 3 is shown in (18).

(18) $l_0 : a_0 : [\mathscr{G}](h)$
$\quad l_1 : a_1 : hand\_shape\_bent(i_1)$
$\quad l_2 : a_2 : palm\_orient\_towards\_down(i_2)$
$\quad l_3 : a_3 : finger\_orient\_towards\_down(i_3)$
$\quad l_4 : a_4 : hand\_location\_lower\_periphery(i_4)$
$\quad l_5 : a_5 : hand\_movement\_circular(i_5)$
$\quad h =_q l_n \ where \ 1 \leq n \leq 5$

Each predicate has a label, an anchor, and a semantic index, as is standard in RMRS. Since a predication mapped from depicting gesture could resolve in context to an event $e$ or an individual $x$, its semantic index is a metavariable $i$ that generalises over $e$ or $x$. The predicate symbols underspecify the particular constructor and its arity in the LF. For instance, a feature-value pair like $\begin{bmatrix} \text{HAND-MOVEMENT} & \text{circular} \end{bmatrix}$ would map to $l_1 : a_1 : hand\_movement\_circular(i)$. Resolving these predicates happens outside the grammar as a byproduct of discourse processing (Lascarides and Stone 2009a). In particular, each underspecified predicate (such as $hand\_movement\_circular(i)$) is a root to a type hierarchy of increasingly specific predications of content. This is roughly analogous to constructing a specific lexical meaning out of a polysemous lexical entry (Copestake and Briscoe 1995), but here the type hierarchy captures constraints on interpretation that are imposed by the requirement for iconicity – i.e., a resemblance between the form of the gesture and its meaning. This type hierarchy is designed so that a circular hand movement can never resolve to, say, a rectangular concept. To illustrate the idea, in Section 2.2 we claimed that one of the interpretations of the circular hand movement in (1) was the mud being mixed. This is achieved by resolving $hand\_movement\_circular(i)$ to a conjunction of predications: $substance(x') \land rotate(e', x')$, which is a node in the type hierarchy that's rooted at $hand\_movement\_circular(i)$, and is featured in (5). In an alternative interpretation this hand movement is a depiction of the mixing event from the agent's viewpoint: i.e., the underspecified predicate $hand\_movement\_circular(i)$ can resolve to the three-place predicate $rotate(e', j', x')$, featured in (7).

Further, recall from Section 2.1 the constraint that an individual that is introduced in a depicting gesture can't be an antecedent to a pronoun in speech. Lascarides and Stone (2009a) regiment this constraint by introducing the scopal operator $[\mathcal{G}]$: all predicates mapped from depicting gesture fall within its scope (via the scopal condition $h =_q l_n$), and the dynamic semantics Lascarides and Stone assign to $[\mathcal{G}]$ ensures that co-reference across the modalities is suitably constrained.

### 5.3.2                    Deictic gestures

The mapping of deixis form to a ULF captures the fact that deixis provides the spatial reference of an individual or event in the physical space $\vec{p}$ (the complete RMRS logical form mapped from the gesture in Figure 4 is shown in (19)). This is formalised by the two-place predicate $l_{21} : a_2 : sp\_ref(i_1)$ $l_{21} : a_2 : ARG1(v(\vec{p}))$ whose first argument is the underspecified variable $i_1$, and the second argument ARG1 – linked through the anchor $a_2$ – is the actually denoted space $v(\vec{p})$ with $v$ being the function that maps the gesture space to the space in denotation (recall discussion in Section 3.2). The ULF is only a partial description of the resolved LF: e.g., resolving the underspecified referent $i_1$ to an object $x$ and inferring a relation between the deixis denotation and the speech denotation is a matter of pragmatic reasoning. Note how in the prior interpretation of *hand_movement_ciricular(i)*, $i$ resolves to an individual $x$, whereas here it resolves to an event $e$.

To capture how the form of the pointing hand affects its meaning, we map each deixis feature-value pair to a two-place predicate, with the first argument being an event variable ($e_0...e_n$) and the second argument ARG1 being the referent identified by the pointing signal ($i_0...i_n$). This formalisation is similar to the treatment of non-scopal modification in the English Resource Grammar (ERG, Flickinger 2000): a deictic predication (as mapped from form) is a two-place predication whose second argument ARG1 is equated with the semantic index of the modified predication, obtained by equating $i_0 = i_1 = i_2 = i_3 = i_4 = i_5 = i_6$ and whose label is equated with the label of the modified predication, obtained via $l_{21} = l_{22} = l_{23} = l_{24} = l_{25} = l_{26}$. For consistency with ERG where individuals are all bound by quantifiers, we use the *deictic_q* quantifier to quantify over the spatial referent $i_1$.

(19) $l_1 : a_1 : deictic\_q(i_0)\, l_1 : a_1 : RSTR(h_1)\, l_1 : a_1 : BODY(h_2)$
  $l_{21} : a_2 : sp\_ref(i_1)\, l_{21} : a_2 : ARG1(v(\vec{p}))$
  $l_{22} : a_3 : hand\_shape\_flat(e_0)\, l_{22} : a_3 : ARG1(i_2)$
  $l_{23} : a_4 : palm\_orient\_towards\_centre(e_1)\, l_{23} : a_4 : ARG1(i_3)$
  $l_{24} : a_5 : finger\_orient\_away\_centre(e_2)\, l_{24} : a_5 : ARG1(i_4)$
  $l_{25} : a_6 : hand\_movement\_down(e_3)\, l_{25} : a_6 : ARG1(i_5)$
  $l_{26} : a_7 : hand\_location\_c(e_4)\, l_{26} : a_7 : ARG1(i_6)$
  $h_1 =_q l_{21}$
  $l_{21} = l_{22} = l_{23} = l_{24} = l_{25} = l_{26}$
  $i_0 = i_1 = i_2 = i_3 = i_4 = i_5 = i_6$

## 6  GRAMMAR RULES FOR SPEECH AND GESTURE

In this section, we propose grammar construction rules that integrate the form of the gesture and the form of the speech signal into a single syntax tree that in turn provides the basis for deriving a ULF of the speech-gesture action. The construction rules license particular speech-gesture alignments, and constraints on their application make predictions about well-formedness, as motivated via the qualitative observations about speech-gesture data in Section 3.

### 6.1                    *Prosodic word and gesture alignment*

We begin with the straightforward case where gesture aligns with a single lexical item:

**Construction Rule 1** (Situated Prosodic Word Constraint). *A depicting or deictic gesture can attach to a spoken word w of a spoken utterance if (a.) there is an overlap between the temporal performance of the gesture stroke and w; and (b.) w bears a nuclear or a pre-nuclear pitch accent.*

We represent the mulitmodal rules as phrase structure rules equipped with the following information (Figure 5): the speech daughter S-DTR and the gesture daughter G-DTR each introduce a TIME feature, a SYNSEM|CAT feature which captures its syntacic category (note that for gestures, this information includes the form feature-value pairs, discussed in Section 5.1) and a SYNSEM|CONT feature

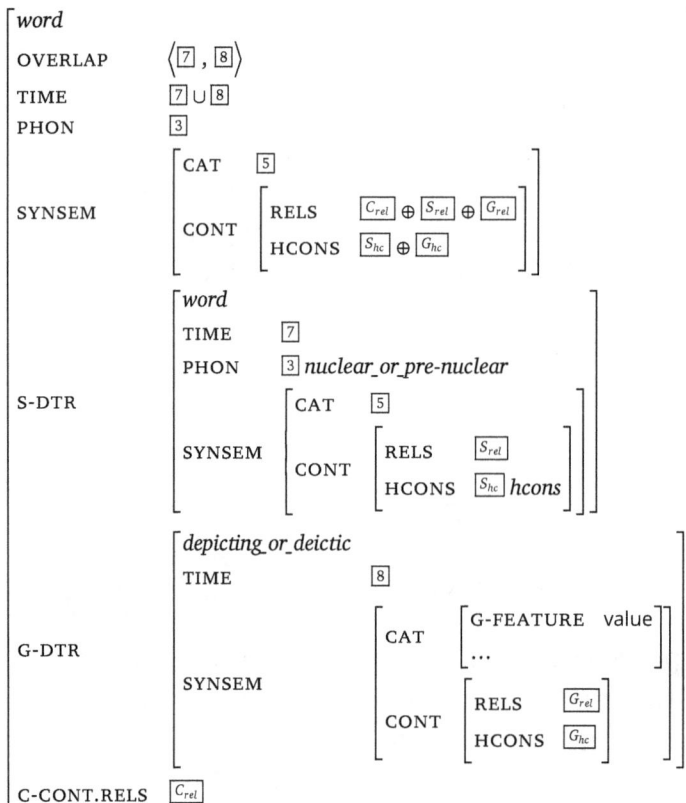

Figure 5: HPSG-based formalisation of the Situated Prosodic Word Constraint aligning gesture and a spoken word

which captures its (underspecified) semantic contribution. The speech daughter also introduces a PHON feature which captures the phonological information. The construction rule introduces a feature OVERLAP whose values are re-entrant with values in the temporal components of the daughters; and also a TIME feature which is the union of the speech daughter's value and the gesture daughter's value. In so doing, we follow previous work where timing is used as a constraint on the integration (Johnston *et al.* 1997). As it is standardly done in ERG, the semantic contribution of the construction rule is captured within C-CONT: here, a depicting gesture introduces an underspecified relation *vis_rel* between the main label of the gesture semantics and the main label of the semantics of the spoken phrase; the underspecified relation introduced by deixis is *deictic_rel* between the semantic index of the speech daughter and the semantic index of the gesture daughter. Multimodal integration happens via unification of these features.

Given the different form-meaning mappings of depicting vs. deictic gestures, we will now provide separate analyses for both gesture types.

### 6.1.1 Situated Prosodic Word Constraint and depicting gesture

To illustrate how the Situated Prosodic Word Constraint works with depicting gestures, consider again example (1). The nuclear accent is on the rightmost word "mud", which licenses an attachment of the gesture to it using Construction Rule 1. The derivation, which attaches the gesture to "mud", is shown in Figure 6.

The prosodic PHON and syntactic CAT information of the speech head daughter gets propagated to the mother node. We do not propagate the gesture form features to the mother node since we do not need to access gesture form any further. The timing of the situated utterance is recorded in the mother's TIME value. This information is necessary in case the (situated) word aligns with another gesture.

The semantic composition follows the standard English Resource Grammar (ERG) process, namely: the individual semantic formulae are decorated with a global label ($h_1$) which demonstrates the derivation of a single LF. Each formula is also augmented with a hook containing the local top label (LTOP, equated to the label of the main predication) and the semantic index. The LTOP of the predicate contributed by the speech daughter $l_6 : a_6 : \_mud\_n\_1(x_1)$ is $l_6$ and the index is $x_1$. The

$$\begin{bmatrix} \text{OVERLAP} & \langle 1, 2 \rangle \\ \text{TIME} & 1 \cup 2 \\ \text{PHON} & \text{nuclear} \\ \text{SYN} & n' \\ \text{CONT} & \begin{bmatrix} \text{TOP} & h_1 \\ \text{HK} & \begin{bmatrix} \text{LTOP} & l_7 \\ \text{IDX} & x_2 \end{bmatrix} \\ \text{RL} & \begin{bmatrix} \text{vis\_rel} \\ \text{LBL} & l_7 \\ \text{ARG0} & e_1 \\ \text{S-LBL} & l_6 \\ \text{G-LBL} & l_0 \\ \text{M-ARG} & x_2 \end{bmatrix}, \boxed{N_{sem}}, \boxed{G_{sem}} \\ \text{HC} & \boxed{G_{=q}} \end{bmatrix} \end{bmatrix}$$

Left daughter:

$$\begin{bmatrix} \text{TIME} & 1 \\ \text{PHON} & \text{nuclear} \\ \text{CAT} & n \\ \text{CONT} & \begin{bmatrix} \text{TOP} & h_1 \\ \text{HK} & \begin{bmatrix} \text{LTOP} & l_6 \\ \text{IDX} & x_1 \end{bmatrix} \\ \text{RL} & \boxed{N_{sem}} \left\langle \begin{bmatrix} \text{\_mud\_n\_1} \\ \text{LBL} & l_6 \\ \text{ARG0} & x_1 \end{bmatrix} \right\rangle \end{bmatrix} \end{bmatrix}$$

$mud$

Right daughter:

$$\begin{bmatrix} \text{TIME} & 2 \\ \text{CONT} & \begin{bmatrix} \text{TOP} & h_1 \\ \text{HK} & \begin{bmatrix} \text{LTOP} & l_0 \\ \text{IDX} & i_{1-5} \end{bmatrix} \\ \text{RL} & \boxed{G_{sem}} \left\langle \begin{bmatrix} [\mathcal{G}] \\ \text{LBL} & l_0 \\ \text{ARG0} & h_0 \end{bmatrix}, \begin{bmatrix} \text{hand\_shape\_bent} \\ \text{LBL} & l_1 \\ \text{ARG0} & i_1 \end{bmatrix}, ..., \begin{bmatrix} \text{hand\_movement\_circular} \\ \text{LBL} & l_5 \\ \text{ARG0} & i_5 \end{bmatrix} \right\rangle \\ \text{HC} & \boxed{G_{=q}} \{ h_0 =_q l_1, ..., h_0 =_q l_5 \} \end{bmatrix} \end{bmatrix}$$

$$\begin{bmatrix} \text{HAND-SHAPE} & \text{bent} \\ ... \\ \text{HAND-MOVEMENT} & \text{circular} \end{bmatrix}$$

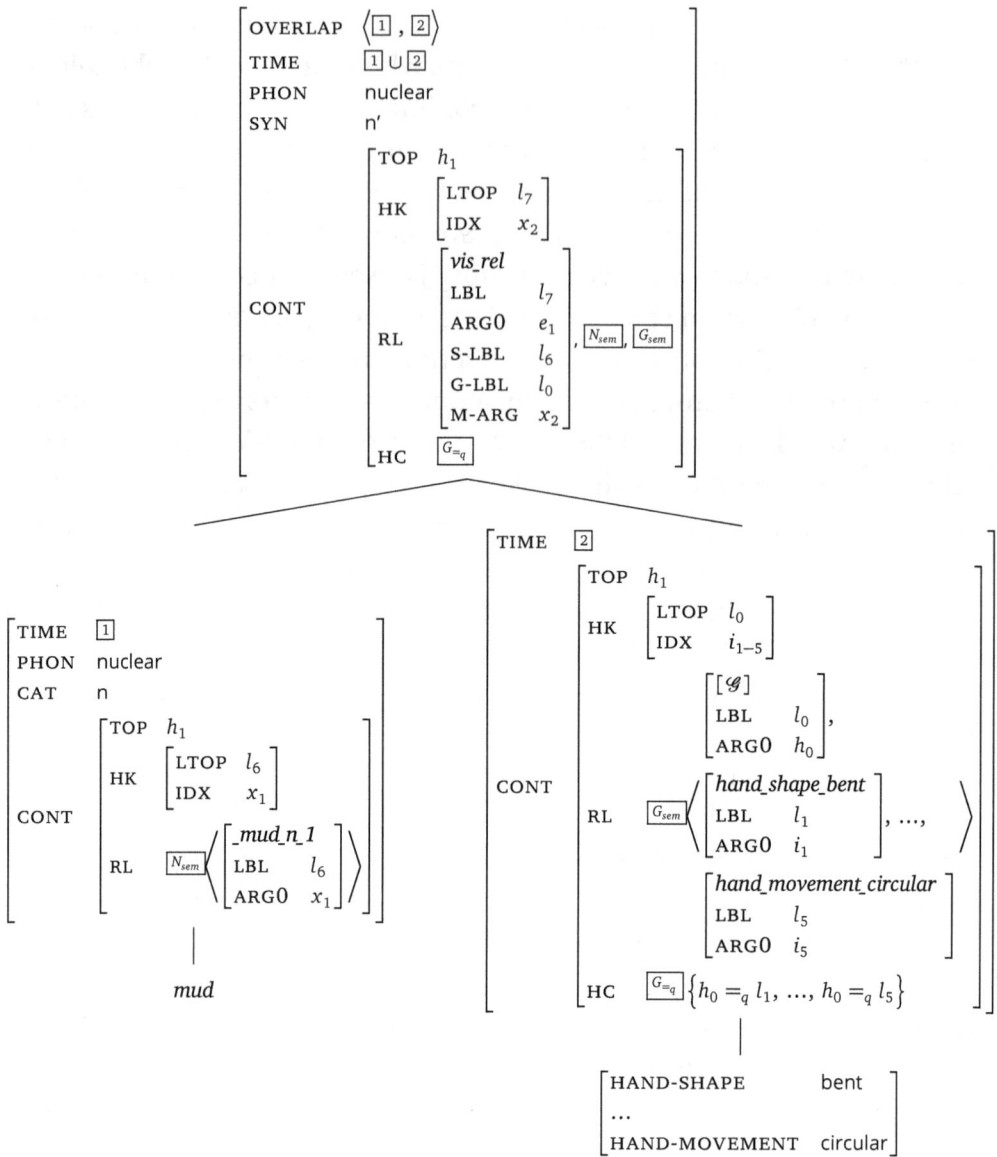

Figure 6: Derivation tree for depicting gesture and the N "mud"

LTOP of the gesture daughter is equated to the label of the $\mathcal{G}$ modality – $l_0$. Regarding the gesture semantic index, the gesture LF is too underspecified to know which of the semantic predications will resolve to the main variable and hence at this stage we have no information as to which is the semantic index of the formula. We therefore use $i_{1-5}$ as a shorter notation for a disjunction of co-indexations to reflect the fact that the underspecified variable $i_1 \ldots i_5$ of each gesture predicate could potentially resolve to the main variable: event $e$ or individual $x$.

Note that the semantic representation CONT of the situated utterance which features the underspecified relation *vis_rel* between the top label $l_6$ of the speech daughter and the top label $l_0$ of the gesture daughter to designate that the speech and gesture are coherently connected. In RMRS, labels denote the scopal position of an elementary predication. We therefore code the arguments of *vis_rel* as S-LBL and G-LBL to designate that their values are labels of spoken and gestural predications, respectively. As illustrated in Section 2.1, *vis_rel* is resolvable at the semantics/pragmatics interface to a specific value – e.g., Depiction, Elaboration – that is dependent on resolving the gestural denotation. Here, the attachment to "mud" would support an interpretation where the gesture designates some substance and the fact that it was going round, which in turn would resolve *vis_rel* to Elaboration, as featured in the LF in (5). The truth conditional contribution of the gesture will thus ultimately be roughly analogous to an appositive or a non-restrictive relative clause modifying the noun. Note that given constraints on reference on the semantics/pragmatics interface, this attachment blocks the gesture referring to anything that is bridging related to "mixes" or "he".

The CONT of the mother is obtained by equating the TOP of the mother to the TOP of the daughters. The relations (abbreviated as RL) of the situated phrase are equal to the append of the predications of the gesture daughter $\boxed{G_{sem}}$ and the speech daughter $\boxed{N_{sem}}$, and also *vis_rel*. Further, *vis_rel* introduces a multimodal argument M-ARG which serves as a semantic index of the integrated speech-gesture signal (the hook's index is therefore equated to the index of M-ARG – $x_2$), and so it can be taken as an argument by any external predicate. Here, for instance, the verb "mix" would take two arguments: ARG1 – corresponding to the subject – would be identified with ARG0 of "he", and ARG2 – corresponding to the object – would be identified with M-ARG of the situated word, consisting of "mud" and the gesture.

### 6.1.2    Situated Prosodic Word Constraint and deictic gesture

We illustrate the syntactic derivation and the semantic composition for deixis and a spoken word using utterance (14). The derivation tree is shown in Figure 7. The Situated Prosodic Word Constraint licenses an attachment of the deictic gesture to the verb "enter": it is marked by a pre-nuclear accent, and it temporally overlaps the gesture.

$$
\begin{bmatrix}
\text{OVERLAP} & \langle \boxed{1}, \boxed{2} \rangle \\
\text{TIME} & \boxed{1} \cup \boxed{2} \\
\text{PHON} & \text{pre-nuclear} \\
\text{SYN} & v' \\
\text{CONT} & \begin{bmatrix}
\text{TOP} & h_0 \\
\text{HK} & \begin{bmatrix} \text{LTOP} & l_4 \\ \text{IDX} & e_5 \end{bmatrix} \\
\text{RL} & \begin{bmatrix} deictic\_rel \\ \text{LBL} \ l_4 \\ \text{ARG0} \ e_5 \\ \text{ARG1} \ e_5 \\ \text{ARG2} \ e_7 \end{bmatrix}, \begin{bmatrix} deictic\_q \\ \text{LBL} \ l_1 \\ \text{ARG0} \ e_6 \\ \text{RSTR} \ h_1 \\ \text{BODY} \ h_2 \end{bmatrix}, \begin{bmatrix} sp\_ref \\ \text{LBL} \ l_{21} \\ \text{ARG0} \ e_7 \\ \text{ARG1} \ v(\vec{p}) \end{bmatrix}, \begin{bmatrix} hand\_shape\_flat \\ \text{LBL} \ l_{22} \\ \text{ARG0} \ e_0 \\ \text{ARG1} \ e_8 \end{bmatrix}, ..., \begin{bmatrix} hand\_location\_c \\ \text{LBL} \ l_{26} \\ \text{ARG0} \ e_4 \\ \text{ARG1} \ i_{12} \end{bmatrix}, \boxed{V_{sem}} \\
\text{HC} & \boxed{D_{=q}} \\
\text{EQS} & \{ l_{21} = l_{22} = ... = l_{26};\ e_6 = e_7 ... = e_{12} \}
\end{bmatrix}
\end{bmatrix}
$$

$$
\begin{bmatrix}
\text{TIME} & \boxed{1} \\
\text{PHON} & \text{pre-nuclear} \\
\text{SYN} & v \\
\text{CONT} & \begin{bmatrix}
\text{TOP} & h_0 \\
\text{HK} & \begin{bmatrix} \text{LTOP} & l_4 \\ \text{IDX} & e_5 \end{bmatrix} \\
\text{RL} & \boxed{V_{sem}} \Bigg\langle \begin{bmatrix} \_enter\_v\_1) \\ \text{LBL} \ l_4 \\ \text{ARG0} \ e_5 \\ \text{ARG1} \ u_1 \\ \text{ARG2} \ u_2 \end{bmatrix} \Bigg\rangle
\end{bmatrix}
\end{bmatrix}
$$

*enter*

$$
\begin{bmatrix}
\text{TIME} & \boxed{2} \\
\text{CONT} & \begin{bmatrix}
\text{TOP} & h_0 \\
\text{HK} & \begin{bmatrix} \text{LTOP} & l_3 \\ \text{IDX} & i_1 \end{bmatrix} \\
\text{RL} & \Bigg\langle \begin{bmatrix} deictic\_q \\ \text{LBL} \ l_1 \\ \text{ARG0} \ i_0 \\ \text{RSTR} \ h_1 \\ \text{BODY} \ h_2 \end{bmatrix}, \begin{bmatrix} sp\_ref \\ \text{LBL} \ l_{21} \\ \text{ARG0} \ e_7 \\ \text{ARG1} \ v(\vec{p}) \end{bmatrix}, \begin{bmatrix} hand\_shape\_flat \\ \text{LBL} \ l_{22} \\ \text{ARG0} \ e_0 \\ \text{ARG1} \ i_2 \end{bmatrix}, ..., \begin{bmatrix} hand\_location\_c \\ \text{LBL} \ l_{26} \\ \text{ARG0} \ e_4 \\ \text{ARG1} \ i_6 \end{bmatrix} \Bigg\rangle \\
\text{HC} & \boxed{D_{=q}} \{ h_1 =_q l_{21} \} \\
\text{EQS} & \{ l_{21} = l_{22} = ... = l_{26},\ i_0 = i_1 ... = i_6 \}
\end{bmatrix}
\end{bmatrix}
$$

$$
\begin{bmatrix}
deictic\text{-}abstract \\
\text{HAND-SHAPE} \quad \text{flat} \\
... \\
\text{HAND-LOCATION} \quad \vec{c}
\end{bmatrix}
$$

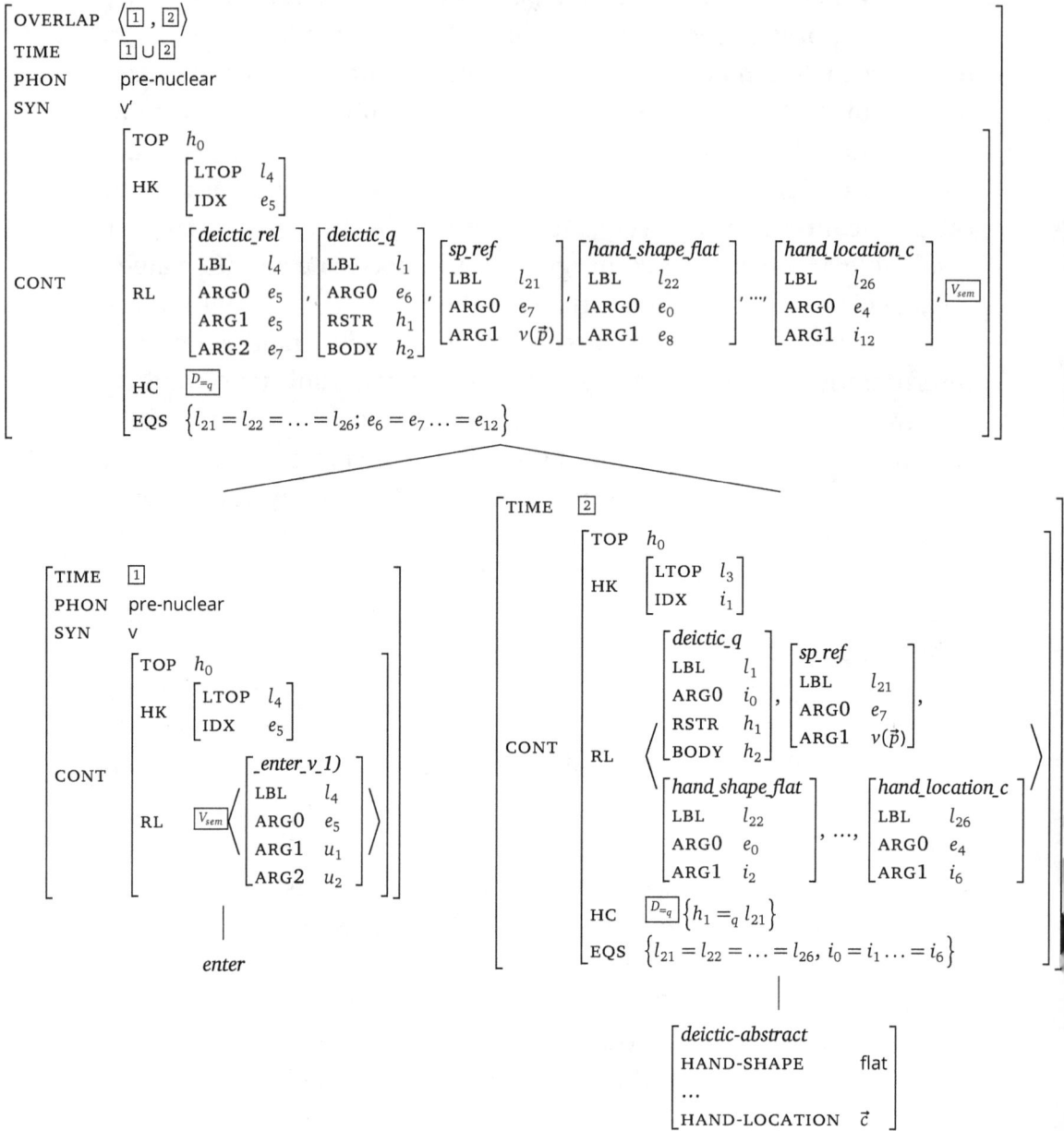

Figure 7: Derivation tree for deictic gesture and the V "enter"

The semantic composition proceeds in the same way as with depicting gestures. Since the gesture semantics features a quantifier (*deictic_q*), the local top of gesture is distinct from the label of the quantifier. The semantic index is the underspecified variable $i_1$ bound by *sp_ref*. In composition, the deixis semantic predicates (as shown

in 19) append to the semantic predicate $\boxed{V_{sem}}$ of the speech daughter
– $l_4 : a_9 : \_enter\_v\_1(e_5)$ $l_4 : a_9 : ARG1(u_1)$ $l_4 : a_9 : ARG2(u_2)$. In so
doing, the underspecified semantic index $i_1$ of the deixis unifies with
the semantic index $e_5$ of the speech, and so the underspecified gesture
variable $i_1$ of $sp\_ref(i_1)$ resolves to an event $(e_7)$.

Like depicting gestures, deictic gestures are connected in semantics to their aligned speech via an (underspecified) relation. The
construction rule therefore introduces the underspecified relation
$deictic\_rel(e_5, e_7)$ between the semantic index $e_5$ of the speech predication and the semantic index $e_7$ of the deictic gesture. Pragmatics
must then resolve this relation to a specific value: one possible resolution would be VirtualCounterpart – i.e., the deictic gesture denotes a
virtual counterpart of the coordinates of entering the apartment door.
Similarly to the treatment of non-scopal modification in language, this
relation shares the same label as the speech head daughter since it further restricts the referent introduced by the gesture. Informally, the
gesture here functions as an appositive in language and a rough linguistic paraphrase is "the entering event, the event at the coordinates
pointed at".

## 6.2          *Speech phrase and gesture alignment*

One of our central claims is that ambiguities as to which speech phrase
a co-speech gesture aligns with are best modelled as attachment ambiguities within the grammar. As we demonstrated in Section 2.2, the
relative timing of speech and gesture is not the only constraint on using
such construction rules; also, temporal constraints should be weaker
than *simultaneity*, contrary to McNeill (1992). Rather, we argued that
the gesture should temporally overlap with its aligned speech (if it
didn't, then by definition it wouldn't be co-speech gesture!) and furthermore temporally overlap with an *accented element* in the (aligned)
speech unit. Thus a single utterance such as (1) or (14) can licence
different speech-gesture alignments, each of them supporting a distinct range of plausible pragmatic interpretations in accordance with
constraints on reference (see Section 2.1). Likewise, it is perfectly acceptable for the gesture in (1) to be performed only while uttering the
accented word "mud", and still interpret the gesture in all the ways
proposed in Section 2.2. In this section we provide the formal methodology of how to arrive at these interpretations.

As proposed in Section 2.2, we introduce construction rules that allow a gesture to align with an *entire constituent* – that is, a head combined with its arguments – in contrast to Rule 1 that aligns gesture with a (temporally overlapping, accented) word. From a descriptive perspective, the inclusion of more context into the speech aligned with gesture is grounded in the "synthetic" nature of gesture versus the "analytic" nature of the spoken words (McNeill 2005). For instance, in example (1) the information about the direction of the mixing event (i.e., clockwise, downwards), the manner of performing the mixing action (i.e., using the entire hand) is denoted by a single visual performance and by several linearly ordered lexical items ("mixes", "mud"). For the purposes of a multimodal grammar it is essential to distinguish between temporal synchrony and alignment: whereas the former is a quantitative measurement of when the two modalities happen, the latter is a qualitative, linguistic notion pertaining to the syntax tree of speech and gesture and the meaning representation it corresponds to. By setting apart these two notions, we also ensure that the physical termination of the gesture does not enable attachment to a midpoint of a speech constituent.

With all this in mind, we now define the construction rule that allows a gesture to attach to a constituent larger than a single prosodic word:

**Construction Rule 2** (Situated Spoken Phrase Constraint). *A depicting or deictic gesture can attach to any of the higher projections in the derivation tree of the nuclear/pre-nuclear accent element, which also form a syntactic and/or prosodic constituent xp, no matter what the syntactic label is if there is an overlap between the temporal performance of the gesture stroke and xp.*

The attachment of the gesture to any projection in the tree would allow for saturating the head with its selected arguments before the attachment takes place. This means that the attachments are licensed at each saturation step. In this way, we account for the fact that gesture can co-refer to any or all of these arguments in the fully resolved pragmatic interpretation. Note also that Rule 2 used 'syntactic and/or prosodic constituent' to refer to any phrase of a hierarchical organisation: prosodic or syntactic. Assuming an analysis where there is no isomorphism between syntax and prosody, this flexibility is necessary whenever there are mismatches between prosodic structure and syntactic structure.[8]

Since the attachments of depicting gesture to a speech phrase are analogous to the attachments of deixis to the speech phrase, we illustrate the possible attachments using the depicting gesture in utterance (1). Recall from Section 2.2 that the resolved LFs for this speech-gesture action featured coherence relations between: (i) the NP's denotation and the 'rotating' gesture, and (ii) between the VP's (or S's) denotation and the 'rotating' gesture. We discussed (i) in the previous section and we therefore forego any further details about it. Given the construction rule in 2, interpretation (ii) is supported as follows: attach the gesture to VP "mixes mud" (or to the S "he mixes mud"). In both cases, the gesture stroke temporally overlaps the nuclear prominent "mud", and so the gesture can attach to its VP projection or S projection. Both of these attachments force the gesture to qualify "mixes" (for the second argument to the underspecified coherence relation that's introduced by the construction rule must outscope $mix(e, y, x)$). They underspecify, however, the relative scope of the coherence relation with respect to the predication $mud(x)$ and $pron(y)$. If these resolve to being within the scope of the coherence relation, then the resolved interpretation of the gesture can co-refer to *he* and to the mud; if not, it can't.

Further to this, we claimed that utterance (10) was ill-formed since the gesture was performed along a non-accented item in an all-rheme utterance. Having introduced the construction rules 1 and 2, we are now in a position to account for the utterance's ill-formedness: the form of (10) doesn't meet the constraints for either of our construction rules. On the other hand, if the gesture was performed in a way that temporally overlaps the prosodic word "mother", then the rules we've proposed license attachments to the N "mother", the NP "your mother" and even to the S "your mother called".

---

[8] In prior work on HPSG-based analysis of prosody (Klein 2000), prosodic structures are analysed in parallel with syntactic structures.

6.3                    *Spoken word and gesture alignment:*
                       *temporal and prosodic relaxation*

The two construction rules we've proposed allow a co-speech gesture to align with a prosodic word or with a constituent that contains
prosodic element(s) that overlap the temporal performance of the gesture. These constructions, however, are not sufficient as they do not
reflect an important finding from our data. We used examples (12) and
(13) to illustrate that when the referent of the deictic gesture is visually
salient, the deictic gestures does *not* necessarily overlap a prosodically
prominent word and/or temporally overlap the semantically related
word. The following rule takes this into account.

**Construction Rule 3** (Deictic Prosodic Word with Defeasible Constraint). *The constraints on temporal overlap in 1 and 2 are defeasible,*
*i.e., a deictic gesture attaches to a word that is not prosodically promi-*
*nent and/or whose temporal performance is adjacent to that of the deictic*
*stroke if: (a.) the mapping v from gestured space $\vec{p}$ to space in denotation*
*$v(\vec{p})$ resolves to equality; and (b.) the temporal performance of the gesture*
*overlaps (some portion of) the spoken utterance containing the word.*

This temporal/prosodic relaxation rule integrates a defeasible
constraint with the view of producing LFs that in context resolve to
the intended meaning. As attested by (13),[9] the relaxation of this con-
traint depends on the salience of co-present individuals and it is thus
necessary only in utterances where the gesture denotation is physically present in the visible space, i.e., there is an equality between the
physical space that the hand points at and the gesture referent. This
rule accounts for the fact that certain characteristics of the context
(i.e., salience of the individual pointed at) are required for the rule
to apply. Otherwise, the interpretation could be infelicitous. Similar
issues occur with deictic expressions and other referential expressions
which require a salient individual in context for the utterance to be
felicitous (see Lücking *et al.* 2006a).

Note also that this rule constrains the alignment to temporal overlap between (some portion of) the utterance and the gesture. This
means that the grammar does not handle gestures performed either
before or after the temporal performance of the utterance since any-

---

[9] Many more examples can be found in the AMI corpus.

thing beyond the clausal level is a matter of relating discourse units. For instance, while the temporal overlap between the gesture and the speech signal in (13) takes care of aligning the gesture and the semantically related element – i.e., "she" in (13) – the gesture in (12) does not overlap any portion of the utterance containing "mouse" and hence the grammar rule cannot attach the gesture to the noun "mouse". Similarly to relating purely linguistic discourse segments, relating the gesture in (12) with the noun "mouse" is a matter of discourse processing that lies beyond the scope of the (syntactic) grammar.

With this constraint in mind, let us examine the possible derivations of utterance (13). The Situated Prosodic Word 1 would license attachments to the temporally overlapping prosodically prominent "said". Although syntactically well-formed, this attachment would not produce the contextually preferred (and the most intuitive) interpretation: namely, an identity between the gesture referent and the speech referent. An alternative attachment is provided by Construction Rule 3: the deictic gesture may attach to "she" thereby providing an interpretation where the gesture denotation is identical to the denotation of the pronoun "she".

## 7          IMPLEMENTATION AND EVALUATION

The main challenge for the grammar implementation stems from the non-linear input of speech-and-gesture actions. Existing grammar engineering platforms for unification-based grammars typically only parse linearly ordered strings, and so they do not handle multimodal signals whose input comes from separate channels connected through temporal relations. Also, these parsing platforms do not support quantitative comparison operations over the time stamps of the input tokens. This is essential for our grammar since temporal overlap constraints choices of attachment.

To solve this, we pre-processed the XML-based Feature Structure (FS) input so that overlapping TIME values were 'translated' into identical start and end edges of the speech token and the gesture token as follows:

```
<edge source="v0" target="v1">
       <fs type="speech_token">
<edge source="v0" target="v1">
       <fs type="gesture_token">
```

This pre-processing step is sufficient since the only temporal relation required by the grammar is *overlap*, an abstraction over more fined-grained relations between speech (S) and gesture (G) such as (*precedence(start(S), start(G)) ∧ identity (end(S), end(G))*).

The linking of gesture to its temporally overlapping speech segment happens prior to parsing via chart-mapping rules (Adolphs *et al.* 2008) which involve re-writing chart items into FSs. The `gesture-unary-rule` (Figure 8) rewrites an input (I) speech token in the context (C) of a gesture token into a combined speech + gesture token where the + GEST and + PROS values of the speech and gesture tokens are copied onto the output (O).

```
gesture-unary-rule := cm_rule &
  [+CONTEXT <gesture_token & [+GEST #gest]>,
   +INPUT <speech_token & [+PROS #pros]>,
   +OUTPUT <speech+gesture_token &
         [+GEST #gest, +PROS #pros]>,
   +POSITION "O1@I1, I1@C1" ].
```

Figure 8: Definition of `gesture-unary-rule`

The + PROS attribute contains prosodic information and the + GEST attribute is a feature-structure representation. The + POSITION constraint restricts the position of the I, O and C items to an overlap (@), i.e., the edge markers of the gesture token should be identical to those of the speech token, and also identical to the speech + gesture token. This chart-mapping rule recognises the gesture token overlapping the speech token and it records this by "augmenting" the speech token with the gesture feature-values.

Gestures overlapping more than one speech token were handled by further chart-mapping rules that distributed the gestural information onto multiple speech tokens within the temporal span of the gesture. So a gesture overlapping, say, three speech tokens, would get split into three gesture tokens. Then, the `gesture-unary-rule` was applied so as to instantiate a speech + gesture token for each speech token temporally overlapping the gesture. The result of this chart-mapping operation is multiple gesture-marked speech tokens whose span is identical to the span of the gesture.

A separate rule was also required for concrete deixis to account for the permitted precedence and sequence relations between the speech token and the concrete deictic gesture token. This rule (which we omit for the sake of space) remains neutral about the positional (and hence temporal) relation between the gesture token and the speech token, thus allowing a gesture token of type *deictic-concrete* to attach to each speech token from the input chart.

In the grammar, we extended the ERG word and phrase rules with prosodic and gestural information where the + PROS and + GEST features of the input token are identified with the PROS and GEST of the word and/or lexical phrase in the grammar. We then added a gesture lexical rule (Figure 9) which projects a gesture daughter to a complex gesture-marked entity for which both the PROS and GEST features are appropriate.

```
gesture_lexrule := phrase_or_lexrule &
  [ ORTH [ PROS #pros,
           GEST no-gesture],
    ARGS <[ ORTH [ GEST gesture-form,
                   PROS p-word & #pros ]]>].
```

Figure 9: Definition of `gesture_lexrule`

In line with Definition 1, this rule constrains PROS to a prosodically prominent word of type *p-word* thereby preventing a gesture from plugging into a prosodically unmarked word. The *gesture-form* value is a supertype over the distinct gesture types – depicting and deictic. The GEST feature of the mother is of type *no-gesture* to block any further recursive instantiation of this rule. The `gesture_lexrule` is inherited by a lexical rule specific to depicting gestures, and by a lexical rule specific to deictic gestures. In this way, we can encode the semantic contribution of depicting gestures which is different from the semantic contribution of deixis. For the sake of space, Figure 10 presents only the `depicting_lexrule`. The semantic information contributed by the rule is encoded within C-CONT.

The rule introduces an underspecified *vis_rel* between the main label #dltop of the spoken sign (via the HCONS constraints) and the main label #glbl of the gesture semantics (via the HCONS constraints). Note that these two arguments are in a *geq* (greater or equal) constraint. This means that *vis_rel* can operate over any projection of the speech word; e.g., attaching the gesture to "mud" in (1) means that the relation is not restricted to the EPs contributed by "mud" but it can be also be over the EPs of a higher projection. Here, the implemented analysis differs from the theoretical one in that we formalise

```
depicting_lexrule := gesture_lexrule &
[ARGS <[ SYNSEM.LOCAL.CONT.HOOK.LTOP #dltop,
          ORTH [ GEST depicting] >,
  C-CONT [ RELS <![ PRED vis_rel,
                    S-ARG #arg1,
                    G-ARG #arg2 ],
                  [ PRED G_mod,
                    LBL #glbl,
                    ARG1 #harg ],
                  [ LBL #larg1 ],...!>,
          HCONS <!geq&[ HARG #arg1,
                        LARG #dltop ],
                  qeq&[ HARG #arg2,
                        LARG #glbl ],
                  qeq&[ HARG #harg,
                        LARG #larg1 ],
                  ...!>]].
```

Figure 10: Definition of `depicting_lexrule`

in semantics the gesture attachment ambiguities as per Situated Spoken Phrase Constraint: that is, *vis_rel* can operate over any projection of the gesture-marked sign.

The gesture's semantics is a bag of EPs, all of which are outscoped by the gestural modality $[\mathcal{G}]$. The rule therefore introduces in RELS a label (here `#larg1`) for an EP which is in *qeq* constraints with $[\mathcal{G}]$. The instantiation of the particular EPs comes from the gestural lexical entry. In the real implementation, the number of these labels corresponds to the number of features.

The evaluation was performed in the tradition of testing wide-coverage grammars, by means of a manually crafted test suite (Oepen *et al.* 1997). We created a test suite covering different gesture types, prosody and the following linguistic phenomena: intransitivity, transitivity, complex NPs, modification, negation and coordination. The test set contained 471 speech-gesture items (71.5% well-formed; 28.5% ill-formed) covering the full range of prosodic (prosodic markedness and unmarkedness) and gesture (the span of depicting/deictic gesture and its temporal relation to the prosodically marked elements) permutations. The gestural vocabulary was limited since a larger gesture lexicon has no effects on the performance. To test the grammar, we used the [incr tsdb()] competence and performance tool (Oepen 2001) which enables batch processing of test items and which creates a cov-

Table 1: Gesture grammar coverage profile of test items generated by [incr tsdb()]

| Aggregate | total items ♯ | positive items ♯ | word string φ | lexical items φ | distinct analyses φ | total results ♯ | overall coverage % |
|---|---|---|---|---|---|---|---|
| $90 \leq$ *i-length* $< 95$ | 126 | 91 | 93.00 | 26.41 | 1.89 | 91 | 100.0 |
| $70 \leq$ *i-length* $< 75$ | 78 | 53 | 71.00 | 12.00 | 1.00 | 53 | 100.0 |
| $60 \leq$ *i-length* $< 65$ | 249 | 179 | 60.00 | 9.42 | 1.00 | 179 | 100.0 |
| $45 \leq$ *i-length* $< 50$ | 18 | 14 | 49.00 | 7.00 | 1.00 | 14 | 100.0 |
| Total | 471 | 337 | 70.18 | 14.31 | 1.24 | 337 | 100.0 |

erage profile of the test set (see Table 1). The values are as follows: the left column separates the items per aggregation criterion (the length of test items);[10] the next column shows the number of test items per aggregate; then we have the number of grammatical items; average length of test item; average number of lexical items; average number of distinct analyses and total coverage.

We manually verified the coverage. While the grammar successfully parses all well-formed examples, the inclusion of a separate chart-mapping rule for concrete deixis results in overgeneration. We believe that the alternative method of enforcing strict precedence or strict sequence is too restrictive with respect to the possible interpretations supported by the distinct attachment configurations.

Finally, we also verified that the newly introduced rules did not change the coverage or increase the ambiguity of the existing broad-coverage grammar. We therefore ran both the ERG grammar and the gesture grammar on the ERG testsuite. The results shown in Table 2 were generated by both the ERG grammar and by the grammar equipped with the gesture rules. In other words, the gesture rules had no effects on the existing rules.

## 8        CONCLUSIONS

The work presented here advances a new theory in which the form-meaning mapping of speech-gesture actions was analysed using well-established methods from linguistics such as constraint-based syntactic derivation and semantic composition. In particular, we cap-

---

[10] Note the length here does not correspond to the actual length of tokens in each test item, since the tool also counts the XML tags.

| Aggregate | total items ♯ | positive items ♯ | word string φ | lexical items φ | distinct analyses φ | total results ♯ | overall coverage % |
|---|---|---|---|---|---|---|---|
| 55 ≤ *i-length* < 60 | 3 | 3 | 55.00 | 108.00 | 2.00 | 3 | 100.0 |
| 45 ≤ *i-length* < 50 | 7 | 7 | 49.00 | 69.00 | 16.86 | 7 | 100.0 |
| 40 ≤ *i-length* < 45 | 17 | 17 | 43.00 | 69.50 | 4.94 | 16 | 94.1 |
| 35 ≤ *i-length* < 40 | 32 | 32 | 37.00 | 41.87 | 2.84 | 32 | 100.0 |
| 30 ≤ *i-length* < 35 | 30 | 30 | 31.00 | 32.57 | 2.37 | 30 | 100.0 |
| 25 ≤ *i-length* < 30 | 13 | 13 | 25.00 | 42.00 | 1.67 | 12 | 92.3 |
| 15 ≤ *i-length* < 20 | 13 | 13 | 19.00 | 15.58 | 1.83 | 12 | 92.3 |
| Total | 115 | 115 | 34.13 | 43.99 | 3.63 | 112 | 97.4 |

(generated by [incr tsdb()] at 8-jul-2005 (04:42 h))

Table 2:[incr tsdb()] coverage profile of ERG test items parsed by ERG and gesture grammar

tured the mapping of form of speech-gesture actions to their meanings within a constraint-based grammar: the construction rules were inspired by examining real data and were further implemented within a wide-coverage grammar for English. The highly ambiguous gesture form was captured using underspecified semantics, which allowed us to account for the range of specific interpretations that a given gesture can take in its context of use. The ambiguities notwithstanding, we demonstrated that the speech-gesture attachments are constrained by the form of the speech signal, thus showing that the difference in ambiguity between linguistic input and gesture input is more a matter of degree than a difference in kind.

## ACKNOWLEDGEMENTS

The authors are very grateful to Elżbieta Hajnicz and the anonymous reviewers, Daniel Loehr, Matthew Stone, Mark Steedman, Emily Bender, Bob Ladd, Michael Johnston, Jonathan Kilgour, Ulrich Schäfer, Stephan Oepen, and also EPSRC for funding this work, as well as ERC (grant number 269427).

## REFERENCES

Dorit ABUSCH (2014), Temporal Succession and Aspectual Type in Visual Narrative, in Luka CRNIČ and Uli SAUERLAND, editors, *The Art and Craft of Semantics: A Festschrift for Irene Heim*, volume 1, pp. 9–29, MIT Working Papers in Linguistics, Cambride, MA.

Peter ADOLPHS, Stephan OEPEN, Ulrich CALLMEIER, Berthold CRYSMANN, Daniel FLICKINGER, and Bernd KIEFER (2008), Some Fine Points of Hybrid Natural Language Parsing, in *Proceedings of the Sixth International Language Resources and Evaluation*, ELRA.

Stergos AFANTENOS, Eric KOW, Nicholas ASHER, and Jeremy PERRET (2015), Discourse parsing for multi-party chat dialogues, in *Proceedings of the 2015 Conference on Empirical Methods in Natural Language Processing, Association for Computational Linguistics*, pp. 928–937, Lisbon.

Hiyan ALSHAWI (1992), *The Core Language Engine*, Cambridge: MIT Press.

Nicholas ASHER and Alex LASCARIDES (1998), Bridging, *Journal of Semantics*, 15(1):83–113.

Nicholas ASHER and Alex LASCARIDES (2003), *Logics of Conversation*, Cambridge University Press.

Janet Beavin BAVELAS and Nicole CHOVIL (2006), Hand gestures and facial displays as part of language use in face-to-face dialogue, in V. MANUSOV and M. PATTERSON, editors, *Handbook of Nonverbal Communication*, pp. 97–115, Thousand Oaks, CA: Sage.

Johan BOS (2004), Computational Semantics in Discourse: Underspecification, Resolution, and Inference, *J. of Logic, Lang. and Inf.*, 13(2):139–157, ISSN 0925-8531, doi:10.1023/B:JLLI.0000024731.26883.86, `http://dx.doi.org/10.1023/B:JLLI.0000024731.26883.86`.

Jean CARLETTA (2006), Announcing the AMI Meeting Corpus, *The ELRA Newsletter*, 11(1):3–5.

Jean CARLETTA (2007), Unleashing the killer corpus: experiences in creating the multi-everything AMI Meeting Corpus, *Language Resources and Evaluation*, 41(2):181–190.

Justine CASSELL, David MCNEILL, and K.E. MCCULLOUGH (1999), Speech-Gesture Mismatches: Evidence for One Underlying Representation of Linguistic and Non-Linguistic Information, *Pragmatics and Cognition*, 7(1):1–33.

Ann COPESTAKE (2007), Semantic composition with (robust) minimal recursion semantics, in *DeepLP '07: Proceedings of the Workshop on Deep Linguistic Processing*, pp. 73–80, Association for Computational Linguistics, Morristown, NJ, USA.

Ann COPESTAKE and Ted BRISCOE (1995), Semi-Productive Polysemy and Sense Extension, *Journal of Semantics*, 12:15–67.

Ann COPESTAKE, Dan FLICKINGER, Ivan SAG, and Carl POLLARD (2005), Minimal Recursion Semantics: An introduction, *Journal of Research on Language and Computation*, 3(2–3):281–332.

Ann COPESTAKE, Alex LASCARIDES, and Dan FLICKINGER (2001), An Algebra for Semantic Construction in Constraint-based Grammars, in *Proceedings of the*

*39th Annual Meeting of the Association for Computational Linguistics (ACL/EACL 2001)*, pp. 132–139, Toulouse.

Markus EGG, Alexander KOLLER, and Joachim NIEHREN (2001), The Constraint Language for Lambda Structures, *Journal of Logic, Language and Information*, 10:457–485, ISSN 0925-8531, doi:10.1023/A:1017964622902, http://portal.acm.org/citation.cfm?id=595849.596040.

Randi ENGLE (2000), *Toward a Theory of Multimodal Communication: Combining Speech, Gestures, Diagrams and Demonstrations in Structural Explanations*, Stanford University, PhD thesis.

Dan FLICKINGER (2000), On Building a More Efficient Grammar by Exploiting Types, *Natural Language Engineering*, 6 (1) (Special Issue on Efficient Processing with HPSG):15–28.

Ellen FRICKE (2008), *Foundations of a Multimodal Grammar for German: Syntactic Structures and Functions (Grundlagen einer multimodalen Grammatik des Deutschen: Syntaktische Strukturen und Funktionen)*, Europa-Universität Viadrina Frankfurt (Oder), Habilitation, Manuskript. Original document in German.

Gianluca GIORGOLO (2012), Integration of Gesture and Verbal Language: A Formal Semantics Approach, in Eleni EFTHIMIOU, Georgios KOUROUPETROGLOU, and Stavroula-Evita FOTINEA, editors, *Gesture and Sign Language in Human-Computer Interaction and Embodied Communication*, volume 7206 of *Lecture Notes in Computer Science*, pp. 216–227, Springer Berlin Heidelberg, ISBN 978-3-642-34181-6, doi:10.1007/978-3-642-34182-3_20, http://dx.doi.org/10.1007/978-3-642-34182-3_20.

Gianluca GIORGOLO and Ash ASUDEH (2011), Multimodal Communication in LFG: Gestures and the Correspondence Architecture , in Miriam BUTT and Tracy Holloway KING, editors, *The Proceedings of the LFG 2011 Conference*, pp. 257–277, Hong Kong, http://cslipublications.stanford.edu/LFG/16/abstracts/lfg11abs-giorgoloasudeh2.html.

Gianluca GIORGOLO and Frans VERSTRATEN (2008), Perception of speech-and-gesture integration, in *Proceedings of the International Conference on Auditory-Visual Speech Processing 2008*, pp. 31–36.

Erving GOFFMAN (1963), *Behavior in Public Places: Notes on the Social Organization of Gatherings*, The Free Press.

Alex GRZANKOWSKI (2015), Pictures Have Propositional Content, *Review of Philosophy and Psychology*, 6(1):151–163, ISSN 1878-5158, doi:10.1007/s13164-014-0217-0, http://dx.doi.org/10.1007/s13164-014-0217-0.

Florian HAHN and Hannes RIESER (2010), Explaining Speech Gesture Alignment in MM Dialogue Using Gesture Typology, in Paweł ŁUPKOWSKI and Matthew PURVER, editors, *Aspects of Semantics and Pragmatics of Dialogue. SemDial 2010, 14th Workshop on the Semantics and Pragmatics of Dialogue*, pp. 99–109, Polish Society for Cognitive Science, Poznań.

Jerry R HOBBS (1985), On the Coherence and Structure of Discourse, Technical report, Stanford University, Center for the Study of Language and Information.

Michael JOHNSTON (1998a), Multimodal Language Processing, in *Proceedings of the International Conference on Spoken Language Processing (ICSLP)*, Sydney, Australia.

Michael JOHNSTON (1998b), Unification-based Multimodal Parsing, in *Proceedings of the 36th Annual Meeting of the Association for Computational Linguistics and 17th International Conference on Computational Linguistics - Volume 1*, ACL 1998, pp. 624–630, Association for Computational Linguistics, Stroudsburg, PA, USA, doi:http://dx.doi.org/10.3115/980845.980949, http://dx.doi.org/10.3115/980845.980949.

Michael JOHNSTON, Philip R. COHEN, David MCGEE, Sharon L. OVIATT, James A. PITTMAN, and Ira SMITH (1997), Unification-Based Multimodal Integration, in Philip R. COHEN and Wolfgang WAHLSTER, editors, *Proceedings of the 35th Annual Meeting of the Association for Computational Linguistics and 8th Conference of the European Chapter of the Association for Computational Linguistics*, pp. 281–288, Association for Computational Linguistics, Somerset, New Jersey.

David KAPLAN (1989), Demonstratives, in J. ALMOG, J. PERRY, and H. WETTSTEIN, editors, *Themes from Kaplan*, Oxford.

Andrew KEHLER (2002), *Coherence, Reference, and the Theory of Grammar*, CSLI Publications.

Ruth KEMPSON, Wilfried MEYER-VIOL, and Dov M GABBAY (2000), *Dynamic syntax: The flow of language understanding*, Wiley-Blackwell.

Adam KENDON (1972), Some relationships between body motion and speech, in A. SEIGMAN and B. POPE, editors, *Studies in Dyadic Communication*, pp. 177–216, Pergamon Press, Elmsford, New York.

Adam KENDON (2004), *Gesture. Visible Action as Utterance*, Cambridge University Press, Cambridge.

Ewan KLEIN (2000), A constraint-based approach to English prosodic constituents, in *ACL '00: Proceedings of the 38th Annual Meeting on Association for Computational Linguistics*, pp. 217–224, Association for Computational Linguistics, Morristown, NJ, USA, doi:http://dx.doi.org/10.3115/1075218.1075246.

Alexander KOLLER, Michaela REGNERI, and Stefan THATER (2008), Regular tree grammars as a formalism for scope underspecification, in *Proceedings of the 46th Annual Meeting of the Association for Computational Linguistics: Human Language Technologies (ACL-08: HLT)*, Columbus, Ohio.

Stefan KOPP, Paul TEPPER, and Justine CASSELL (2004), Towards integrated microplanning of language and iconic gesture for multimodal output, in *ICMI '04: Proceedings of the 6th international conference on Multimodal interfaces*, pp. 97–104, State College, PA, USA, ACM, New York, NY, USA, ISBN 1-58113-995-0, doi:http://doi.acm.org/10.1145/1027933.1027952.

Stefan KOPP, Paul A. TEPPER, Kimberley FERRIMAN, Kristina STRIEGNITZ, and Justine CASSELL (2007), *Trading Spaces: How Humans and Humanoids Use Speech and Gesture to Give Directions*, pp. 133–160, John Wiley & Sons, Ltd, ISBN 9780470512470, doi:10.1002/9780470512470.ch8, http://dx.doi.org/10.1002/9780470512470.ch8.

Peter KÜHNLEIN, Manja NIMKE, and Jens STEGMANN (2002), Towards an HPSG-based Formalism for the Integration of Speech and Co-Verbal Pointing, in *Proceedings of Gesture – The Living Medium*, Austin, Texas.

Alex LASCARIDES and Matthew STONE (2006), Formal Semantics for Iconic Gesture, in *Proceedings of Brandial'06, the 10th International Workshop on the Semantics and Pragmatics of Dialogue (SemDial10)*, pp. 125–132, Universitätsverlag Potsdam, Potsdam, Germany.

Alex LASCARIDES and Matthew STONE (2009a), Discourse Coherence and Gesture Interpretation, *Gesture*, 9(2):147–180.

Alex LASCARIDES and Matthew STONE (2009b), A Formal Semantic Analysis of Gesture, *Journal of Semantics*, 26(4):393–449.

Stephen C. LEVINSON (1983), *Pragmatics*, Cambridge University Press, Cambrdige.

Daniel LOEHR (2004), *Gesture and Intonation*, Georgetown University, Washington DC, doctoral dissertation.

Andy LÜCKING, Hannes RIESER, and Marc STAUDACHER (2006a), Multi-modal Integration for Gesture and Speech, in David SCHLANGEN and Raquel FERNÁNDEZ, editors, *brandial'06 – Proceedings of the 10th Workshop on the Semantics and Pragmatics of Dialogue*, pp. 106–113, Universitätsverlag Potsdam, Potsdam.

Andy LÜCKING, Hannes RIESER, and Marc STAUDACHER (2006b), SDRT and Multi-modal Situated Communication, in David SCHLANGEN and Raquel FERNÁNDEZ, editors, *brandial'06 – Proceedings of the 10th Workshop on the Semantics and Pragmatics of Dialogue*, pp. 72–79, Universitätsverlag Potsdam, Potsdam.

David MCNEILL (1992), *Hand and Mind. What Gestures Reveal about Thought*, University of Chicago Press, Chicago.

David MCNEILL (2005), *Gesture and Thought*, University of Chicago Press, Chicago.

Richard MONTAGUE (1988), The Proper Treatment of Quantification in Ordinary English, in Jack KULAS, James H. FETZER, and Terry L. RANKIN, editors, *Philosophy, Language, and Artificial Intelligence*, volume 2 of *Studies in Cognitive Systems*, pp. 141–162, Springer Netherlands, ISBN 978-94-010-7726-2,

doi:10.1007/978-94-009-2727-8_7,
http://dx.doi.org/10.1007/978-94-009-2727-8_7.

Cornelia MÜLLER, Jana BRESSEM, and Silva H. LADEWIG (2013), Towards a grammar of gesture – a form based view, *Body–Language–Communication: An International Handbook on Multimodality in Human Interaction. (Handbooks of Linguistics and Communication Science 38.1)*, pp. 707–733.

Stephan OEPEN (2001), [incr tsdb()] — Competence and Performance Laboratory. User Manual, Technical report, Computational Linguistics, Saarland University, Saarbrücken, Germany.

Stephan OEPEN, Klaus NETTER, and Judith KLEIN (1997), TSNLP — Test Suites for Natural Language Processing, in John NERBONNE, editor, *Linguistic Databases*, pp. 13–36, CSLI Publications, Stanford, CA.

Patrizia PAGGIO and Costanza NAVARRETTA (2009), Integration and representation issues in the annotation of multimodal data, in Costanza NAVARRETTA, Patrizia PAGGIO, Jens ALLWOOD, Elisabeth ALSÉN, and Yasuhiro KATAGIRI, editors, *Proceedings of the NODALIDA 2009 workshop Multimodal Communication — from Human Behaviour to Computational Models*, volume 6, pp. 25–31, Northern European Association for Language Technology (NEALT).

Thies PFEIFFER, Florian HOFMANN, Florian HAHN, Hannes RIESER, and Insa RÖPKE (2013), Gesture Semantics Reconstruction Based on Motion Capturing and Complex Event Processing: a Circular Shape Example, in *Proceedings of the SIGDIAL 2013 Conference*, pp. 270–279, Association for Computational Linguistics, http://aclweb.org/anthology/W13-4041.

Livia POLANYI (1985), A Theory of Discourse Structure and Discourse Coherence, in *Proceedings of the 21st Meeting of the Chicago Linguistics Society*, Chicago, Illinois: Linguistics Department, University of Chicago.

Uwe REYLE (1993), Dealing with Ambiguities by Underspecification: Construction, Representation and Deduction, *Journal of Semantics*, 10:123–179.

I. A. SAG and T. A. WASOW (1999), *Syntactic Theory: A Formal Introduction*, Center for the Study of Language and Information, Stanford, California, ISBN 1575861615 (hard cover), 1575861607 (paper).

Mark STEEDMAN (2000), *The Syntactic Process*, The MIT Press.

Francis & Mark Turner STEEN (2013), Multimodal Construction Grammar, *Language and the Creative Mind*, pp. 255–274.

# 5

# A probabilistic model of Ancient Egyptian writing

*Mark-Jan Nederhof and Fahrurrozi Rahman*
School of Computer Science
University of St Andrews
United Kingdom

*Keywords: Ancient Egyptian, writing systems, language models*

## ABSTRACT

This article offers a formalization of how signs form words in Ancient Egyptian writing, for either hieroglyphic or hieratic texts. The formalization is in terms of a sequence of sign functions, which concurrently produce a sequence of signs and a sequence of phonemes. By involving a class of probabilistic automata, we can define the most likely sequence of sign functions that relates a given sequence of signs to a given sequence of phonemes. Experiments with two texts are discussed.

## 1 INTRODUCTION

Ancient Egyptian writing, used in Pharaonic Egypt, existed in the form of *hieroglyphs*, often carved in stone or painted on walls, and sometimes written on papyrus (Allen 2000). Hieroglyphs depict people, animals, plants and various kinds of objects and geographical features. A cursive form of Ancient Egyptian writing, called *hieratic*, was predominantly written on papyrus. Most hieratic symbols can be seen as simplified hieroglyphs, to such an extent that it is difficult for the modern untrained eye to tell what is depicted. Because hieratic handwriting varied considerably over time, with notable differences between regions and scribes, the creation of computer fonts for hieratic is problematic, and consequently scholars commonly resort to publishing hieratic texts in a normalized hieroglyphic font. Since Version 5.2,

Unicode contains a selection of 1071 hieroglyphs. Henceforth we will use the term *sign* to refer to a hieroglyph or a hieratic symbol.

The Ancient Egyptian language is in the family of Afro-Asiatic languages, which includes the Semitic languages (Loprieno 1995). As in writing systems of several Semitic languages (e.g. Hebrew, Arabic, Phoenician), only consonants are written. Modern scholars use 24 or 25 letters to transliterate Ancient Egyptian texts in terms of these consonants. Most are written as Latin characters, some with diacritical marks, plus aleph ꜣ and ayin ꜥ. An equal sign is commonly used to precede suffix pronouns; thus *sḏm* means "to hear" and *sḏm=f* "he hears". A dot can be used to separate other morphemes; for example, in *sḏm.tw=f*, "he is heard", the morpheme *tw* indicates passive.

The Ancient Egyptian writing system itself is a mixture of phonetic and semantic elements. The most important are *phonograms*, *logograms* and *determinatives*. A phonogram is a sign that represents a sequence of one, two or three letters, without any semantic association. A logogram represents one particular word, or more generally the lemma of a word or a group of etymologically related words. A determinative is commonly written at the end of a word, following phonograms, to clarify the meaning of a word; in their most obvious use, determinatives disambiguate between homophones, or more precisely, different words consisting of the same consonants. In addition, there are *typographical* signs, for example, three strokes that indicate the plural form of a noun (also used for collective nouns). These and more classes of signs are discussed in detail in Section 2.

What makes automatic analysis of Ancient Egyptian writing so challenging is that there was no fixed way of writing a word, so that table-lookup is largely ineffective. Even within a single text, the same word can often be found written in several different ways. Moreover, one sign can often be used in different functions, e.g. as phonogram or as determinative. Some signs can be used as different phonograms with different sound values. Together with the absence of word boundary markers, this makes it even hard to segment a text into words.

Generalizing statements can be made about writings of words. Typically, either a word starts with a number of phonograms, covering all the letters of the stem, possibly some covered more than once, followed by one or more determinatives, or a word starts with a logogram, possibly followed by one or more phonograms, possibly followed by one or more determinatives. More phonograms can follow the determinatives for certain suffixes. This coarse description is inadequate however to model the wide spectrum of writings of words, nor would it be sufficient to disambiguate between alternative analyses of one sequence of signs.

These factors motivate the search for an accurate and robust model that can be trained on data, and that becomes more accurate as more data becomes available. Ideally, the model should be amenable to unsupervised training. Whereas linguistic models should generally avoid unwarranted preconceptions, we see it as inevitable that our model has some knowledge about the writing system already built in, for two reasons. First, little training material is currently available, and second, the number of signs is quite large, so that the little training material is spread out over many parameters. The *a priori* knowledge in our model consists of a sign list that enumerates possible functions of signs and a formalization of how these functions produce words. This knowledge sufficiently reduces the search space, so that probabilistic parameters can be relatively easily estimated.

In our framework, a *sign function* is formally identified by the combination of (a) the one or more signs of its writing, (b) its class, which could be 'phonogram', 'logogram', 'determinative', etc., and (c) a sequence of letters or a description of a semantic value, depending on the class. One example is the phonogram function for sign ⬤ with sound value $r$. There is a logogram function for the same sign, with as value the transliteration of the lemma $r\beta$, which means "mouth". A typographical function for the three strokes may have a semantic value 'plurality or collectivity'.

The first attempt to systematically classify functions of signs in context may have been Schenkel (1984). The proposed system used a notation that is close to traditional transliteration, but with additional elements, capturing *some* functional aspects of *some* used signs. For example, for each determinative in the writing of a word, a superscript giving the name of the sign is added to the transliteration. Use of logograms was indicated by capitalizing letters of the stem in the transliteration. It is not possible however to reconstruct a complete hieroglyphic writing from an instance of this notation, and moreover this system does not seem to lend itself to formalization.

The problem we will address in the experiments is guessing the sign functions given the signs and the letters. This is related to the problem of automatically obtaining transliteration from hieroglyphic text. As far as we are aware, the earliest work to attempt this was Billet-Coat and Hérin-Aime (1994), which focussed on a multi-agent architecture to combine expert knowledge about signs, words and clauses. Another approach to automatic transliteration, by Tsukamoto (1997), used Unix applications such as 'grep' and 'sed'. The approach by Rosmorduc (2008) used manually produced rewrite rules. Further work along these lines by Barthélemy and Rosmorduc (2011) used two approaches, namely cascades of binary transducers and intersections of multitape transducers, with the objective to compare the sizes of the resulting automata.

A more modest task is to automatically align given hieroglyphic text and transliteration, as considered by Nederhof (2008), who used an automaton-based approach with configurations, similar to that in Section 5, except that manually determined penalties were used instead of probabilities. As we will demonstrate, the use of probabilities allows training of parameters of the model.

Relating hieroglyphic texts and their Egyptological transliteration is an instance of relating two alternative orthographic representations of the same language. The problem of mechanizing this task is known as machine transliteration. For example, Knight and Graehl (1998) consider translation of names and technical terms between English and katakana, and Malik *et al.* (2008) consider transliteration between Hindi and Urdu. Another very related problem is conversion between graphemes and phonemes, considered for example by Galescu and Allen (2002).

Typical approaches to solve these tasks involve finite-state transducers. This can be justified by the local dependencies between input and output, that is, ultimately the transliteration can be broken down into mappings from at most $n$ to at most $m$ symbols, for some small $n$ and $m$. For Ancient Egyptian however, it is unclear what those bounds on $n$ and $m$ would be. We therefore depart from finite-state methods, and propose a model that involves a tape, with a tape head that can jump left as well as right. This idea is reminiscent of alignment models of machine translation (Brown *et al.* 1993) and of the Operation Sequence Model (Durrani *et al.* 2015).

Sproat (2000) formulates the *Regularity* hypothesis, stating that orthographic processes can be realized in terms of finite-state methods. For Ancient Egyptian, he singles out two isolated phenomena, namely a particular writing of plurality (cf. Section 2.6) and honorific transposition (cf. Section 4). He argues that whereas their realization requires extra care, they can be realized in terms of finite-state methods nonetheless. He ignores more problematic phenomena however, such as phonetic complements (cf. Section 2.2) and phonetic determinatives (cf. Section 2.4), which are core elements of the writing system and form the main motivation for our non-finite-state automaton model. Thereby, Ancient Egyptian remains a significant challenge to the Regularity hypothesis.

In the sequel, we let 'Egyptian' refer to 'Ancient Egyptian'. The structure of this paper is as follows. Section 2 explains in more detail the sign functions that are distinguished in our model of Egyptian writing. An annotated sign list couples sign functions to signs, as explained in Section 3. The annotated texts themselves, which were used for training and testing, are presented in Section 4. A formal model of Egyptian writing is the subject of Section 5, extended with probabilities in Section 6. Experiments are discussed in Section 7.

## 2                        SIGN FUNCTIONS

In our formal framework, we distinguish the sign functions that are explained in the following sections. Except for 'spurious' functions, each function has exactly one value, specified at the end of each section.

### 2.1                        *Logograms*

A *logogram* is a sign that represents a word, or more accurately, the lemma of a word, or possibly a group of etymologically related words with closely related meanings. Often a logogram depicts the word it represents. For example, the aforementioned sign ⬯ can be a logogram for *r₃*, "mouth". In other cases, a logogram may represent an idea that can be associated with the thing that is depicted, rather than the thing itself. For example, ⬫ depicts a (standing) leg, while its meaning is the word *bw*, "place". A related example is the sign ⬫ depicting (walking) legs, with meaning *jw*, "to come".

An example where we would include etymologically related words is the following. The sign 🐝 can literally mean the thing that is depicted, namely *bjt*, "bee", but the same sign is used in much the same way for the etymologically related word *bjt*, "honey".

The value of a logogram is the transliteration of the lemma that it represents.

2.2                           *Phonograms*

Much of the Ancient Egyptian writing system evolved via the principle of *rebus writing* (Daniels and Bright 1996), that is, the use of a sign solely for its sound value, derived from one or more sounds that occur in the word expressing what the sign depicts. For example, from the logographic use of sign ⅃ for *bw*, "place", the use as *phonogram* evolved, allowing it to represent the letter *b* in the writing of any word.

For each letter, there is at least one phonogram that represents that letter in isolation. We call such a phonogram *uniliteral*. There are also several dozens of phonograms for sequences of two or three letters. For example, 🪶 is a (biliteral) phonogram with sound value *wn* and 🐦 is a (triliteral) phonogram with sound value *tjw*.

A word is often written using several phonograms, which together cover some letters more than once. A uniliteral phonogram representing a letter that is also represented by a neighboring biliteral or triliteral phonogram is known as a *phonetic complement*; there are examples in Figure 3 that will be discussed later.

As pointed out by e.g. Schenkel (1984), it can be very hard to distinguish between logograms and phonograms, especially in the case of triliteral phonograms that can by themselves write a whole word. For example, ⅃ can stand for the word *wḥmt*, "hoof", and in this use it is obviously a logogram, but it can also stand for the word *wḥm*, "to repeat". (The *t* in *wḥmt* is the feminine ending.) It is plausible that the two words are etymologically related, as the depicted cloven hoof 'repeats' a toe. However, traditionally the use of ⅃ in "to repeat" is analyzed as phonogram, as if its use was motivated by accidental similarity of the pronunciations of the two words. We have adopted that view.

One more example is the sign ⅂, which is primarily used as logogram for *nṯr*, "god". It is also used in the writing of the word *snṯr*, "incense", and one may naively interpret it as phonogram there. However, it is very likely that the sign is not merely chosen for its sound value, but for its semantic relationship to *nṯr*, "god", in combination with the causative prefix *s-*. An alternative etymology suggested by de Vartavan (2010) involves the verb *sn*, "to smell", in combination with *nṯr*, but either way, the sign ⌐ in *snṯr* is best analyzed as logogram.

In later stages of Egyptian, some pairs of sounds from earlier stages merged together. As a result, the corresponding signs were sometimes confused. One example is the use of a sign representing the sound *t* for writing a word whose historical pronunciation had a different sound *ṯ*. In our framework, we let the value of a phonogram be its historical sound value, regardless of how it is used. However, we follow Hannig (1995) in not distinguishing *s* from *z*. In Middle Egyptian, these two sounds had merged together to such an extent that even the (conservative) writing system treated both as largely exchangeable. Both sounds are therefore transliterated as *s*.

2.3                              *Determinatives*

A *determinative* is a sign that derives a semantic value from what is depicted, much like many logograms. However, determinatives are not used in isolation to form writings of words. Instead they must be combined with logograms and phonograms together covering all the letters. Typically, determinatives occur at the end of a writing, following the logograms and phonograms.

Most determinatives do not pertain to any particular word. For example, the "tree" determinative ◊ is used with various nouns related to trees, plants and wood. Another example is ▭, depicting a papyrus scroll with ties, which is used as determinative for words that express abstract notions. Thus we have ⌐△⌐, *jqr*, "excellent", where the first three signs are each uniliteral phonograms for the three letters in that word.

The sign 𓀀 can be used as determinative with the general meaning "man and his occupations". For example, it is used in ⌐⌐𓀀, *šmsw*, "follower" (someone accompanying the king). Here the first sign is a logogram for the verb *šms*, "to follow" and the second sign is a uniliteral phonogram with value *w*, a suffix which turns the verb into a masculine noun.

The distinction between determinatives and logograms is illustrated by the word *pryt*, "settlement", written as ⬚⬚. The first sign (reading left-to-right and top-to-bottom for stacked signs) is a logogram depicting the plan of a house, with meaning *pr*, "house", and derivatives. The next four signs are phonograms together covering the letters *r*, *y* and *t*. Note the *r* in *pryt* is covered by both the logogram and the first phonogram, which makes ⬡ here a phonetic complement. The second occurrence of ⬚ has a different function from the first. Here it is a determinative, clarifying that the written word has something to do with buildings.

A determinative may also be specific to one lemma. For example, ⎮ is generally used only for the noun *mnjt*, "mooring post", and its derivatives. One may ask what distinguishes such a determinative from a logogram, which is by definition also specific to one lemma. The answer lies in the different roles that logograms and determinatives fulfil in the writing of words, as illustrated above for *pryt*, "settlement".

When a determinative is specific to one lemma, the same sign can often be used as logogram as well, that is, the sign can be used to write a word without accompanying phonograms. For example, 🐾 can as logogram stand on its own for *ḫr*, "to fall", but it is determinative in the alternative writing ⬡ 🐾, *ḫr*, where it is preceded by two uniliteral phonograms.

The value of a determinative specific to a word is the transliteration of that word, such as *mnjt* for ⎮. The value of other determinatives is a general description of the kinds of concepts that are covered, such as "building, seat, place" for ⬚.


2.4                    *Phonetic determinatives*

A *phonetic determinative* is similar to a determinative in that it tends to be placed near the end of a word, next to normal determinatives. However, its value is phonetic, repeating letters already written by logograms and phonograms.

An example is given by the writing of the word *mnḫt*, "splendid (fem.)" in Figure 1. The phonetic determinative 𓏠 here has phonetic reading *mnḫ*. Note that unlike the phonograms, it occurs near the end of the word, even following the feminine *t* ending.

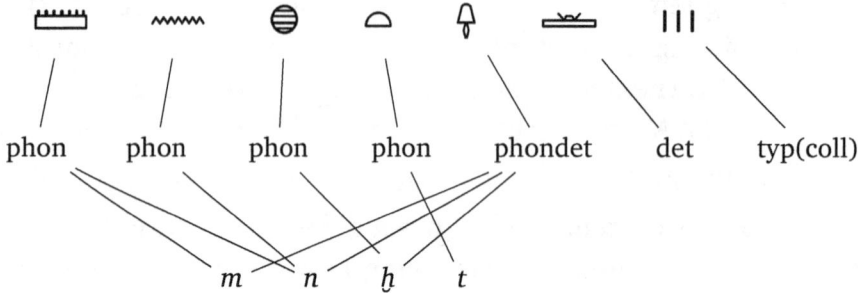

Figure 1:Use of a phonetic determinative

Many signs can be both phonograms and phonetic determinatives, even with the same sound value. We then classify an occurrence as the latter only if the corresponding letters have already been accounted for by earlier signs.

The value of a phonetic determinative is its (earliest historical) sound value.

### 2.5                    *Typographical signs*

Signs that fall outside any of the classes above will be called *typographical*. One example is the single stroke written under, or next to, another sign, most often a logogram. Often its function is to indicate that the meaning of that other sign is what is depicted, rather than, say, the sound value of that sign. We then call the single stroke a *semogram marker*. For example, $\ominus$ might mean *r₃*, "mouth", while $\ominus$, without semogram marker, might stand for the preposition *r*, "to". The sign $\ominus$ here is logogram or phonogram, respectively.

The function of the single stroke is not always clear however. More often than not, it acts as *space filler*; at this point we should explain that Egyptian writing is often influenced by aesthetical considerations, in particular the desire to fill up empty spaces between signs. As a consequence, 𓁷 can either mean *ḥr*, "face", or *ḥr*, "on". In the first case, the single stroke is clearly a semogram marker, but in the second it is merely a space filler.

Further typographical symbols consist of a combination of two or three strokes. These are typically written at the end of a noun as marker of duality or plurality. (Egyptian had a dual form next to a plural.) The three strokes were however also used for singular nouns with collective meanings, such as *rmṯ*, "people" and *jmnt*, "what is hidden". The three strokes are also written behind plural personal pronouns. Similarly, two strokes can be used for singular words whose meaning involves the idea of pairing two things or two people. An example is

[hieroglyphs], *snnw = f*, "his fellow".

There are also *false* dual and *false* plural writings, with two or three strokes for words that happen to end on -*wj*, -*tj* or -*w*, the masculine and feminine dual and masculine plural endings, while these words are not grammatically dual or plural. In these cases the group of two or three strokes is analyzed as phonogram with sound value *wj*, *j* (without the feminine ending *t*) or *w*. It is not always easy however to determine whether words ending on -*wj*/-*tj*/-*w* are (historically) dual or plural.

Further typographical symbols include the numerals. We analyze a number written using a sequence of numerals as one sign function. Egyptian numerals are a topic by themselves (Ifrah 1981) and further discussion here would not be productive.

A peculiar typographical function exists in a combination of signs that indicates the preceding (phrase, word or sequence of letters) should be read twice. An example is [hieroglyphs], *sksk*, "to destroy". Here the first three signs are phonograms together accounting for the first two letters *sk* of *sksk*. The following group [hieroglyph] then indicates the letters *sk* should be read a second time.

As value of a typographical function we take a description, which can be, for example, "semogram marker", "space filler", "duality", "plurality or collectivity", "replaces human figure, or sign difficult to draw" and "number".

2.6                              *Multiplication of signs*

We discussed above that duality and plurality (and collectivity) can be expressed by two or three strokes. There is an alternative way to express the same, by repeating a sign once or twice. For example, the logogram [hieroglyph] stands for *nṯr*, "god". By repeating it twice, we obtain [hieroglyphs], *nṯrw*, "gods". We recall -*w* is the masculine plural ending.

Typically only the last sign of a singular writing is repeated to obtain a dual or plural writing, but sometimes larger groups of signs are repeated. For example, ⬡ stands for *rn*, "name", written with two uniliteral phonograms for *r* and *n*, respectively. The plural can be written ⬡⬡⬡, *rnw*, "names".

Also determinatives may be repeated. An example is the writing of "the two lands (Upper and Lower Egypt)" as ▦, *t꜡wj*. We recall *-wj* is the masculine dual ending. A typical writing for the singular is | ▦, *t꜡*, "land", written with a logogram for *t꜡*, depicting a strip of land with three grains of sand, a semogram marker, and a determinative depicting irrigated land.

We have chosen a modeling of such writings that allows straight-forward automatic processing. This consists in taking all repeated signs together to correspond to a single function indicating plurality. In the example of "names", the first occurrences of ⬡ and ⌇ are analyzed as phonograms *r* and *n*, respectively, as they would be in the singular writing of the word. The two remaining occurrences each of ⬡ and ⌇ together indicate plurality. An example for duality, as illustrated in Figure 2a, will be discussed later.

As in the case of the dual and plural strokes (Section 2.5), there are false dual and false plural writings using duplication of signs. Common examples concern the nisbe form. A *nisbe* is an adjective derived from a noun by adding the ending *-j*. For example, ⊗, *njwt* means "town" while *njwtj* means "concerning the town; local". The latter word is typically written as ⊗⊗, which should be read "local" and not "the two towns".

There are cases of plural and collective nouns that are written us-ing three similar but *distinct* signs. For example, the word that means "cattle" can be accompanied by three determinatives depicting differ-ent kinds of cattle, and the word that means "birds" can be accompa-nied by three determinatives depicting different species of birds. These cases are rare enough to be ignored for the purposes of our model in Section 5. At this point we should emphasize that playfulness and cre-ativity are important features of Egyptian writing, and this precludes existence of an exhaustive list of orthographic phenomena.

The value of a multiplicative function is a number, which can be 2 for dual and 3 for plural. In rare cases, we also find multiplicative functions for the numbers 4 and 9.

### 2.7 *The spurious functions*

Occasionally we find signs that do not have a clear function. Some can be plausibly attributed to scribal errors. There are also cases however for which a historical explanation can be given. For example, the two signs 𓊖, representing crossing streets, and 𓏏, the phonogram for *t*, are often written as one 'frozen' group. This makes sense in the writing of the word *njwt*, "town", which has the (feminine) ending -*t*, with 𓊖 being a logogram. However, where 𓊖 is used as determinative with meaning "inhabited area" at the end of a masculine word (not ending on -*t*), we sometimes also find 𓏏. We then classify 𓏏 as spurious.

The spurious functions also contribute to creating a robust model. By interpreting some signs as 'spurious', the model can complete the analysis of a problematic writing as fall-back option if nothing else works. We return to this matter in Section 5.

### 2.8 *Combinations of signs having a function*

In the above, we have seen a few instances of a group of signs together having one function, in the case of multiplications of signs and in the case of typographical signs. Another example is 𓇗𓆼, which together represents the logogram *tꜣwj*, "the two lands". The signs in isolation represent two different plants, lily and papyrus, symbolizing Upper and Lower Egypt, respectively.

The group 𓇒𓇒 has a single function as phonogram with sound value *nn*. An isolated 𓇒 can only be a phonogram *nḫbt*. Similarly, the combination of signs 𓀀𓁐𓏥 has a single function as a determinative for a "group of people".

## 3 SIGN LIST

Essential to the application of our model is an annotated sign list. We have created such a list in the form of a collection of XML files.[1]

[1] http://mjn.host.cs.st-andrews.ac.uk/egyptian/unicode/

Apart from being machine-readable, these files can also be converted to human-readable web pages. Among other things, the files contain knowledge about the various functions of the 1071 signs from the Unicode repertoire, gathered from a number of sources, the foremost of which is Gardiner (1957). The annotated sign list is necessarily imperfect and incomplete, which is due to inadequacies of the Unicode set itself (Rosmorduc 2002/3; Polis and Rosmorduc 2013), as well as to the nature of Ancient Egyptian writing, which gave scribes considerable freedom to use existing signs in new ways and to invent new signs where existing signs seemed inadequate. We have furthermore ignored the origins of signs, and distinguish fewer nuances of sign use than e.g. Schenkel (1971). See Polis and Rosmorduc (2015) for a revised taxonomy of hieroglyphic sign functions, motivated by the goal of compiling sign lists.

The items in our annotated sign list most relevant to this article each consist of:

- a sequence of signs (sometimes multiple sequences of alternative writings),
- a sign function class of that sequence,
- a sequence of letters or a semantic value, depending on the class.

As discussed in Section 2, a sign can often be both a logogram or a determinative specific to a lemma. Similarly, sometimes a sign can be both a phonogram or a phonetic determinative. To avoid duplication, we have created two combined classes. Thus, the sign list distinguishes the following:

- logogram, with the transliteration of a lemma,
- determinative, with a description of meaning,
- logogram / determinative, with the transliteration of a lemma,
- phonogram, with a phonetic value,
- phonetic determinative, with a phonetic value,
- phonogram / phonetic determinative, with a phonetic value,
- typographical, with a description of meaning.

Note that multiplication of signs and spurious signs are not included in the sign list, as these are not properties of the signs themselves but consequences of particular use.

Some signs can be used instead of other signs. This happens in particular where one sign is a graphical variant of another. In order to avoid redundancy, the sign list then only contains a listing of the sign functions for the most representative of two or more graphical variants, plus references from less representative to more representative variants. Such a reference can be automatically expanded into the relevant functions of the most representative sign. Also the two combined classes (logogram / determinative, and phonogram / phonetic determinative) can be split into the individual classes for the purposes of the model of Section 5.

The sign list contains (very rudimentary) information about the morphological structure of the lemmas written by logograms, in particular the stem and the gender (of nouns). The motivation is that this is necessary in order to match sign occurrences to transliterations. For example, the information that the word *nmtt*, "step", denoted by the logogram △, is feminine can be used to infer that uses of the logogram in plural writings should be matched to *nmtwt*, "steps", with the feminine plural ending -*wt* in place of the feminine singular ending -*t*. Similarly, the logogram ⤳, for *ḫnj*, "to row", is accompanied by information that its stem is *ḫn*, so we can identify the use in the writing of *ḫn=f*, "he rows", without the weak consonant *j*, which disappears in most inflections.

# 4        CORPUS

There is currently only one comprehensive corpus of Late Egyptian, which is still under development (Polis *et al.* 2013). Corpora of Middle Egyptian, the object of our study, are scarce however. Moreover, we are not aware of any available corpora of hieroglyphic texts in which each sign is annotated with its function. One attempt in that direction was reported by Hannig (1995, p. XXXV), with the objective to determine the ratios of frequencies of four main classes of signs, using the first 40 lines of the text of Sinuhe.

It follows that in order to train and test our model, we had to create our own annotated corpus.[2] As yet, it is of modest size, including

---

[2] as part of the St Andrews corpus: http://mjn.host.cs.st-andrews.ac.uk/egyptian/texts/

just two classical texts, known as The Shipwrecked Sailor (Blackman 1932) and Papyrus Westcar (Blackman 1988). Disregarding damaged parts of the manuscripts, the segmented texts comprise 1004 and 2669 words, respectively.

For the convenience of annotation with sign functions, the texts were linearized, that is, information about horizontal or vertical arrangement of signs was discarded. Whereas the positioning of signs relative to one another can be meaningful, our current models do not make use of this; if necessary in the future, the exact sign positions can be extracted from another tier of annotation.

We normalized the texts by replacing graphical variants, such as ⟨hieroglyph⟩ and ⟨hieroglyph⟩, by a canonical representative, using machine-readable tables that are part of our sign list (Section 3). We also replaced composite signs by smallest graphemic units. For example, we replaced a single sign consisting of three strokes (typographical sign for plurality or collectivity) by three signs of one stroke each. Motivations for this include convenience and uniformity: in typeset hieroglyphic texts one may prefer to use three separate strokes and fine-tune the distance between them to obtain a suitable appearance.

The texts were annotated with functions, using a customized, graphical tool. In this tool one can select known functions for signs, as present in the XML files mentioned in Section 3, but the tool also gives the option to create new functions that are not covered by the sign list. Many such functions were found during annotation.

A peculiar phenomenon in Egyptian writing is *honorific transposition*, which means that a sign or word is written first, even though its linguistic position is further to the end of a word or phrase. This applies in particular to gods and kings. For example, The Shipwrecked Sailor has *dwꜣ.n=f n=j nṯr*, "he thanked the god for me", with the sign for *nṯr*, "god", written before the signs for *dwꜣ.n=f n=j*. Where there is honorific transposition in the corpus spanning more than one word, all these words are put together in one *segment*. Apart from honorific transposition, a segment in the annotated corpus is simply one word.

For each word (or segment), the annotated corpus has:

- the sequence of functions, and
- the sequence of letters of the transliteration.

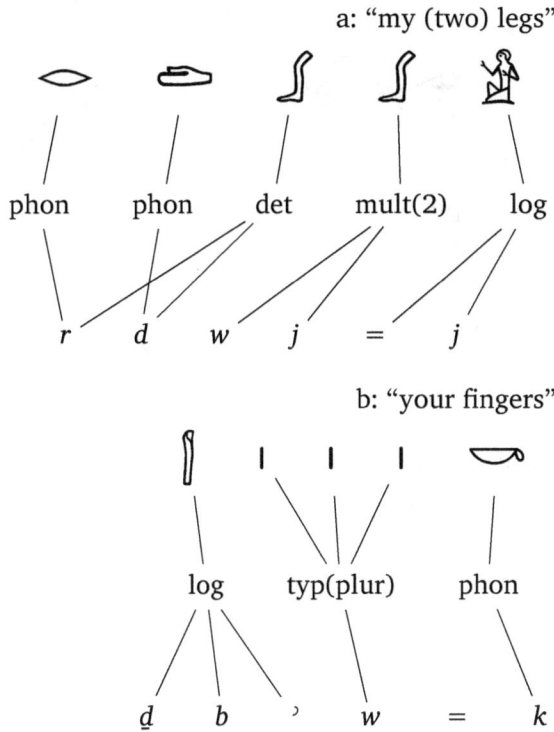

Figure 2: Annotations in the corpus (Shipwrecked Sailor)

The allowable functions are those listed in Section 2. Each function represents one or more signs, which are assumed to occur consecutively. Thereby the sequence of functions specifies the sequence of signs in the hieroglyphic writing. This was made possible by, among other things, our representation of the multiplicative functions (Section 2.6). An example is given in Figure 2a for *rdwj*, "pair of legs". Whereas the first 'leg' sign of the writing is represented by a determinative function, the second such sign is represented by a multiplicative function with value '2', that is, indicating duality.

Depending on their classes, functions may also represent letters, but due to such phenomena as phonetic complements, the sequence of letters of the transliteration is not determined uniquely by the sequence of functions. For this reason, the transliteration is present as separate tier, and functions are linked to the relevant letters of the transliteration, where applicable. In particular, phonograms and phonetic determinatives are linked in this way, and so are logograms and determinatives specific to words.

Also multiplicative functions may be linked to the letters of the dual/plural endings, as exemplified in Figure 2a. The same holds for a: "he is seen"

b: "water"

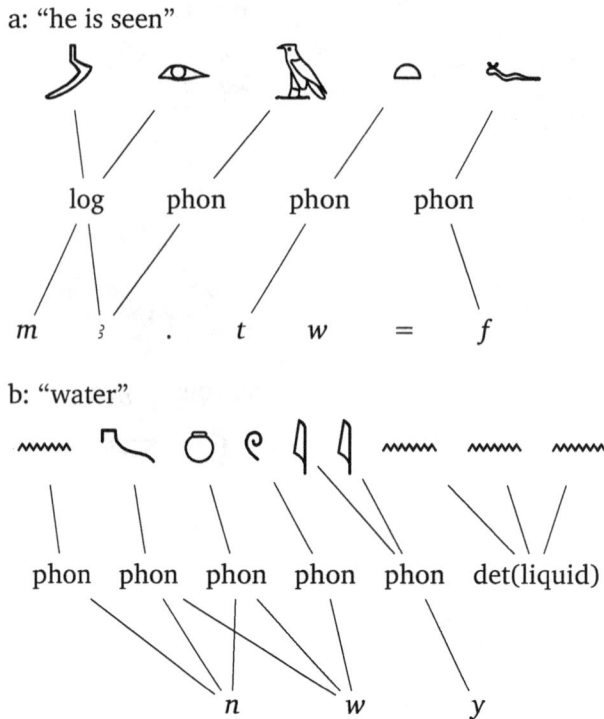

Figure 3: Further annotations (Shipwrecked Sailor)

the two or three strokes that indicate duality/plurality. An example is found in Figure 2b, for the plural of *ḏbꜣ*, "finger". Recall that the masculine plural ending is -*w*. Not linked to letters are determinatives that are not specific to any word, as exemplified in Figure 3b.

In the diagrams, the values of the functions are abbreviated or omitted altogether to avoid clutter. For example, we do not explicitly indicate the sound values of phonograms, which usually follow from the links between functions and letters. Also the lemmas of logograms and determinatives specific to words are not shown in the diagrams. Note that these may not be equal to the relevant letters from the transliteration. For example, the lemma of the first function in Figure 3a is in fact *mꜣꜣ*, "to see"; the second ꜣ disappears in some verb forms. Recall that the morpheme *tw* indicates passive; in this writing the *w* is not written out.

Figure 3b is interesting in that it shows two phonetic complements: both the first and the fourth signs are uniliteral phonograms that cover the letters *n* and *w*, which are also covered by the second and third signs, which are both biliteral phonograms.

An essential document while annotating the corpus was the annotation manual, which helped to disambiguate contentious cases, of which there were many. Examples of such cases were discussed in Section 2.2. We have as far as possible relied on conventional wisdom, but on several occasions we had to resort to informed guesses, making additions to the annotation manual to ensure consistency.

5                         MODEL

In order to motivate our model, we investigate Figure 3a. If we string together the letters coming from the respective functions we obtain *mȝȝtf* rather than the correct transliteration *mȝ.tw=f*. Similarly, for Figure 3b we would obtain *nnwnwwy*. There are two causes for this mismatch. The first is that letters can be written more than once, by several functions. In most cases this is done with phonetic complements, that is uniliteral phonograms, but we also find biliteral and triliteral phonograms as well as phonetic determinatives that cover letters already covered before. The second cause is that some letters in the transliteration, often weak consonants, are not represented by any signs at all. For pragmatic reasons, we will treat the Egyptological punctuation symbols, such as the period and the equal sign, on a par with weak consonants not written by signs.

For the second issue, our solution is to introduce an additional type of function, which we call *epsilon-phonogram*. Such a function acts much like a normal phonogram in the sense that a letter is produced in the transliteration, but it does not correspond to any sign (in other words, it corresponds to the empty, or epsilon string of signs).

For the first issue, that of letters covered several times, we conceive of the transliteration as being produced incrementally, in terms of a tape with a head that can move in both directions. In the simplest case, a function appends letters at the end of the tape, and moves the head a corresponding number of places to the right. This suffices for Figure 2b, as shown in Figure 4. The left column indicates the kind of function that is applied, omitting the associated signs, and the right column indicates the tape content, with the arrow marking the position of the head. Initially the tape is empty, and the tape head is at position 0. The logogram function then puts *ḏbʾ* on the tape, moving the tape head to position 3. Subsequently, the typographical function appends a *w*, moving the head to position 4. After application of an epsilon-phonogram and a phono-

$$
\begin{array}{l|l}
 & \downarrow \\
\log(\underline{d}b^{\backslash}) & \underline{d}\ b\ ^{\backslash}\ \downarrow \\
\text{typ(plur)} & \underline{d}\ b\ ^{\backslash}\ w\ \downarrow \\
\text{eps-phon}(=) & \underline{d}\ b\ ^{\backslash}\ w\ =\ \downarrow \\
\text{phon}(k) & \underline{d}\ b\ ^{\backslash}\ w\ =\ k\ \downarrow
\end{array}
$$

Figure 4: Computation for $\underline{d}b^{\backslash}w = k$

gram function, $=$ and $k$ will have been appended and the head is at position 6.

The situation is only slightly more involved for Figure 2a. Here the determinative specific to $rd$ should only be allowed if $rd$ occurs at the beginning of the tape. This 'lookback' amounts to a check of validity of the computation, but it does not alter the fact that the tape is written strictly from left to right, and the tape head always moves rightward.

However, a different approach is needed for cases such as those in Figure 3, which involve phonograms that cover letters more than once, some appending more letters to the tape at the same time. Our solution is to add one more type of function, which we call *jump*. This decrements (or increments) the position of the head, so a string of letters can be written starting from a position other than the end of the tape. The computation for $m_3.tw = f$ is given by Figure 5. Here a jump one position back allows another occurrence of $_3$ corresponding to a phonogram, after $_3$ was already seen as part of the logogram. Recall that the second $_3$ of the lemma $m_{33}$, "to see", is omitted in many verb forms. The second feature of '$\log(m_{33}, m_3)$' in our ad hoc notation attempts to convey that we are dealing with a particular use of this logogram that produces only the letters $m_3$ in the transliteration. For writing of other words, in which the full, geminated form is present,

$$
\begin{array}{l|l}
 & \downarrow \\
\log(m_{33}, m_3) & m\ _3\ \downarrow \\
\text{jump}(-1) & m\ \downarrow\ _3 \\
\text{phon}(_3) & m\ _3\ \downarrow \\
\text{eps-phon}(.) & m\ _3\ .\ \downarrow \\
\text{phon}(t) & m\ _3\ .\ t\ \downarrow \\
\text{eps-phon}(w) & m\ _3\ .\ t\ w\ \downarrow \\
\text{eps-phon}(=) & m\ _3\ .\ t\ w\ =\ \downarrow \\
\text{phon}(f) & m\ _3\ .\ t\ w\ =\ f\ \downarrow
\end{array}
$$

Figure 5: Computation for $m_3.tw = f$

|              |             |
|--------------|-------------|
|              | ↓           |
| phon($n$)    | $n$ ↓       |
| jump(-1)     | ↓ $n$       |
| phon($nw$)   | $n\,w$ ↓    |
| jump(-2)     | ↓ $n\,w$    |
| phon($nw$)   | $n\,w$ ↓    |
| jump(-1)     | $n$ ↓ $w$   |
| phon($w$)    | $n\,w$ ↓    |
| phon($y$)    | $n\,w\,y$ ↓ |
| det(liquid)  | $n\,w\,y$ ↓ |

Figure 6: Computation for *nwy*

|               |                   |
|---------------|-------------------|
|               | ↓                 |
| phon($mn$)    | $m\,n$ ↓          |
| jump(-1)      | $m$ ↓ $n$         |
| phon($n$)     | $m\,n$ ↓          |
| phon($ḫ$)     | $m\,n\,ḫ$ ↓       |
| phon($t$)     | $m\,n\,ḫ\,t$ ↓    |
| phondet($mnḫ$)| $m\,n\,ḫ\,t$ ↓    |
| det(abstract) | $m\,n\,ḫ\,t$ ↓    |
| typ(coll)     | $m\,n\,ḫ\,t$ ↓    |

Figure 7: Computation for *mnḫt*

we could use alternatively 'log($m_{33}$, $m_{33}$)'. We will see more examples of functions having additional features later.

The computation for *nwy* is given by Figure 6. Here several jumps are needed to model that *n* and *w* are each covered by three different signs. Note that the determinative has a general description 'liquid' and so does not correspond to any letters.

The computation for *mnḫt* is given by Figure 7. As shown, application of a phonetic determinative does not require a jump. This is motivated by the observation that phonetic determinatives behave similarly to determinatives in that they tend to appear at the end of a word, even after phonograms for subsequent letters (cf. Figure 1). A phonetic determinative with a certain sound value is applicable if that value is a substring of the current content of the tape. Application of the function leaves the tape content and position of the head unchanged.

We impose two constraints on the use of jumps. The first is that jumps with positive values, moving the tape head rightward, should not bring it beyond the end of the (written) tape. This is because the transliteration should be a sequence of letters without any gaps.

The second constraint is that no tape square that already contains a letter can be overwritten with a different letter. This is consistent with the application we are aiming to model, viz. Egyptian writing. This means for example that the first 'phon($nw$)' in Figure 6 is applicable because the tape content to the right of the head, which is $n$, is a prefix of $nw$. Application of the function leaves that existing $n$ unaffected and in addition appends the remaining suffix $w$ at the end of the tape and moves the head to be after that suffix. In general, if the tape content to the right of the head is $\beta$, then we can apply a phonogram with value $\gamma$ if:

- $\beta$ is a prefix of $\gamma$ (as in the case discussed above) or
- $\gamma$ is a prefix of $\beta$ (cf. phonogram for $f$ in Figure 8a below).

Our aim is to complete the above framework to allow a sequence of functions to uniquely determine a sequence of signs and a sequence of letters. The sequence of signs is straightforwardly obtained as we already assumed from Section 1 onward that each function determines one or more consecutive signs. After having added epsilon-phonograms and jumps, we can now also account for letters not represented by signs, and for letters represented by several signs.

At least one more refinement remains to be explained. A phonogram for $t$ or $d$ is sometimes used for letters in a word that historically should have $\underline{t}$ or $\underline{d}$, and vice versa; cf. the discussion in Section 2.2 about historical sound changes in Egyptian. Hence we sometimes need to give a phonogram an additional feature, so that for example 'phon($t,\underline{t}$)' indicates that $t$ is the historical sound value of the sign, say $\frown$, but the sign is used in the writing of a word whose transliteration has $\underline{t}$ instead.

After this and other minor refinements, any sequence of functions corresponds to at most one analysis of a word, in terms of a sequence of signs, a sequence of letters, and the links between them, as exemplified in Figures 1–3, or in other words, in terms of the kinds of annotations that exist in our corpus. We also aim to achieve the converse, namely to translate an annotation of a word to a unique sequence of functions. Part of this is straightforward, as most of the functions and the order in which they occur in a sequence are determined by the order of the signs. However, if there are no further restrictions, jumps may be inserted anywhere, even when they are not useful. In particular, they may be applied just before applying a determinative, even though a determinative does not depend on the input positions. In principle we could even apply a number of jumps in sequence, moving the head back and forth.

We solve this by demanding that jumps only occur just before application of a phonogram, or a related function whose application relies on the input position. The concrete realization is by a flag $\mathbf{fl}_{jump}$, which is set to **true** after a jump. As long as the flag is **true**, no determinative, phonetic determinative, or another jump is applicable. A phonogram and a few other functions reset the flag to **false**. For similar reasons, we use a flag $\mathbf{fl}_{eps}$ that is set of **true** after application of an epsilon-phonogram. As long as this flag is **true**, no jump is allowed. The effect is that epsilon-phonograms are applied as late as possible. Two more flags, $\mathbf{fl}_{fp}$ and $\mathbf{fl}_{end}$, will be discussed later.

To make the preceding more precise, we introduce the concept of *configuration*, which contains:

- the tape content preceding the head position, denoted by $\alpha$,
- the tape content from the head position onwards, denoted by $\beta$,
- the values of the four flags.

Initially, the tape is empty, so $\alpha = \beta = \varepsilon$, where $\varepsilon$ denotes the empty string, and all flags are **false**.

In a given configuration, only a subset of functions is applicable. For example, if $\alpha = \varepsilon$ and $\beta = n$, then a function phon($nw$) would be applicable, but not say a function phon($t$). The flags also restrict the applicable functions, as explained above. In general, every function has a *precondition*, that is, a set of constraints that determines whether it is applicable in a certain configuration, and a *postcondition*, which specifies how its application changes the configuration. The most important functions are characterized in this manner in Table 1, with tape content and position of the head as specified by $\alpha$ and $\beta$.

The precondition of a logogram for lemma $\gamma$ says that $\gamma$ must occur from the position of the head onward, possibly after a prefix of $\gamma$ was written already, e.g. using phonograms. Furthermore, the position of the head must be either 0 or 1, and in the latter case,

Table 1: Preconditions and postconditions

### Logogram for $\gamma$

| | |
|---|---|
| Pre | $\alpha = \varepsilon$ or (for causative; see main text) $\alpha = s$, $\beta$ is prefix of $\gamma$, $\mathbf{fl}_{eps} = \mathbf{false}$. |
| Post | $\alpha := \alpha\gamma$, $\beta := \varepsilon$, $\mathbf{fl}_{jump} := \mathbf{false}$. |

### Phonogram with sound value $\gamma$

| | |
|---|---|
| Pre | $\gamma$ is prefix of $\beta$ or $\beta$ is prefix of $\gamma$. |
| Post | $\alpha := \alpha\gamma$, if $\beta$ was of the form $\gamma\delta$ then $\beta := \delta$ else $\beta := \varepsilon$, $\mathbf{fl}_{jump} := \mathbf{false}$, $\mathbf{fl}_{eps} := \mathbf{false}$. |

### Determinative not specific to any word

| | |
|---|---|
| Pre | $\mathbf{fl}_{jump} = \mathbf{false}$, $\mathbf{fl}_{eps} = \mathbf{false}$. |
| Post | - |

### Determinative specific to $\gamma$

| | |
|---|---|
| Pre | $\alpha\beta = \gamma\delta$ or (for causative) $\alpha\beta = s\gamma\delta$ for some $\delta$, $\mathbf{fl}_{jump} = \mathbf{false}$, if $\mathbf{fl}_{eps} = \mathbf{true}$ then $\delta = \varepsilon$. |
| Post | $\mathbf{fl}_{eps} := \mathbf{false}$. |

### Phonetic determinative with sound value $\gamma$

| | |
|---|---|
| Pre | $\alpha\beta = \delta_1\gamma\delta_2$ for some $\delta_1$ and $\delta_2$, $\mathbf{fl}_{jump} = \mathbf{false}$, if $\mathbf{fl}_{eps} = \mathbf{true}$ then $\delta_2 = \varepsilon$. |
| Post | $\mathbf{fl}_{eps} := \mathbf{false}$. |

### Spurious

| | |
|---|---|
| Pre | $\mathbf{fl}_{jump} = \mathbf{false}$, $\mathbf{fl}_{eps} = \mathbf{false}$ |
| Post | - |

### Jump with value $j$

| | |
|---|---|
| Pre | $\mathbf{fl}_{jump} = \mathbf{false}$, $\mathbf{fl}_{eps} = \mathbf{false}$, $\delta = \alpha\beta$, $i = |\alpha|$, $0 \leq i + j \leq |\delta|$. |
| Post | $\alpha := \alpha'$, $\beta := \beta'$ for some $\alpha'$ and $\beta'$ such that $\alpha'\beta' = \delta$ and $|\alpha'| = i + j$, $\mathbf{fl}_{jump} := \mathbf{true}$. |

### Epsilon-phonogram for letter $\ell$

| | |
|---|---|
| Pre | $\beta = \varepsilon$. |
| Post | $\alpha := \alpha\ell$, $\mathbf{fl}_{eps} := \mathbf{true}$. |

the first letter on the tape must be *s*. This is because in Egyptian, the prefix *s*- can be used to derive causative verbs from other verbs. The writing may then consist of a phonogram for *s* followed by a logogram for the original verb. The postcondition for logograms says simply that $\gamma$ is written to the tape and the head moves rightward by $|\gamma|$ positions.

The precondition of a phonogram with value $\gamma$ was discussed before. The postcondition is slightly complicated by the need to distinguish between two cases, where $\gamma$ is a prefix of $\beta$ or where $\beta$ is a prefix of $\gamma$ (if $\gamma = \beta$, the two cases collapse).

The preconditions and postconditions of determinatives not specific to any words are straightforward. For a determinative specific to word $\gamma$, we merely need to check whether $\gamma$ is present near the beginning of the tape, possibly after the causative prefix *s*-; if the previous function was an epsilon-phonogram, then $\gamma$ must be a suffix of the tape content (recall that we want epsilon-phonograms to be applied as late as possible). Phonetic determinatives are similar, except that the required string $\gamma$ need not occur near the beginning of the tape.

Spurious functions require that the previously applied function is not a jump or epsilon-phonogram. A jump with value $j$, which can be positive or negative, is allowed for current position $i$ of the head provided the previously applied function was not a jump or epsilon-phonogram, and provided the new position $i + j$ is not preceding the beginning of the tape nor beyond the end of the tape. An epsilon-phonogram is only allowed if the head is at the end of the tape.

Our model has a number of specialized functions in place of the generic typographical functions as they occur in the corpus. For example, the three strokes, for 'plurality or collectivity', in the model correspond to three different functions with different preconditions and postconditions. First, the three strokes may be purely semantic, in the writing of a collective noun in singular form, where they do not represent any letters. This function behaves much like a determinative not specific to any word, except that it can only occur at the end of a word. For this reason, the flag $\mathbf{fl}_{end}$ is set to **true**. The purpose of this flag is to prevent that further letters are appended behind the end of the tape, until possibly an Egyptological '=' symbol marks the end of the current word proper, before a suffix pronoun.

The plural strokes may also signify plurality in the grammatical sense, in which case it corresponds to the -w ending of masculine plural, or to the -wt ending of feminine plural. A separate function is needed for the two genders, both of which set $fl_{end}$ to **true**. Apart from the flag $fl_{end}$, the function of three strokes for masculine plural has preconditions and postconditions identical to those of the phonograms. The case of feminine plural will be discussed further below.

Similarly, our model distinguishes between three uses of the multiplicative functions with value '3', with different preconditions and postconditions. As in the case of the plural strokes, their meaning may be purely semantic, without a word being grammatically plural, or they may be used as markers of either masculine plural or feminine plural.

In our corpus we have linked functions marking plural only to the w from the ending, whether it is the -w ending of masculine plural or the w that is the first letter of the -wt ending of feminine plural. This is because the t of the feminine ending would normally be accounted for already by another sign, which could be a phonogram or logogram, as illustrated in Figures 8a and 8b.

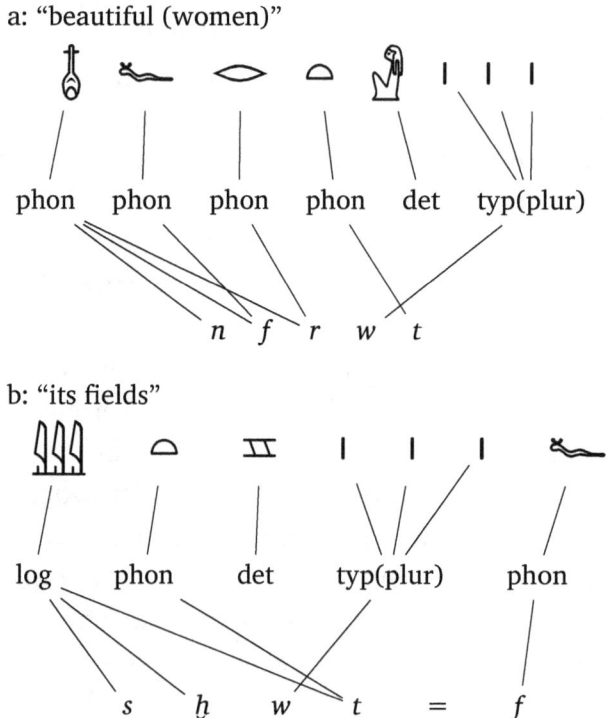

a: "beautiful (women)"

phon   phon   phon   phon   det   typ(plur)

n   f   r   w   t

b: "its fields"

log   phon   det   typ(plur)   phon

s   ḫ   w   t   =   f

Figure 8: Annotations of feminine plural words (Papyrus Westcar)

The same two examples also illustrate the challenge that feminine plural poses to a left-to-right automaton model. When the feminine $t$ is written to the tape, the function justifying the $w$ in front of the $t$ is not seen until many steps later. The use of jumps to handle this seems inappropriate, as jumps were designed for phonetic complements. Another potential solution is to use lookahead, but this appears difficult to extend with probabilities.

We have chosen for a different solution, using the flag $\mathbf{fl}_{fp}$, for 'feminine plural'. This flag is set to **true** when a feminine plural is predicted by (nondeterministically) putting an extra $w$ on the tape, in one of two cases. The first is if a logogram of a feminine word is seen, and the second is if a phonogram for $t$ is seen.

The rest of the computation then has the obligation to reset $\mathbf{fl}_{fp}$ to **false**, and this can only happen if a function for plurality (either the three strokes or a multiplicative function with value '3') is seen later. While $\mathbf{fl}_{fp} = \mathbf{true}$, analysis of the current word cannot be completed.

Concretely for Figure 8a, we now have two functions 'phon($t,t,$**false**)' and 'phon($t,wt,$**true**)'. Both correspond to a phonogram for the letter $t$ (the first feature), but realized as $t$ or $wt$ in the transliteration (the second feature), while possibly predicting feminine plural (the third feature). The first function has the preconditions and postconditions of a normal phonogram (cf. Table 1), while the second writes $wt$ on the tape instead of just $t$ and sets $\mathbf{fl}_{fp}$ to **true**. The resulting computation is in Figure 9.

Similarly for Figure 8b, we now have two functions 'log($sḫt,sḫt,$**false**)' and 'log($sḫt,sḫwt,$**true**)'. Both are logograms for the same sign for lemma $sḫt$ (first feature) while they are realized differently in the transliteration (second feature), possibly predicting feminine plural (the third feature). The first function behaves like a normal logogram, but the second writes $sḫwt$ on the tape and sets $\mathbf{fl}_{fp}$ to **true**. The resulting computation is in Figure 10.

Our model presently has no special provisions for the phenomenon of honorific transposition (Section 4). This implies that accuracy is poor for the (few) cases of honorific transposition in the corpus. To address this, one may consider refinements of the model that allow 'gaps' in the hieroglyphic writing to be filled in later, along the lines of the Operation Sequence Model (Durrani *et al.* 2015).

| | ↓ | $\text{fl}_{fp}$ = false, $\text{fl}_{end}$ = false |
|---|---|---|
| phon(*nfr*) | *n f r* ↓ | $\text{fl}_{fp}$ = false, $\text{fl}_{end}$ = false |
| jump(-2) | *n* ↓ *f r* | $\text{fl}_{fp}$ = false, $\text{fl}_{end}$ = false |
| phon(*f*) | *n f* ↓ *r* | $\text{fl}_{fp}$ = false, $\text{fl}_{end}$ = false |
| phon(*r*) | *n f r* ↓ | $\text{fl}_{fp}$ = false, $\text{fl}_{end}$ = false |
| phon(*t, wt*, fp = **true**) | *n f r w t* ↓ | $\text{fl}_{fp}$ = **true**, $\text{fl}_{end}$ = **true** |
| det(female) | *n f r w t* ↓ | $\text{fl}_{fp}$ = **true**, $\text{fl}_{end}$ = **true** |
| typ(plur) | *n f r w t* ↓ | $\text{fl}_{fp}$ = false, $\text{fl}_{end}$ = **true** |

Figure 9: Computation for *nfrwt*

| | ↓ | $\text{fl}_{fp}$ = false, $\text{fl}_{end}$ = false |
|---|---|---|
| log(*sḫt,sḫwt*, fp = **true**) | *s ḫ w t* ↓ | $\text{fl}_{fp}$ = **true**, $\text{fl}_{end}$ = **true** |
| jump(-1) | *s ḫ w* ↓ *t* | $\text{fl}_{fp}$ = **true**, $\text{fl}_{end}$ = **true** |
| phon(*t,t*,fp = **false**) | *s ḫ w t* ↓ | $\text{fl}_{fp}$ = **true**, $\text{fl}_{end}$ = **true** |
| typ(plur) | *s ḫ w t* ↓ | $\text{fl}_{fp}$ = false, $\text{fl}_{end}$ = **true** |
| phon(=) | *s ḫ w t* = ↓ | $\text{fl}_{fp}$ = false, $\text{fl}_{end}$ = false |
| phon(*f*) | *s ḫ w t* = *f* ↓ | $\text{fl}_{fp}$ = false, $\text{fl}_{end}$ = false |

Figure 10: Computation for *sḫwt=f*

## 6          PROBABILITIES

After having captured the relation between sequences of signs and sequences of letters solely in terms of sequences of functions, the next step is to estimate their probabilities. An obvious candidate is a simple $N$-gram model:

$$P(f_1^n) = \prod_i P(f_i \mid f_1^{i-1}) \approx \prod_i P(f_i \mid f_{i-N+1}^{i-1})$$

Here $f_1, \ldots, f_n$ is a sequence of functions, ending in an artificial end-of-word function, and $f_i^j$ is short for $f_i, \ldots, f_j$. In our experiments, estimation of $P(f_i \mid f_{i-N+1}^{i-1})$ is by relative frequency.

About 4000 functions are compiled out of the entries of the sign list. Added to this are dynamically created functions, such as numbers, epsilon-phonograms and jumps. Because little training material is available, this means a considerable portion of these functions is never observed, and smoothing techniques become essential. We use Katz's back-off (Katz 1987) in combination with Simple Good-Turing (Gale and Sampson 1995).

Functions are naturally divided into a small number of classes, such as the class of all phonograms and the class of all logograms. Using these classes as states, we obtain a second type of model in terms of (higher-order) HMMs (Rabiner 1989; Vidal *et al.* 2005). For fixed $N$, and with $c_i$ denoting the class of function $f_i$, we have:

$$P(f_i|f_{i-N+1}^{i-1}) \quad \approx \quad P(c_i|c_{i-N+1}^{i-1}) * P(f_i|c_i)$$

Estimation of both expressions in the right-hand side is again by relative frequency estimation, in combination with smoothing.

It should be noted that not all sequences of functions correspond to valid writings. Concretely, in the configuration reached after applying functions $f_1^{i-1}$, the preconditions of function $f_i$ may not hold. As a result, some portion of the probability mass is lost in invalid sequences of functions. We see no straightforward way to avoid this, as the model discussed in Section 5, which allows jumps of the tape head, cannot be captured in terms of finite-state machinery.

## 7                             RESULTS

In our experiments, the training corpus was Papyrus Westcar and the test corpus was The Shipwrecked Sailor. We have considered but rejected the possibility of taking two disjoint parts of both texts together as training and test corpora, for example taking all odd words from both texts for training and all even words for testing. The argument against this is that many words occur repeatedly in the same text, and therefore there would be a disproportionate number of words that occur in both training and test material, potentially leading to skewed results.

Our objective is now to guess the correct sequence of functions, given the sequence of signs and the sequence of letters of a word. We determined recall, precision, and F-measure, averaged over all words in the test corpus. This was done after removing jumps and epsilon-phonograms, so that we could take the annotations from the corpus as gold standard. We have also ignored how functions are linked to letters; the main motivation for this was to be able to define a suitable baseline, as described next.

Among all sequences of functions that correspond to a given sequence of signs, the baseline model yields the one that maximizes the product of the (unigram) probabilities of those functions. Note that a function can correspond to one, two or more signs, so that all relevant partitions of the given sequence of signs need to be considered.

As this ignores the letters altogether, the baseline is independent of the model of Section 5, avoiding the intricacies of preconditions and postconditions.

For a concrete example, consider Figure 2b as gold standard. The 'relevant' items are (1) the logogram function of ⸜ for the lemma $\underline{d}b$', "finger", tied to the first sign, (2) the typographical function of the three strokes, with meaning 'plural' and realized as letter $w$, tied to the next three signs, and (3) the phonogram function of ⸜ with sound value $k$, tied to the last sign. Recall and precision are 100% if 'retrieved' are exactly these three items.

We implemented the $N$-gram models and HMMs from Section 6. An acyclic finite automaton is first created, with states representing configurations together with the last $N - 1$ functions or classes. Transitions are labelled by functions, and have weights that are negative log probabilities determined by the chosen probabilistic model. Most of the functions directly come from the sign list. Other functions are dynamically constructed, on the basis of the input signs, as for example typographical functions representing numbers. Another example is the class of multiplicative functions, which are generated if a pattern of one or more signs occurs two or more times. Final states correspond to configurations reached after processing all the signs of a word, with $\alpha$ equal to the transliteration of that word, $\beta = \varepsilon$, $\mathbf{fl}_{jump} = \mathbf{false}$ and $\mathbf{fl}_{fp} = \mathbf{false}$. A final state always exists, in the worst case by analyzing all signs as spurious, and applying one epsilon-phonogram for every letter.

The shortest path from the initial state to a final state is extracted using the shortest-path algorithm of Dijkstra (1959). The labels on this path then give us the list of functions on the basis of which we compute recall and precision.

Results are given in Table 2. It is unsurprising that the models with $N = 1$ improve over the baseline. Although the baseline is also defined in terms of unigram probabilities, it ignores consistency of the sequence of functions relative to the letters. The first-order HMM performs better than the unigram model. This can be attributed to smoothing. For example, the unigram model will assign the same low probability to a spurious function unseen in the training material as to an unseen phonogram, although phonograms overall are far more

|  | R | P | F1 |
|---|---|---|---|
| baseline | 86.0 | 86.0 | 86.0 |
| *N*-gram | | | |
| $N = 1$ | 90.6 | 90.6 | 90.6 |
| $N = 2$ | 94.4 | 94.4 | 94.4 |
| $N = 3$ | 94.4 | 94.4 | 94.4 |
| HMM | | | |
| $N = 1$ | 91.4 | 91.4 | 91.4 |
| $N = 2$ | 91.8 | 91.8 | 91.8 |
| $N = 3$ | 92.0 | 92.0 | 92.0 |
| interpolation of *N*-gram and HMM | | | |
| $N = 1$ | 90.5 | 90.5 | 90.5 |
| $N = 2$ | 94.8 | 94.8 | 94.8 |
| $N = 3$ | **95.0** | **94.9** | **94.9** |

Table 2: Experimental results: recall, precision, F-measure

likely. The first-order HMM however suitably models the low probability of the class of spurious functions.

For *N* greater than 1, the HMMs perform less well than the *N*-gram models. This suggests that the probabilities of functions depend more on the exact identities of the preceding functions than on their classes. The best results are obtained with linear interpolation of the *N*-gram model and the HMM, weighted 9:1, for $N = 3$.

## 8      CONCLUSION AND OUTLOOK

Our contributions include the design of an annotated corpus of sign use, allowing quantitative study of the writing system, and serving to document rare uses of signs. The second main contribution is a probabilistic model of how signs follow one another to form words. The model is amenable to supervised training. Unsupervised training will be the subject of future investigation.

The probabilistic model is evaluated through computation of the most probable sequence $F$ of functions given the sequence $S$ of signs and the sequence $L$ of letters, or formally $\text{argmax}_F P(F \mid S, L) = \text{argmax}_F P(F, S, L)$, where $P(F, S, L)$ is the joint model of Section 6. The model could also be the starting point for other tasks, such as automatic transliteration. However, evaluating $\text{argmax}_L P(L \mid S) = \text{argmax}_L \sum_F P(F, S, L)$, using the same model $P(F, S, L)$ as before, is not likely to give satisfactory results. This is because, in general, a shorter sequence $F$ tends to have a higher probability than a longer one, and handling of, for example, phonetic complements typically requires longer sequences involving jumps. As a consequence, overly long transliterations will be produced with repeated letters.

The solution we propose is to let the automaton model compute conditional probabilities $P(F, S \mid L)$, in combination with a prior model $P(L)$. This model would involve a probability distribution over the lengths of stems (most nouns and verbs have stems of two or three letters) and simple forms of morphosyntactic knowledge, including the Egyptological punctuation symbols. In the ideal case it would also include a lexicon. This is yet to be implemented and evaluated.

## ACKNOWLEDGMENTS

This work evolved out of intense discussions of the first author with Serge Rosmorduc and François Barthélemy, in the summer of 2012. Gratefully acknowledged are the anonymous referee reports, which provided many insightful and useful suggestions.

## REFERENCES

J.P. ALLEN (2000), *Middle Egyptian: An Introduction to the Language and Culture of Hieroglyphs*, Cambridge University Press.

F. BARTHÉLEMY and S. ROSMORDUC (2011), Intersection of multitape transducers vs. cascade of binary transducers: the example of Egyptian Hieroglyphs transliteration, in *Proceedings of the 9th International Workshop on Finite State Methods and Natural Language Processing*, pp. 74–82, Blois, France.

S. BILLET-COAT and D. HÉRIN-AIME (1994), A Multi-Agent Architecture for an Evolving Expert System Module, in *Database and Expert Systems Applications, 5th International Conference*, volume 856 of *Lecture Notes in Computer Science*, pp. 581–590, Springer-Verlag, Athens, Greece.

A.M. BLACKMAN (1932), *Middle-Egyptian Stories – Part I*, Fondation Égyptologique Reine Élisabeth.

A.M. BLACKMAN (1988), *The Story of King Kheops and the Magicians*, J.V. Books.

P.F. BROWN, S.A. DELLA PIETRA, V.J. DELLA PIETRA, and R.L. MERCER (1993), The Mathematics of Statistical Machine Translation: Parameter Estimation, *Computational Linguistics*, 18(4):263–311.

P.T. Daniels and W. Bright, editors (1996), *The World's Writing Systems*, Oxford University Press, New York.

C.T. de Vartavan (2010), Snt[r]/snt̲[r] means '[Divine/Godly] Scent', *Advances in Egyptology*, 1:5–17.

E.W. Dijkstra (1959), A Note on Two Problems in Connexion with Graphs, *Numerische Mathematik*, 1:269–271.

N. Durrani, H. Schmid, A. Fraser, P. Koehn, and H. Schütze (2015), The Operation Sequence Model — Combining N-Gram-Based and Phrase-Based Statistical Machine Translation, *Computational Linguistics*, 41(2):157–186.

W.A. Gale and G. Sampson (1995), Good-Turing Frequency Estimation Without Tears, *Journal of Quantitative Linguistics*, 2(3):217–237.

L. Galescu and J.F. Allen (2002), Pronunciation of proper names with a joint n-gram model for bi-directional grapheme-to-phoneme conversion, in *Proceedings of the Seventh International Conference on Spoken Language Processing (ICSLP-2002)*, pp. 109–112, Denver, CO, USA.

A. Gardiner (1957), *Egyptian Grammar*, Griffith Institute, Ashmolean Museum, Oxford.

R. Hannig (1995), *Grosses Handwörterbuch Ägyptisch-Deutsch: die Sprache der Pharaonen (2800-950 v.Chr.)*, Verlag Philipp von Zabern, Mainz.

G. Ifrah (1981), *Histoire Universelle des Chiffres*, Editions Seghers, Paris.

S.M. Katz (1987), Estimation of probabilities from sparse data for the language model component of a speech recognizer, *IEEE Transactions on Acoustics, Speech, and Signal Processing*, 35(3):400–401.

K. Knight and J. Graehl (1998), Machine Transliteration, *Computational Linguistics*, 24(4):599–612.

A. Loprieno (1995), *Ancient Egyptian: a linguistic introduction*, Cambridge University Press.

M.G.A. Malik, C. Boitet, and P. Bhattacharyya (2008), Hindi Urdu machine transliteration using finite-state transducers, in *The 22nd International Conference on Computational Linguistics*, volume 1, pp. 537–544, Manchester, UK.

M.-J. Nederhof (2008), Automatic Alignment of Hieroglyphs and Transliteration, in N. Strudwick, editor, *Information Technology and Egyptology in 2008, Proceedings of the meeting of the Computer Working Group of the International Association of Egyptologists*, pp. 71–92, Gorgias Press.

S. Polis, A.-C. Honnay, and J. Winand (2013), Building an Annotated Corpus of Late Egyptian, in S. Polis and J. Winand, editors, *Texts, Languages & Information Technology in Egyptology*, pp. 25–44, Presses Universitaires de Liège.

S. Polis and S. Rosmorduc (2013), Réviser le codage de l'égyptien ancien. Vers un répertoire partagé des signes hiéroglyphiques, *Document Numérique*, 16(3):45–67.

S. POLIS and S. ROSMORDUC (2015), The Hieroglyphic Sign Functions. Suggestions for a Revised Taxonomy, in H. AMSTUTZ, A. DORN, M. MÜLLER, M. RONSDORF, and S. ULJAS, editors, *Fuzzy Boundaries: Festschrift für Antonio Loprieno*, volume 1, pp. 149–174, Widmaier Verlag, Hamburg.

L.R. RABINER (1989), A Tutorial on Hidden Markov Models and Selected Applications in Speech Recognition, *Proceedings of the IEEE*, 77(2):257–286.

S. ROSMORDUC (2002/3), Codage informatique des langues anciennes, *Document Numérique*, 6:211–224.

S. ROSMORDUC (2008), Automated Transliteration of Egyptian Hieroglyphs, in N. STRUDWICK, editor, *Information Technology and Egyptology in 2008, Proceedings of the meeting of the Computer Working Group of the International Association of Egyptologists*, pp. 167–183, Gorgias Press.

W. SCHENKEL (1971), Zur Struktur der Hieroglyphenschrift, *Mitteilungen des deutschen archäologischen Instituts, Abteilung Kairo*, 27:85–98.

W. SCHENKEL (1984), *Aus der Arbeit an einer Konkordanz zu den altägyptischen Sargtexten*, volume 12 of *Göttinger Orientforschungen, IV. Reihe*, Harrassowitz.

R. SPROAT (2000), *A Computational Theory of Writing Systems*, Cambridge University Press, Cambridge.

A. TSUKAMOTO (1997), Automated Transcription of Egyptian Hieroglyphic Texts: via transliteration using computer, *Journal of the Faculty of Culture and Education*, 2(1):1–40, Saga-University.

E. VIDAL, F. THOLLARD, C. DE LA HIGUERA, F. CASACUBERTA, and R.C. CARRASCO (2005), Probabilistic Finite-State Machines — Part II, *IEEE Transactions on Pattern Analysis and Machine Intelligence*, 27(7):1026–1039.

# 6

# A type-logical treebank for French

*Richard Moot*
CNRS (LaBRI), Bordeaux University

*Keywords: type-logical grammar, categorial grammar, semi-automatic grammar extraction*

## ABSTRACT

This paper describes the TLGbank, a treebank developed in the framework of (multimodal) type-logical grammar. Using the French Treebank as a starting point, a combination of automated and manual techniques are applied to obtain type-logical derivations (parses) corresponding to the phrases of the French Treebank. The TLGbank has been developped with applications to wide-coverage semantics in mind. This means that the TLGbank has richer structure than the original French Treebank, especially where it concerns semantically relevant information such as passives, coordination, extraction and gapping.

## 1             INTRODUCTION

Categorial grammars have interesting theoretical advantages, most notably their very clean syntax-semantics interface. In the last decade, research in Combinatory Categorial Grammar has shown that this is not merely a *theoretical* advantage, but that, with the appropriate resources and tools – an annotated treebank, the CCGbank (Hockenmaier and Steedman 2007), a very efficient parser (Clark and Curran 2004) and a semantic lexicon (Bos *et al.* 2004) – we can use categorial grammars for wide-coverage, deep semantic analysis. Applications of the resulting wide-coverage semantics include natural-language question-answering (Bos *et al.* 2007) and recognising textual entailments (Bos and Markert 2005).

The development of the CCGbank, which has allowed parameter optimization for the wide-coverage parser and provided a framework (in types and in derivations) for the semantic applications, has been a key element for these applications.

Categorial grammars in the logical tradition initiated by Lambek (1958) (Moortgat 2011; Morrill 2011; Moot and Retoré 2012) have stayed somewhat behind in terms of their application to large-scale linguistic data. The goal of the current paper is to describe the TLGbank, a semi-automatically extracted treebank containing type-logical proofs, created with the explicit goal of making similar wide-coverage parsing and semantics possible in the type-logical context.

The work described in this paper extends and refines a much earlier version of the TLGbank (Moot 2010b). Lefeuvre *et al.* (2012) and Moot (2012) discuss some initial applications of the treebank to wide-coverage semantics.

## 2                    TYPE–LOGICAL GRAMMAR

This section is a very short introduction to (multimodal) type-logical grammars. For more detailed introductions, see Oehrle (2011), Moortgat (2011, Section 2.4) or Moot and Retoré (2012, Chapter 5).

Although the treebank is annotated using multimodal type-logical grammar, the annotation has been chosen in such a way that derivations in the treebank can easily be translated into derivations of the Displacement calculus (Morrill *et al.* 2011) or of first-order linear logic (Moot and Piazza 2001; Moot 2014). Translations to other versions of categorial grammar are conceivable, but will probably require significantly more work.

The atomic formulas are $n$ (for nouns), $np$ (for noun phrases), $pp_x$ (for prepositional phrases, with $x$ the preposition heading the phrase) and $s_x$ for sentences, where we distinguish between several types of sentences/phrases: $s_{main}$ for main, tensed sentence, $s_{whq}$ for a wh-question, $s_q$ for a sentence introduced by "que" (*that*) and further types for passives $s_{pass}$, infinitives $s_{inf}$,[1] and past $s_{ppart}$ and present $s_{ppres}$ participles; this is inspired by the French Treebank annotation –

---

[1] Like prepositions, $s_{inf}$ is further subdivided into categories for infinitive phrases headed by a preposition: $s_{inf_a}$, $s_{inf_{de}}$, $s_{inf_{pour}}$, $s_{inf_{par}}$. This allows us to distinguish, for example, between "finir de" (*to* finish *doing something*) and "finir par" (*to* end up *doing something*). The infinitive headed by "pour" occurs in constructions like "trop tôt pour ..." (*too early to ...*).

Table 1: Logical rules for multimodal categorial grammars

$$\frac{}{w \vdash A} \; Lex \qquad\qquad\qquad \frac{}{x \vdash A} \; Hyp$$

$$\frac{X \vdash A/B \quad Y \vdash B}{X \circ Y \vdash A} \; /E \qquad\qquad \frac{X \vdash B \quad Y \vdash B\backslash A}{X \circ Y \vdash A} \; \backslash E$$

$$\frac{\begin{array}{c} x \vdash B \\ \vdots \\ X \circ x \vdash A \end{array}}{X \vdash A/B} \; /I \qquad\qquad \frac{\begin{array}{c} x \vdash B \\ \vdots \\ x \circ X \vdash A \end{array}}{X \vdash B\backslash A} \; \backslash I$$

$$\frac{X[Y] \vdash B \quad Z \vdash B\backslash_1 A}{X[Y \circ_1 Z] \vdash A} \; \backslash_1 E \qquad \frac{\begin{array}{c} x \vdash B \\ \vdots \\ X[Y \circ x] \vdash A \end{array}}{X[Y] \vdash A/\Diamond_1 \Box_1 B} \; /\Diamond_1 \Box_1 I$$

though passives are not annotated as such in this treebank – and the categorial treatments of Carpenter (1991) and Hockenmaier and Steedman (2007). The different subtypes of $s$ and $pp$ are implemented using first-order variables and unification, following Moot (2014) and Morrill (1994, Section 2.1).

An intransitive verb is assigned $np \backslash s_{main}$, indicating that it requires a noun phrase to its left in order to form an inflected sentence. Similarly, transitive verbs are assigned the formula $(np \backslash s_{main})/np$, requiring a noun phrase to their right in order to form an intransitive verb. In what follows, we will often simply write $s$ instead of $s_{main}$.

To make this article understandable to the reader not intimately familiar with modern type-logical grammars, all examples in the text use the simplified presentation of Table 1. The intrepid reader interested in the full technical details can find the complete presentation in Appendix A, with further applications in Appendix B.

We will abbreviate the lexicon rule as $\frac{w}{A}$. The rule for $/E$ simply states that whenever we have shown an expression $X$ to be of type $A/B$ and we have shown an expression $Y$ to be of type $B$, then the tree with $X$ as its immediate subtree on the left and $Y$ as its immediate subtree of the right is of type $A$ (the $\backslash E$ rule is symmetric).

An easy instantiation of the $/E$ rule (with $X := the$, $Y := student$, $A := np$, $B := n$) would be the following.

$$\frac{the \vdash np/n \quad student \vdash n}{the \circ student \vdash np} \, /E$$

The two rules at the bottom row of the table require some special attention. The $\backslash_1 E$ rule is an *infixation rule*. This rule is used for adverbs (and other VP modifiers) occurring after the verb. Like the $\backslash E$ rule, it takes a $B$ formula as its argument, but infixes itself to the right of any subtree $Y$ of $X$ ($X[Y]$ denotes a tree $X$ with a designated subtree $Y$). This tree $Y$ can occur at any depth in the tree $X[Y]$, including the root, i.e. $Y$ can be equal to $X[Y]$.[2]) An example is shown below for the VP *"impoverishes the CGT dangerously"*. The interest of this rule is that it allows a uniform type assignment for adverbs occurring post-verbally, regardless of other verb arguments.

$$\frac{\dfrac{appauvrit \vdash (np\backslash s)/np \quad la \circ CGT \vdash np}{appauvrit \circ (la \circ CGT) \vdash np\backslash s} \, /E \quad dangereusement \vdash (np\backslash s)\backslash_1(np\backslash s)}{(appauvrit \circ_1 dangereusement) \circ (la \circ CGT) \vdash np\backslash s} \, /E$$

Each occurrence of the introduction rules $/I$, $\backslash I$ and $/\Diamond_1\Box_1$ uses a distinct syntactic variable $x$ which is unique to the proof; therefore, in the case of a proof containing multiple introduction rules, the hypothesis corresponding to an introduction rule can always be uniquely determined by this variable name (we can use any naming convention to ensure this; common choices are $x_0, x_1, \dots$ or, for shorter proofs, $x, y, z$).

The $/\Diamond_1\Box_1$ rule is an *extraction* rule, extracting a $B$ constituent from any right branch inside an $X$ constituent.[3] Comparing the rule $/\Diamond_1\Box_1 I$ to the rule $/I$, we can see that $/I$ is the special case of $/\Diamond_1\Box_1 I$ where the context $X[]$ is empty (i.e. where $X[Y]$ is equal to $Y$). From the point of view of semantics the two rules are the same — both correspond to abstraction over the semantic variable assigned to the $B$ formula which is withdrawn by the rule — but the rule $/\Diamond_1\Box_1 I$ can

---

[2] For adverbs, as here, $Y$ is typically the verb, but in principle infixation is possible anywhere (an admitted oversimplification, which can be remedied by a more sophisticated treatment of mode information).

[3] For readers familiar with the Displacement calculus (Morrill *et al.* 2011), the infixation construction $A\backslash_1 B$ corresponds to $\breve{\ }B \downarrow A$ and the extraction construction $A/\Diamond_1\Box_1 B$ to $\breve{\ }(A \uparrow B)$.

apply in a larger number of syntactic contexts. As an example, in the following sentence

(1)　　l'　argent dont　　elle est responsable
　　　　the money for which she is　responsible

the relativizer "dont" is assigned the formula $(n\backslash n)/(s/\Diamond_1\Box_1 pp_{de})$ meaning it is looking to its right for a sentence missing a prepositional phrase headed by the preposition "de" (*for*). The subformula $\Diamond_1\Box_1 pp_{de}$ should be seen as a special type of $pp_{de}$ formula. Unlike a normal $pp_{de}$ argument, it can occur on *any* right branch, no matter how deeply nested (unlike the rules for $/I$ in Table 1, which apply only when the argument is the immediate right daughter). This means "dont" can take a phrase such as "elle est responsable" (*she is responsible*), where "responsable" is analysed as an adjective which first selects a $pp_{de}$ to its right, as an argument since we can assign it $s/\Diamond_1\Box_1 pp_{de}$ as follows.

$$
\cfrac{\cfrac{elle}{np}\,Lex \quad \cfrac{\cfrac{est}{(np\backslash s_{main})/(n\backslash n)}\,Lex \quad \cfrac{\cfrac{\cfrac{responsable}{(n\backslash n)/pp_{de}}\,Lex \quad \cfrac{}{x \vdash pp_{de}}\,Hyp}{responsable \circ x \vdash n\backslash n}\,/E}{est \circ (responsable \circ x) \vdash np\backslash s_{main}}\,/E}{\cfrac{elle \circ (est \circ (responsable \circ x)) \vdash s_{main}}{elle \circ (est \circ responsable) \vdash s_{main}/\Diamond_1\Box_1 pp_{de}}\,/\Diamond_1\Box_1 I}}{}\,\backslash E
$$

As shown in the proof, the extraction analysis starts by assuming a $pp_{de}$ hypothesis (corresponding to a $pp_{de}$ gap in a mainstream generative grammar analysis) then derives a sentence $s_{main}$ using the elimination rules. Finally, the introduction rule "binds" the gap: it removes the leaf $x$ corresponding to the $pp_{de}$ hypothesis and binds it semantically. The proof above also shows why the assignment of the simpler formula $(n\backslash n)/(s/pp_{de})$ to the word "dont" doesn't suffice: in the penultimate step of the proof, we have derived $elle \circ (est \circ (responsable \circ x))$ of type $s_{main}$, whereas for the $/I$ rule to apply we would need a differently bracketed structure such as $(elle \circ (est \circ responsable)) \circ x$, with $x$ the immediate right daughter of the root node.[4] Appendix A gives a

---

[4] To be precise, this example only shows the need for a form of associativity, but slightly more complicated examples like "for which she was responsible in 1992" show that associativity alone is no solution. Examples of this kind have been a driving force in the development of extensions of the Lambek calculus.

detailed treatment of the unabbreviated version of this proof, showing notably how to *derive A* from $\Diamond_1 \Box_1 A$. To summarize, formulas of the form $\Diamond_1 \Box_1 A$ are special types of *A* formulas that can be extracted from deeply embedded positions.

## 3          THE FRENCH TREEBANK

The French Treebank (FTB, Abeillé *et al.* 2000) is a set of syntactically annotated news articles from the newspaper *Le Monde*. The FTB consists of 12,891 annotated sentences with a total of 383,227 words. The FTB has previously been used to extract phrase structure grammars (Arun and Keller 2005), dependency grammars (Candito *et al.* 2009; Guillaume and Perrier 2012), lexical-functional grammars (Schluter and van Genabith 2008), and tree adjoining grammars (Dybro-Johansen 2004).

For its annotation, the FTB uses simple, rather flat trees with some functional syntactic annotation (subject, object, infinitival argument, etc.). Consecutive multiword-expressions have been merged in the annotation and neither traces nor discontinuous dependencies have been annotated.

Consider the following sentence from the French Treebank.

(2)     À  cette  époque,  on  avait  dénombré  cent_quarante  candidats
        at that  time,    we had   counted    hundred-forty  candidates
        'At that time, there were 140 candidates.'

Its FTB annotation is shown in Figure 1. We can see that verb clusters are treated as constituents (labelled *VN*) and that the arguments of the verb occur as sisters of this verbal cluster. For example, the object noun phrase in Figure 1 is the sister of the *VN*. However, as we will see in Section 4.3, we obtain a much neater analysis when we treat the object as an argument of "dénombré" (*counted*), which is the past participle of a transitive verb.

## 4          GRAMMAR EXTRACTION

Grammar extraction algorithms for categorial grammars follow a general methodology – see, for example, Buszkowski and Penn (1990),

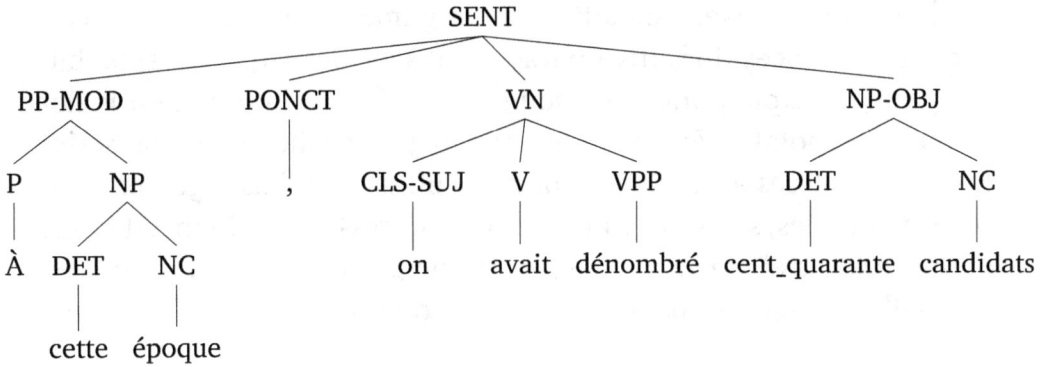

Figure 1: An example sentence from the French Treebank

Moortgat and Moot (2001), Hockenmaier and Steedman (2007) and Sandillon-Rezer (2013), shown as item 2 below – with some additional rules to deal with the quirks of the format of the input treebank. A high-level description of the grammar extraction algorithm used to convert the FTB into the TLGbank is given below.

1. split multiword expressions,

2. binarize the tree, keeping track of the distinction between modifiers and arguments; arguments are assigned formulas based on their syntactic label (e.g. $np$ for a noun phrase argument, $np\backslash s_{inf}$ for an infinitival argument, etc.)

3. reattach verb cluster arguments,

4. rearrange coordinations,

5. insert traces in the appropriate places and assign the appropriate formulas to relative pronouns and clitics.[5]

All steps are done by a single Prolog tree transformation, then verified and corrected manually (either by writing an ad hoc tree transformation script or by manually editing the output, then verifying that the result remains a valid derivation). Since the FTB annotation makes

---

[5] Subject clitics are treated as normal $np$ subjects. Object clitics, such as the object clitic "l" in "Marie l'aime" (Marie him-clitic loves, *Marie loves him*) are assigned the formula $(np\backslash s)/((np\backslash s)/\Diamond_1\Box_1 np)$ following the analysis of Moot and Retoré (2006). By assigning these higher-order formulas to the clitics, we can assign a normal transitive verb formula to "aime" (*loves*). Only the reflexive clitic "se" and the clitic "y" in the construction "il y a" (*there is/are*) are treated as arguments of the verb (with formulas $cl_{se}$ and $cl_y$, respectively).

the distinction between modifiers and arguments only for certain categories (sentences, infinitive phrases, present participle phrases, but
not past participle phrases or noun phrases), this information is not
explicitly annotated for many major categories (the extraction script
treats these cases as modifiers for noun phrases and as arguments for
other categories, such as past participle phrases). In addition, all forms
of the verb "être" (*to be*) with a past participle as argument have been
manually changed to passive whenever this was a passive construction.[6]

In Step 4, which harmonizes the annotation of coordinations,
many simple coordinations are treated correctly by the extraction
script. Special care has been taken of the punctuation symbols, which
in many cases are manually given a coordination-like formula assignment, and of gapping, which must be treated manually as well (the
treatment of gapping is presented in detail in Appendix B.4).

Finally, relative pronouns are treated by the extraction script as
arguments of the immediately following verb, which is correct in many
cases but needs to be manually verified for all occurrences.

In sum, after a pass of the extraction script, many constructions
are manually verified and corrected. To give an indication of the
amount of manual cleanup done: simply running the Prolog script on
the treebank results in a lexicon with 5,240 distinct formulas assigned
to the words of the lexicon (Moot 2010b) (note that this is without a
distinction between passives and past participles), but after cleanup
there are 1,101.

From Section 4.1 to Section 4.5, we will treat each of the stages
of the extraction algorithm in turn.

## 4.1          *Splitting multiword expressions*

The French Treebank treats many multiword expressions as single
nodes in the annotation. For example, the expression "dépôt de bilan"
(*voluntary liquidation*) occurs as "dépôt_de_bilan"; similarly, as shown
in Figure 1, numbers such as "cent_quarante" (*140*) are analysed as

---

[6] Not all occurrences of passives are accompanied by a form of "to be": adjectival uses of passive (e.g. in English "books written by Stephen King") are treated
automatically, whereas extraposed passive phrases, such as "Elaborated with the
greatest discretion, this project...", are handled during the manual correction of
coordination/punctuation.

a single word. Though very good solutions exist to detect these automatically in a separate preprocessing step (see, for example, Constant *et al.* 2011), we have decided to split all these into their separate words in order not to have to depend on additional components.

Fortunately, the French Treebank also annotates the internal structure for many of these complex lexical lemmas, so we can find that "dépôt de bilan" has the internal structure [noun, preposition, noun] and use this to automatically annotate the expression according to the basic case discussed below, so this step requires little human intervention.

4.2                         *The basic case*

The heart of the algorithm binarizes the trees from the French Treebank and separates the daughters of a node into functors/heads, arguments, and modifiers. This step is done automatically, using a version of the classic "head percolation" table (Magerman 1994) similar to the ones used for other categorial grammar extraction algorithms (Hockenmaier and Steedman 2007; Moortgat and Moot 2001; Moot 2010a).

The automated part of the extraction algorithm recursively descends each node and successively performs each of the different transformations described here, as well as the refinements described in Sections 4.3 to 4.5. Thus, even though these cases are described separately for ease of exposition, they apply together at each node.

For example, the following sentence

(3)     le   score correspondait à peine au   tiers de l'   objectif
        the score corresponded  barely   to a third of the goal
        mensuel
        monthly
        'the score barely corresponded to a third of the monthly goal'

has the French Treebank annotation shown in Figure 2. In the figure, the multiword expression "à peine" (*hardly*) has already been separated into its component words in the previous step of the algorithm.

The binarization step first selects the head of the constituent (the head percolation table first tries to find a verbal group VN as the head of a sentence SENT) and then combines it first with the sisters to its right, then with the sisters to its left, as shown in the figure below.

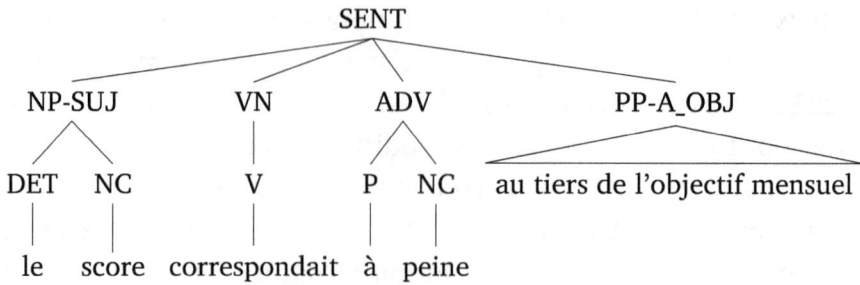

Figure 2: Initial French Treebank tree.

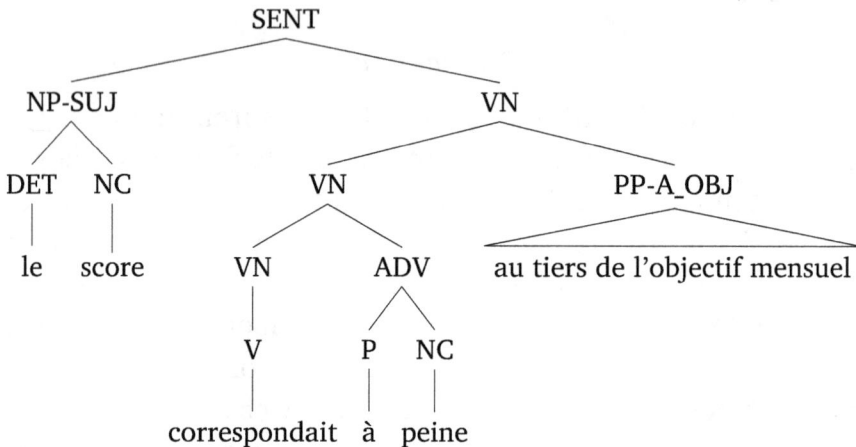

Figure 3: The tree of Figure 2 after binarization.

The label of the newly created nodes remains the same; VN in this case. The resulting tree, shown in Figure 3 has only unary and binary branches.

Next, a similar table of defaults decides for each binary branch if the pair of nodes concerned are a functor and its argument or a modifier and a category it modifies. So in the current example ADV is treated as a modifier whereas PP-A_OBJ is treated as an argument. A functor and argument are given the formulas $F/A$ and $A$, if the argument occurs on the right, or $A$ and $A\backslash F$ if the argument occurs on the left, where $F$ is the formula assigned to the parent node and $A$ is the formula corresponding to the syntactic label of the argument node (this is again performed by looking up the values in a table, which indicates for example, that NP corresponds to $np$ and PP-A_OBJ corresponds to $pp_a$). For modifiers, the modifier is assigned $F/F$ if it occurs on the left and $F\backslash F$ if it occurs on the right, where $F$ is the formula assigned to the parent node; the sister node of the modifier will therefore be assigned the same formula $F$ as the parent node.

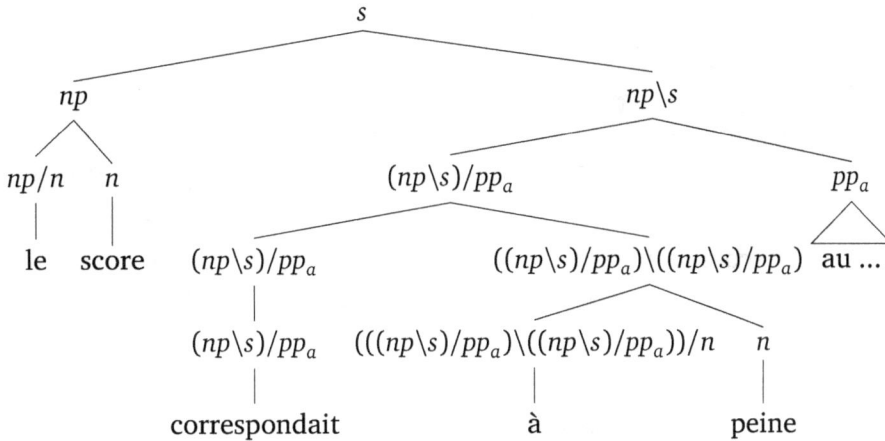

Figure 4: First derivation corresponding to Figure 3, using only elimination rules.

This translates the binarized tree of Figure 3 into the tree shown in Figure 4. This tree gives a full description of a derivation using only the elimination rules $/E$ and $\backslash E$: suppressing the unary modes, we can label each pair of sisters uniquely with one of these rules by looking only at their formulas, either $F/A$ and $A$ or $A$ and $A\backslash F$; the distinction between modifiers and other functors is no longer relevant now, modifiers are simply those formulas where $F = A$.

So far, the extraction algorithm has followed the classic categorial grammar extraction methodology of Buszkowski and Penn (1990) and Moortgat and Moot (2001). However, the tree above gives a rather complicated formula to the modifier "à peine" (*hardly*). Moreover, this formula would change with the formula assigned to the verb it modifies – requiring a different formula for transitive verbs, intransitive verbs, auxiliary verbs, etc. – resulting in unnecessary duplication of lexical entries for all adverbs. As we have seen in Section 2 with the adverb "dangereusement" (*dangerously*), we can choose an infixation solution and treat all adverbs as VP modifiers as shown in Figure 5.

From this tree, we can again obtain a complete derivation, this time using the $/E$, $\backslash E$ and $\backslash_1 E$ rules of Table 1, though we now need the word order of the original sentence to determine the position of the adverb. The $\backslash_1 E$ rule essentially plays the role of the crossing composition rules used for similar situations in the CCGbank (Hockenmaier and Steedman 2007). This simplification is performed automatically whenever a complex verb-modifier formula would be assigned to an adverb.

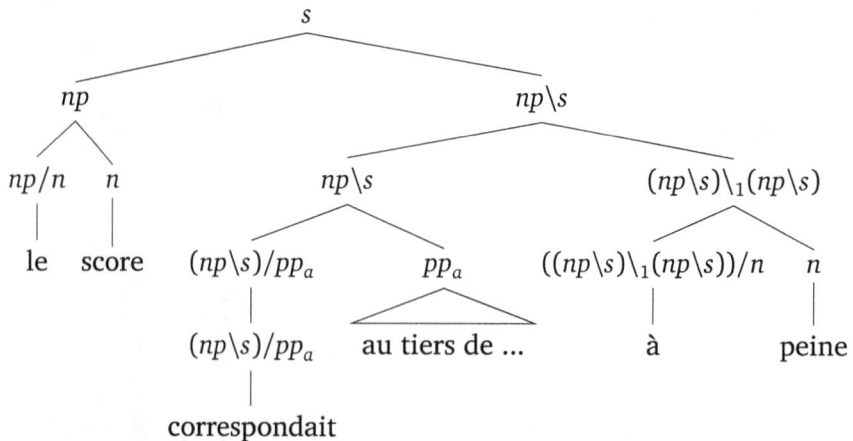

Figure 5: A version of the derivation of Figure 4 using a simpler lexical entry for the adverb "à peine"

## 4.3           *Verb clusters*

As discussed in Section 3, verb clusters (which include clitics and some adverbs) and the arguments of verbs are sisters in the FTB annotation trees. While this wasn't a problem for the simple cases treated in the previous section, this becomes problematic in the case of a complex verbal group. Figure 6 shows an example corresponding to sentence (4) (Figure 1 back on page 235 requires a similar treatment).

(4)     Ils    ont   déjà     pu            constater que (...)
        they   have   already   been   able   to   note      that

In a categorial setting, we obtain a much simpler analysis if the VN arguments are arguments of the embedded verbs instead: in the current case, we'd like the infinitival group to be the argument of the past participle "pu" (past participle of the verb "pouvoir", *can*). At the bottom of Figure 6 we see the rightward branching structure which results from the corpus transformation. Note also how the adverb "déjà" (*already*) is assigned the VP-modifier formula $(np\backslash s_x)/(np\backslash s_x)$ which is parametric for the type of sentence (in essence, this is a formula with an implicit first-order quantifier ranging over the different sentence types, see Moot 2014 or Moortgat 2011, Section 2.7; in the figure, $x$ is instantiated to *ppart*).

The extraction script automatically rebrackets the verb clusters as indicated above and treats any arguments of the verb cluster as arguments of the final verb in the cluster. This step requires very few manual corrections.

## 4.4 *Coordination and punctuation symbols*

The sentences below illustrate some of the problems with coordination which we will discuss in this section.

(5)  Elles reprennent et   amplifient des programmes existants
     they resume      and amplify        programs    existing
     ou en cours d'      adaptation
     or currently being adapted

(6)  Les lieux  où    les deux derniers morts  ont   été
     the places where the two   last     deaths have been
     recensés, lundi    30 décembre, La Yougoslavie et   La
     reported, Monday 30 December,    Yugoslavia   and
     Colombie, (...)
     Colombia,

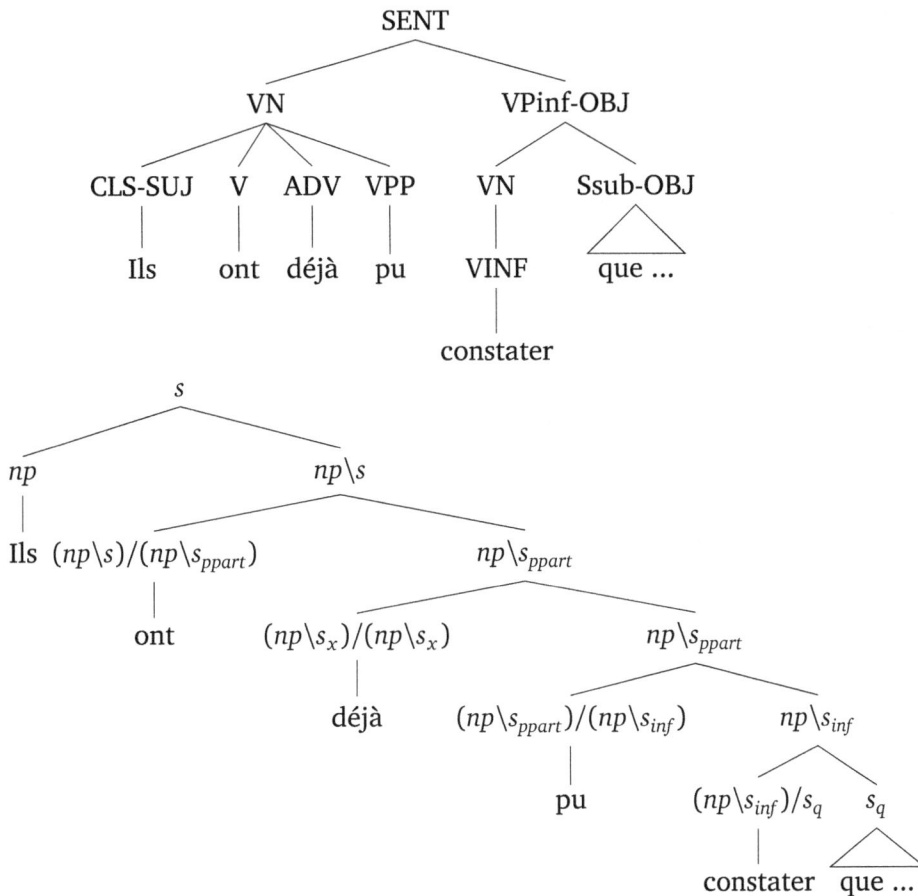

Figure 6: Rebracketing a verbal group and its arguments

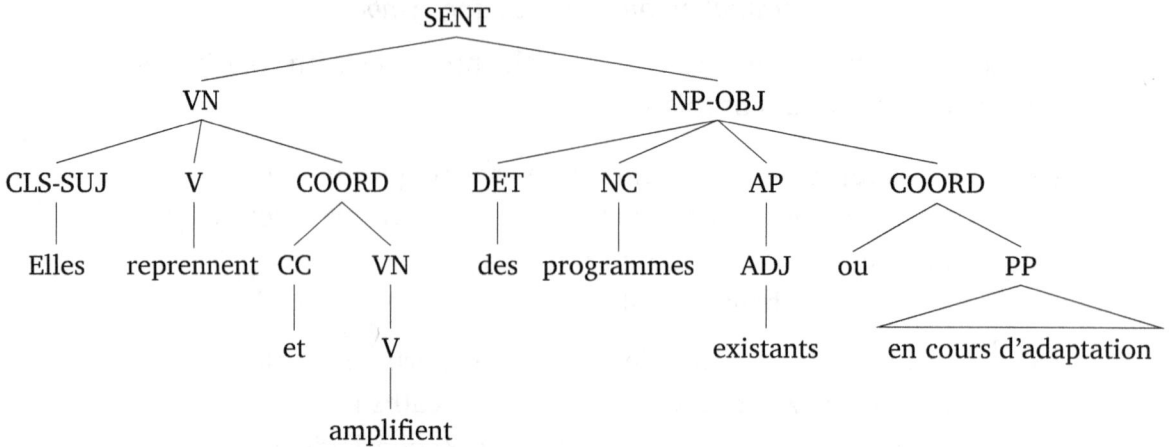

Figure 7: Coordination

Figure 7 shows the FTB syntactic structure of sentence (5). In categorial grammars, conjunctions like "ou" (*or*) are generally assigned instances of the formula $(X\backslash X)/X$ (for a contextually appropriate choice of the formula $X$). The first conjunction is of the two transitive verbs (instantiating $X$ with the formula $(np\backslash s_{main})/np$) that share both the subject and the object. For the second coordination it is the adjective and the prepositional phrase which are conjoined (though this is not so clear from the annotation only, where it seems to be an unlike coordination between an $np$ and a $pp$). As is standard in categorial grammars, we assign both the adjective and the PP the formula $n\backslash n$ (this is the standard assignment for a PP modifying a noun), turning this seemingly unlike coordination into a trivial instance of the general coordination scheme.

The (somewhat simplified) FTB annotation of sentence (6) of Figure 8 shows another problem: appositives, which are treated by assigning a coordination-like formula to the punctuation symbol preceding them (a similar solution is used for parentheticals and for most extrapositions).[7] An additional complication in this example is that we have

---

[7] Not all extrapositions can be analysed as coordinations this way. In the example below

(i)      A celà s'ajoute      une considération générale : (...)
           to that adds-itself a      general consideration

"A celà" is assigned $s/(s/\Diamond_1\Box_1 pp_a)$ allowing it to function as a long-distance $pp$ argument to "s'ajoute", as we have seen for the $s/\Diamond_1\Box_1 pp_{de}$ argument of "dont" in Section 2.

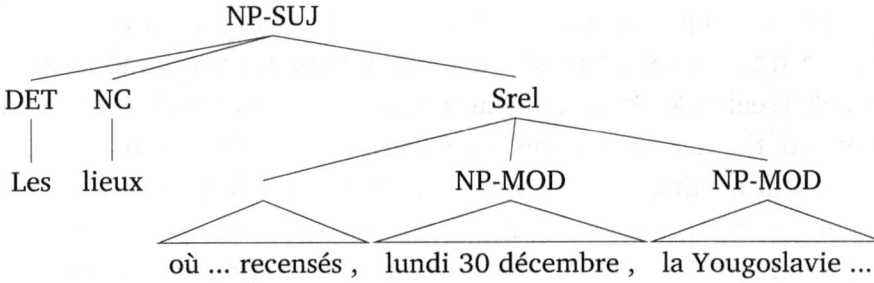

Figure 8: Appositives

to distinguish between the NP-MOD temporal adverb, which modifies the verb "recensés" (*reported*), and the NP-MOD for the appositive, which conjoins to "Les lieux" (*the places*) with the NP containing "la Yougoslavie" (*Yugoslavia*).

As the example shows, these cases are difficult to infer from the information provided by the FTB annotation alone, and therefore must be annotated manually; in total a bit more than 20% of the punctuation symbols – over ten thousand punctuation symbols – are assigned coordination-like categories. This complicated treatment of punctuation is not necessary for standard phrase structure parsers but given that in a categorial grammar analysis we want coordination-like punctuation to behave *semantically* like coordination, some special treatment of coordination is necessary.

More complex forms of coordination, such as right-node raising and gapping, require a more sophisticated treatment, which is discussed in Appendix B.

4.5            *Traces and long-distance dependencies*

As an example of a simple long-distance dependency in the corpus, consider the example below.

(7)    Premier handicap auquel    il convenait   de s'attaquer:
       first      handicap to which it was agreed to  attack:
       l'inflation
       the inflation

Figure 9 shows how the insertion of traces works. In the input structure on the top of the figure, "auquel" (*to which*) is assigned a preposition + pronoun POS-tag and assigned the role of a prepositional object with the preposition "à" (*to*). However, this preposition is an argument of the verb "s'attaquer à" (*to attack*), which occurs much lower in the annotation tree. Since none of these dependencies are annotated in the French Treebank, the default automatic treatment assigns them as arguments of the next occurring verb. Even though this is a reasonable default, it still produces many errors. In the example above, it would assign the $pp_a$ as argument of the main verb "convenait" (*to agree*), which is a possible assignment for this verb but is incorrect in the current case. As a consequence all relative pronouns, wh-pronouns, and clitics – a total of over 3,000 occurrences in the corpus – have been manually verified and, where necessary, corrected with the appropriate long-distance dependencies. At the bottom of Figure 9, the manually added long-distance dependency is shown (for reasons of horizontal space, the subproof of "de s'attaquer $pp_a$" has been stretched, as indicated by the dots).

## 5                     ANALYSIS

Categorial grammars, much like lexicalized tree adjoining grammars and other strongly lexicalized formalisms, use very construction-specific lexical entries. This means, for example, that when a verb can be used both as transitive and intransitive, it will have (at least) two distinct lexical entries. For extracted grammars, this generally means a very high level of lexical ambiguity.

Using the most detailed extraction parameters, the final lexicon uses 1,101 distinct formulas, though only 800 of these occur more than once and, 684 more than twice and 570 at least five times. The lion's share of these rare formulas are assigned to frequently occurring words, such as "et" (*and*) and verbs, appearing in unusual syntactic constructions.

Using a slightly less detailed extraction (which, for example, distinguishes only $pp_{de}$, $pp_a$ and $pp_{par}$ and uses simply $pp$ for prepositional phrases headed by other prepositions) there are 761 different formulas used in the lexicon (of which only 684 occur more than once, 546 occur more than twice and 471 occur at least five times).

Even in this second lexicon, many frequent words have a great number of lexical assignments. The conjunction "et" (*and*) has 86 different lexical formulas, the comma "," (which, as we have seen, often functions much like a conjunction) is assigned 72 distinct formulas, the adverb "plus" (*more*) has 44 formulas (in part because of possible combinations with "que", *than*), the prepositions "pour" (*for/to*), "en" (*in/while*) and "de" (*of/from*) have 43, 42 and 40 formulas respectively, and the verb "est" (*is*) has 39 formulas.

Although this kind of lexical ambiguity may seem like an important problem when using the extracted lexicon for parsing, well-known techniques such as *supertagging* (Bangalore and Joshi 2011), which assign the contextually most likely set of formulas (supertags) to each word, can be used to reduce the lexical ambiguity to an acceptable level. To give an idea of how effective this strategy is in the current context and with the reduced lexicon of 761 formulas: using the supertagger of Clark and Curran (2004) and assigning only the most

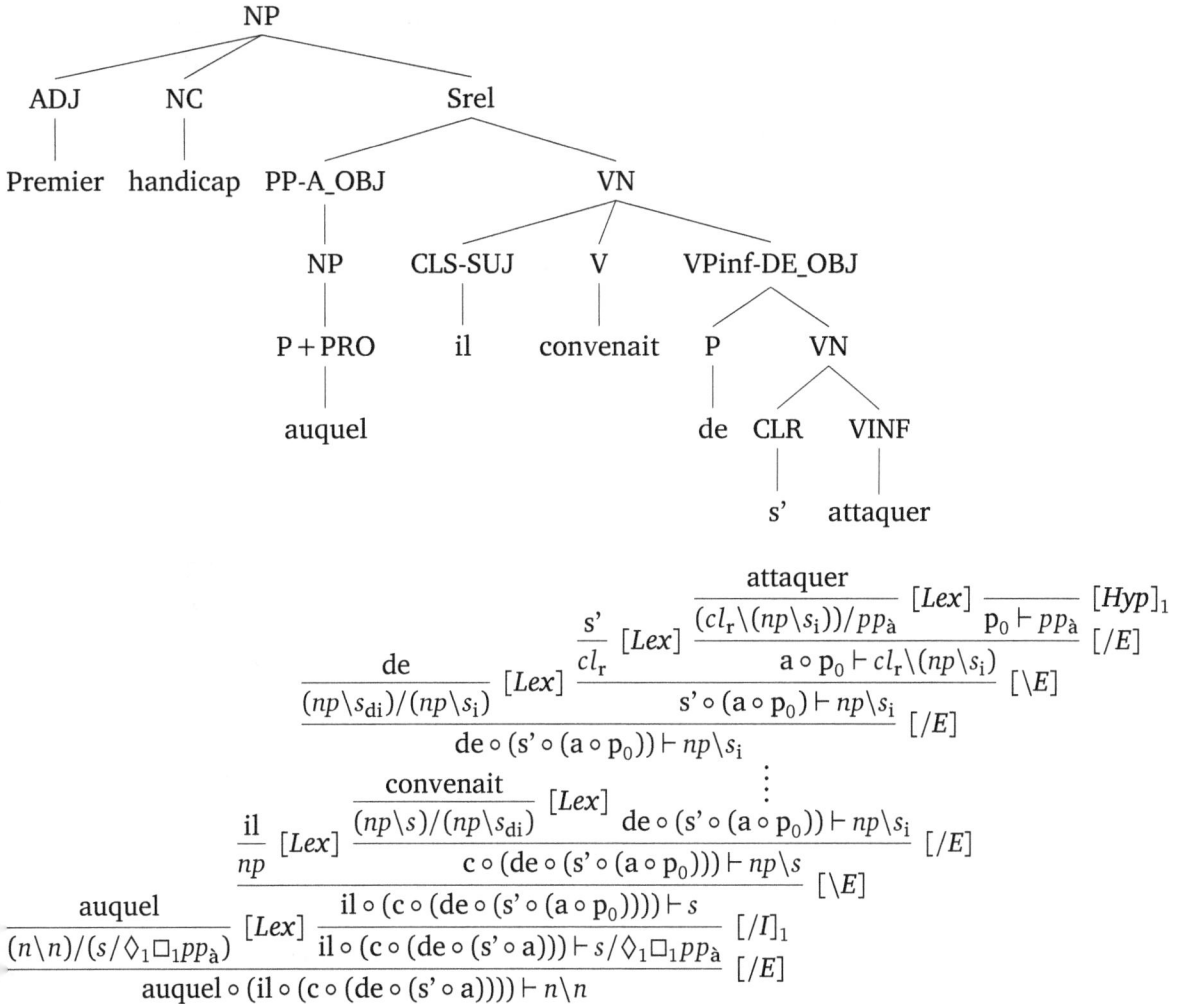

Figure 9: Adding traces to the output

likely formula to each word, 90.6% of the words are assigned the correct formula. When assigning each word all formulas with probability greater than 1% of the most likely supertag (for an average of 2.3 formulas per word), the supertagger assigns the correct formula to 98.4% of all words (for the FTB section of the TLGbank, using ten-fold cross-validation).

Supertagging does not solve the problem of data sparseness: for the supertagger, formulas which are seen only once or twice in the training data are not fundamentally different from formulas which do not occur at all. However, since these are exceptional cases, this has little effect on the coverage of the parser: Clark and Curran (2007) use only categories occurring at least 10 times for their parser based on the CCGbank and still obtain 99.58% coverage on unseen sentences.

We will discuss the performance of the supertagger in more detail, especially on sentences *outside* of the French Treebank, while discussing bootstrapping in Section 7.1.


6          COMPARISON WITH THE CCGBANK

Apart from the obvious theoretical differences between CCG and type-logical grammars and the different treatment of certain linguistic phenomena – such as extraction – that this implies, it is worth spending some time on some of the less obvious differences between the two treebanks.

Whereas the CCGbank uses a certain number of rules besides the standard combinatory schemata – notably for extraposition and coordination,[8] but also to transform passives $np\backslash s_{pass}$ into adjectives $n\backslash n$ and (bare) nouns $n$ into noun phrases $np$ – the TLGbank uses no non-logical rules. As a result, the lexicon of the type-logical treebank does more of the work. The lexicon is bigger and consequently, the tasks of the supertagger and the parser are more difficult in comparison with the CCG supertagger (Clark and Curran 2007). The supertagger's precision is similar – 98.4% correct in both cases – though the number

---

[8] To give an idea of the form of these rules, there is an extraposition rule transforming "$np$" (that is, a noun phrase followed by a comma) into a sentence modifier $s/s$ and a set of rules transforming constructions like "$X$ and $X$" (that is, the word "and" occurring between two expression of the same category $X$) to $X$, see Section 2.5.5 of Hockenmaier and Steedman (2005) for more details.

of lexical formulas per word is higher – 2.3 for the TLGbank versus 1.7 for the CCGbank. The number of lexical formulas per word is an important factor for parsing speed.

If we want to reduce the size of the lexicon in a way similar to the CCGbank, there are two basic options:

1. the first option is to allow non-logical rules of the same style as those used for the CCGbank,

2. the second option, more in line with the general spirit of type-logical grammars, is to exploit the derivability relation and to replace the analysis of passives by a formula $F$ such that $F \vdash n\backslash n$ (see Section 4.4.2 of Morrill 2011 for a particularly nice solution).

Since reducing the lexical ambiguity increases parsing speed but adding rules (as in option 1) or complicating the formulas (as in option 2) will reduce it, a careful evaluation of the benefits should be made. We leave to future research the transformation of the TLGbank in these two ways.

# 7            TOOLS AND RESOURCES

To facilitate annotation, correction, and parsing, several tools have been developed, using a combination of Prolog and TclTk. In addition, several well-known tools have been used for the exploitation of the corpus: the Stanford Tregex tool (Levy and Andrew 2006) for browsing and querying the French Treebank (as well as some of its transformations), Lefff (Sagot 2010) for lemmatizing and related tasks, the C&C tools (Clark and Curran 2004) for training POS-tag and supertag models using the annotated corpus, and a chart parser strongly inspired by Shieber *et al.* (1995) for parsing with the resulting grammar.

Figure 10 shows a screenshot of the interface to the supertagger and parser. This "horizontal" interface allows the user to type in sentences and see the resulting semantic output from the parser. The darker-shaded percentage of the block to the left of the formula gives a visual indication of the probability assigned to the formula (the exact numbers can be seen by moving the mouse over the corresponding area). Apart from some configuration options, this interface is not interactive.

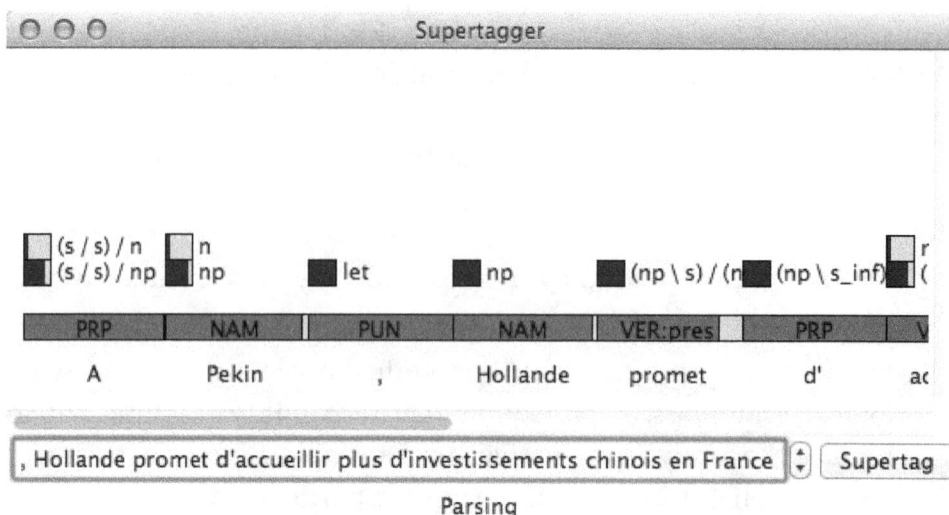

Figure 10: Screenshot of the supertagger interface

Figure 11 shows a screenshot of the "vertical" interface to the parser and supertagger. This is an interactive interface, allowing the user to select (or type in) the desired formula – to help prevent errors, the current frequency of the chosen formula for the current word is displayed after a manual choice of the formula – as well as allowing the user to select the parser rule applications by clicking on one of the premises for a rule (an additional dialog pops up if the rule choice is ambiguous, which happens infrequently). The weight column shows the log-probability of the item.[9]

## 7.1                                   *Bootstrapping*

Given that the French Treebank is somewhat small compared to other treebanks and given that the conversion of the FTB to the type-logical treebank was rather labour-intensive, it makes sense to look at more efficient ways of increasing the size of the treebank. The tools described in the previous section, interfacing with the supertagger and the parser for the core corpus are useful in this respect.

Currently, slightly over 1,600 additional sentences have been annotated (for a total annotated corpus of 14,539 sentences and 421,348

---

[9] The current implementation of the parser is not statistical in the sense that the rule applications do not have a probability assigned to them (the supertags do, so the parser outputs the first parse found for the most probable combination of supertags which allows a parse). However, the source code has the required hooks to add a probability model for the rule applications, whereas the required probabilities can be estimated from the treebank itself.

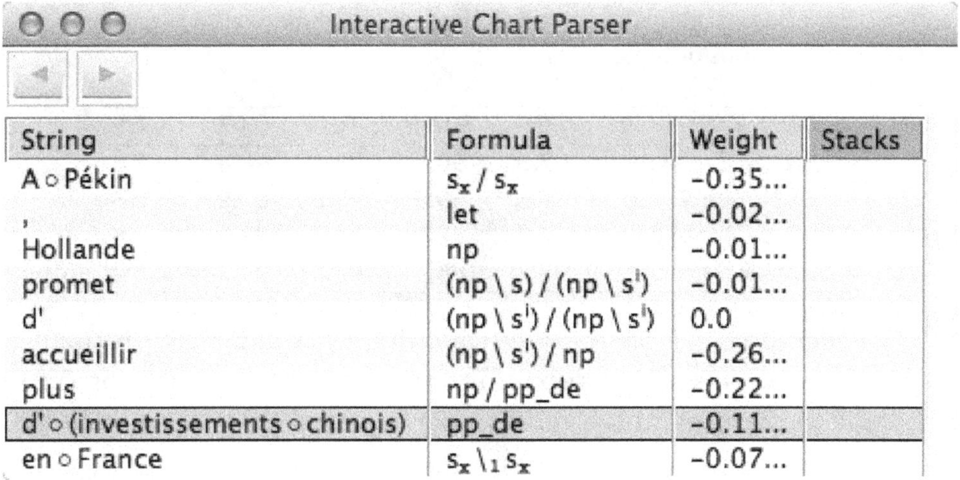

| String | Formula | Weight | Stacks |
|---|---|---|---|
| A ∘ Pékin | $s_x / s_x$ | −0.35... | |
| , | let | −0.02... | |
| Hollande | np | −0.01... | |
| promet | $(np \backslash s) / (np \backslash s^i)$ | −0.01... | |
| d' | $(np \backslash s^i) / (np \backslash s^i)$ | 0.0 | |
| accueillir | $(np \backslash s^i) / np$ | −0.26... | |
| plus | $np / pp\_de$ | −0.22... | |
| d' ∘ (investissements ∘ chinois) | $pp\_de$ | −0.11... | |
| en ∘ France | $s_x \backslash_1 s_x$ | −0.07... | |

Figure 11: Screenshot of the interactive parser

words). Most of these sentences come from the Sequoia treebank (Candito and Seddah 2012) and the French Timebank (Bittar 2010). The observed accuracy of the supertagger for these sentences from the *L'Est Républicain* newspaper is slightly lower than the results reported in Section 5: in 88.1% of cases, the best supertag is correct, and in 97.6% of cases the correct supertag has probability greater than 1% of the best supertag (as compared to 90.6% and 98.4% respectively for the cross-validated results). Part of this difference might be attributable to stylistic differences between the two newspapers (initial experiments with annotating unseen sentences from *Le Monde* seem to confirm this) but it may also be the case that cross-validation gives a somewhat optimistic picture of actual performance on unseen data from other sources (the different training and test sets not being completely independent).

Table 2 shows the accuracy of the Part-of-Speech tagger and of the supertagger for the different sub-corpora. The columns POS and Super list the accuracy of the Part-of-Speech tagger and of the supertagger respectively for the different corpora. Performance degrades gracefully for the different newspaper corpora (the French treebank and more modern articles in *Le Monde* being presumably the most similar, whereas the articles in *L'Est Républicain* from Sequoia and the French Timebank have a slightly reduced supertagger performance) but it shows a somewhat more important reduction for the literary corpus of travelogues in the Pyrenees of Itipy (Lefeuvre *et al.* 2012; Moot 2012).

Table 2: Supertagger and Part-of-Speech tagger performance on
the different sections of the corpus

| Corpus | POS | Super | 0.1 | 0.01 | F/w |
|---|---|---|---|---|---|
| French Treebank | 97.8 | 90.6 | 96.4 | 98.4 | 2.3 |
| Le Monde 2010 | 97.3 | 89.9 | 95.8 | 97.9 | 2.2 |
| L'Est Républicain | 97.3 | 88.1 | 94.8 | 97.6 | 2.4 |
| Itipy/Forbes | 95.7 | 86.7 | 93.8 | 97.1 | 2.6 |

The 0.1 and 0.01 columns indicate the supertagger's performance when all supertags with probability greater than $\beta$ ($=0.1$ or $0.01$) times the probability of the most likely supertag have been included. The column F/w indicates how many supertags this is per word for $\beta = 0.01$ (for $\beta = 0.1$ this number is around 1.4). We can see that even though the supertagger's performance for the best supertag (in the Super column) reduces steadily – from 90.6 on the main corpus to 86.7 on the Itipy corpus, a 3.9 percentage points difference – when using multiple supertags, this difference is greatly reduced (from 98.4 to 97.1, a 1.3 percentage points difference).

Even in the more difficult context of the Itipy corpus, the parser/supertagger combination (with $\beta = 0.01$) finds a complete analysis for 88.6% of the sentences in this subcorpus. We expect this figure to improve when better search heuristics, such as those described by Clark and Curran (2007), are used to deal with the increased number of formulas per word. To give an indication that even the current parser implementation performs well: the only other parsing statistics I've seen for the Itipy corpus are given by Nguyen (2012), who reports that a total of 18.5% of the sentences in the Itipy corpus were successfully parsed using an off-the-shelf parser.

7.2                     *Availability*

All the tools and resources are available from the author under the GNU Lesser General Public License.

```
http://richardmoot.github.io/TLGbank/
```

An unfortunate exception to this is the main part of the Typelogical Treebank itself: being a derived work of the French Treebank, it is available only to those who have a license for the original treebank (contact to author for access to the private Git). The Sequoia part of the treebank and the models derived from the complete treebank are freely available, however.

# 8        CONCLUSION

We have shown how the French Treebank has been semi-automatically transformed into a set of derivations in multimodal type-logical grammars: the TLGbank. This is an important first step in training and evaluating wide-coverage type-logical parsers and we hope to see several competitive type-logical parsers in the future.

# ACKNOWLEDGMENTS

I would like to thank Michael Moortgat and Noémie-Fleur Sandillon-Rezer for our work together on similar grammar extraction tasks. In addition, Michael Moortgat's insights on how to design multimodal type-logical grammars have deeply influenced all aspects of the design of the current treebank.

I also thank Yannick Parmentier and Denys Duchier for organizing the ESSLLI 2013 workshop in Düsseldorf where I presented this material and all workshop participants for their feedback.

I would also like to thank the anonymous referees for their many useful comments.

I, of course, take full responsibility for any remaining errors.

# APPENDIX

## A        COMPLETE LOGICAL RULES

Table 3 lists the full set of rules for multimodal categorial grammars. Binary modes $i$ range over $\{\epsilon, 1, 2, 3, l, r\}$ – although we will continue to write $X \circ_\epsilon Y$ as $X \circ Y$ and $A/_\epsilon B$ as $A/B$, etc. – and unary modes $j$ range over $\{0, 1, l, r\}$.

### A.1        *The unary connectives*

The rules for $\Diamond$ and $\Box$ may require some additional explanation for people unused to multimodal type-logical grammars. Whereas the rules for $\bullet$, $/$, and $\backslash$ produce binary trees labelled by indices — with the $\bullet I$, $/E$, and $\backslash E$ rules *constructing* trees (i.e. combining previously derived trees $X$ and $Y$ into a single tree $X \circ_j Y$) and with the $\bullet E$, $/I$, and $\backslash I$ rules *removing* binary branches — the rules for $\Box$ and $\Diamond$ produce and remove unary branches. So the $\Box E$ rule states that if we have previ-

Table 3: Full set of logical rules for multimodal type-logical grammar

$$\frac{}{w \vdash A} \; Lex \qquad\qquad \frac{}{x \vdash A} \; Hyp$$

$$\frac{X \vdash A/_iB \quad Y \vdash B}{X \circ_i Y \vdash A} \; /E \qquad\qquad \frac{X \vdash B \quad Y \vdash B\backslash_iA}{X \circ_i Y \vdash A} \; \backslash E$$

$$\frac{\begin{array}{c} x \vdash B \\ \vdots \\ X \circ_i x \vdash A \end{array}}{X \vdash A/_iB} \; /I \qquad\qquad \frac{\begin{array}{c} x \vdash B \\ \vdots \\ x \circ_i X \vdash A \end{array}}{X \vdash B\backslash_iA} \; \backslash I$$

$$\frac{Y \vdash A \bullet_i B \quad \begin{array}{c} x \vdash A \quad y \vdash B \\ \vdots \\ X[x \circ_i y] \vdash C \end{array}}{X[Y] \vdash C} \; \bullet E \qquad\qquad \frac{X \vdash A \quad Y \vdash B}{X \circ_i Y \vdash A \bullet_i B} \; \bullet I$$

$$\frac{X \vdash \Box_jA}{\langle X \rangle^j \vdash A} \; \Box E \qquad\qquad \frac{\langle X \rangle^j \vdash A}{X \vdash \Box_jA} \; \Box I$$

$$\frac{Y \vdash \Diamond_jA \quad \begin{array}{c} x \vdash A \\ \vdots \\ X[\langle x \rangle^j] \vdash C \end{array}}{X[Y] \vdash C} \; \Diamond E \qquad\qquad \frac{X \vdash A}{\langle X \rangle^j \vdash \Diamond_jA} \; \Diamond I$$

ously derived $X$ to be of type $\Box_jA$, then $\langle X \rangle^j$ is of type $A$; we remove the $\Box_j$ connective and add a unary branch labelled by the index $j$. Symmetrically, the $\Box I$ rule states that if we have derived $\langle X \rangle^j$ (i.e. we have an initial unary branch labelled $j$ with a daughter subtree $X$) to be of type $A$ then the tree $X$ by itself is of type $\Box_jA$.

The elimination rules for the product $\bullet$ and the diamond $\Diamond$ may appear a bit odd: they are similar to the disjunction elimination rule in intuitionistic logic and involve an arbitrary formula $C$. The $\Diamond E$ rule gives instructions on how to use a formula $\Diamond_jA$ once we have derived it (as the subproof of the left premise of the rule) by stating that if we can use a formula $A$ labelled with a fresh variable $x$ to derive any tree $X$ (of any formula $C$) such that this $x$ corresponding to $A$ occurs as a leaf with a unary branch labelled $j$ as its immediate parent (as indicated by the tree term $X[\langle x \rangle^j]$), then we can conclude that this tree $X$ with the unary branch $j$ and leaf $x$ replaced by $Y$ (the tree corresponding to $\Diamond_jA$) is also a tree

Table 4: Structural rules

**Infixation**

$$\frac{V[(X \circ Y) \circ_1 Z] \vdash C}{V[X \circ (Y \circ_1 Z)] \vdash C} \; MA \qquad \frac{V[(X \circ Y) \circ_1 Z] \vdash C}{V[(X \circ_1 Z) \circ Y] \vdash C} \; MC$$

**Extraction**

$$\frac{V[X \circ (Y \circ \langle Z \rangle^1)] \vdash C}{V[(X \circ Y) \circ \langle Z \rangle^1] \vdash C} \; MA\Diamond_1 \qquad \frac{V[(X \circ \langle Z \rangle^1) \circ Y] \vdash C}{V[(X \circ Y) \circ \langle Z \rangle^1] \vdash C} \; MC\Diamond_1$$

**Left-node raising/right-node raising**

$$\frac{V[(\langle X \rangle^0 \circ Y) \circ Z] \vdash C}{V[\langle X \rangle^0 \circ (Y \circ Z)] \vdash C} \; MA_l\Diamond_0 \qquad \frac{V[X \circ (Y \circ \langle Z \rangle^0)] \vdash C}{V[(X \circ Y) \circ \langle Z \rangle^0] \vdash C} \; MA_r\Diamond_0$$

**In situ binding**

$$\frac{V[X \circ \langle Y \rangle^2] \vdash C}{V[\langle X \rangle^r \circ_2 Y] \vdash C} \; I_{2r} \qquad \frac{V[\langle X \rangle^2 \circ Y] \vdash C}{V[\langle Y \rangle^l \circ_2 X] \vdash C} \; I_{2l}$$

$$\frac{V[X \circ (Y \circ_2 Z)] \vdash C}{V[(X \circ_r Y) \circ_2 Z] \vdash C} \; MA_{2r} \qquad \frac{V[(X \circ_2 Z) \circ Y] \vdash C}{V[(X \circ_l Y) \circ_2 Z] \vdash C} \; MC_{2l}$$

**Quoted speech**

$$\frac{V[(X \circ_3 Y) \circ Z] \vdash C}{V[X \circ_3 (Y \circ Z)] \vdash C} \; MA_3 \qquad \frac{V[Y \circ (X \circ_3 Z)] \vdash C}{V[X \circ_3 (Y \circ Z)] \vdash C} \; MC_3$$

of type $C$. In other words, $X[\langle x \rangle^j]$ becomes $X[Y]$ as indicated in the rule.

As an example, we show that if a tree $Y$ is of type $\Diamond_j \Box jA$ then this tree is also of type $A$ (for all formulas $A$ and unary indices $j$), as already alluded to in Section 2.

$$\frac{Y \vdash \Diamond_j \Box_j A \quad \dfrac{x \vdash \Box_j A}{\langle x \rangle^j \vdash A} \; \Box E}{Y \vdash A} \; \Diamond E$$

If $Y$ is of type $\Diamond_j \Box jA$, then we start the subproof on the right using the hypothesis $x$ of type $\Box_j A$. Then we apply the elimination rule for $\Box$ to produce the tree $\langle x \rangle^j$ of type $A$. But now, we are immediately in the right configuration to apply the $\Diamond E$ rule (it is the special case where the context $X[]$ is empty) and this allows us to replace $\langle x \rangle^j$ by $Y$, thereby proving that $Y$ is of type $A$ as required.

A.2                                   *The structural rules*

Although these patterns of derivability are interesting and can be used to give accounts of case and other forms of subtyping (Bernardi and Moot 2003), our interest here lies in the fact that they give access to structural rules which can rearrange our derived trees in controlled ways. The structural rules are listed in Table 4. The double line for the in situ binding rules indicate that these rules can be applied in both directions: top-to-bottom and bottom-to-top.

   Even though this looks like a rather large list, these are principally instantiations of the well-known universal rule schemata of mixed associativity and mixed commutativity (see Moortgat 2011 and Moot and Retoré 2012 for commentary, and Vermaat 2005 for arguments that these structural rules are truly universal).

   For the grammar engineer, the structural rules give us great flexibility and modularity when designing our grammars (although it could be argued that there is *too* much flexibility to this). However, the account given for different linguistic phenomena follows the conventional wisdom of categorial grammars and, as discussed in the next subsection, our annotation choices have been designed to be compatible with other modern type-logical grammars. So there has been a conscious choice not to create the smallest possible lexicon (at the cost of additional structural rules) but to keep the set of structural rules to the current set of instantiations of well-known schemata.

   The abbreviated proof from Section 2, is repeated below.

$$\cfrac{\cfrac{appauvrit \vdash (np\backslash s)/np \quad la \circ CGT \vdash np}{appauvrit \circ (la \circ CGT) \vdash np\backslash s} \, {/E} \quad dangereusement \vdash (np\backslash s)\backslash_1(np\backslash s)}{(appauvrit \circ_1 dangereusement) \circ (la \circ CGT) \vdash np\backslash s} \, {/E}$$

Using the structural rules of Table 4, this proof looks as follows.

$$\cfrac{\cfrac{\cfrac{appauvrit \vdash (np\backslash s)/np \quad la \circ CGT \vdash np}{appauvrit \circ (la \circ CGT) \vdash np\backslash s} \, {/E} \quad dangereusement \vdash (np\backslash s)\backslash_1(np\backslash s)}{(appauvrit \circ (la \circ CGT)) \circ_1 dangereusement \vdash np\backslash s} \, {/E}}{(appauvrit \circ_1 dangereusement) \circ (la \circ CGT) \vdash np\backslash s} \, {MC}$$

Similarly, we can translate proofs which use the $/\Diamond_1\Box_1 I$ rule of Table 1 into proofs using a combination of $\Diamond E$, $\Box E$, $/I$ and the two extraction rules $MA\Diamond_1$ and $MC\Diamond_1$ as shown below.

$$
\cfrac{
\cfrac{
\cfrac{
\cfrac{elle}{np}\,Lex \quad
\cfrac{
\cfrac{est}{(np\backslash s_{main})/(n\backslash n)}\,Lex \quad
\cfrac{
\cfrac{responsable}{(n\backslash n)/pp_{de}}\,Lex \quad
\cfrac{
\cfrac{x \vdash \Box_1 pp_{de}}{\langle x\rangle^1 \vdash pp_{de}}\,\Box E
}{}
}{responsable \circ \langle x\rangle^1 \vdash n\backslash n}\,/E
}{est \circ (responsable \circ \langle x\rangle^1) \vdash np\backslash s_{main}}\,/E
}{elle \circ (est \circ (responsable \circ \langle x\rangle^1)) \vdash s_{main}}\,\backslash E
}{elle \circ ((est \circ responsable) \circ \langle x\rangle^1) \vdash s_{main}}\,MA\Diamond_1
}{(elle \circ (est \circ responsable)) \circ \langle x\rangle^1 \vdash s_{main}}\,MA\Diamond_1 \quad
\cfrac{y \vdash \Diamond_1\Box_1 pp_{de}}{}\,Hyp
}{
\cfrac{(elle \circ (est \circ responsable)) \circ y \vdash s_{main}}{elle \circ (est \circ responsable) \vdash s_{main}/\Diamond_1\Box_1 pp_{de}}\,/I
}\,\Diamond E
$$

Given that the goal formula is $s_{main}/\Diamond_1\Box_1 pp_{de}$, we apply the introduction rule for $/$ to obtain a hypothesis $y$ of type $\Diamond_1\Box_1 pp_{de}$, then immediately the $\Diamond E$ rule to obtain a hypothesis $x$ of type $\Box_1 pp_{de}$. Given this hypothesis we can continue the proof using the elimination rules for $/$, $\backslash$, and $\Box$ to derive $elle \circ (est \circ (responsable \circ \langle x\rangle^1))$ of type $s_{main}$.

Applying the $\Diamond E$ rule immediately will cause our derivation to fail, since it simply substitutes $y$ for $\langle x\rangle^1$ and for the correct application of the $/I$ rule, we need $y$ to be the immediate right daughter of the tree. Our goal is therefore to move the $\langle x\rangle^1$ subterm to the top of the tree and then apply the $\Diamond E$ rule immediately followed by the $/I$ rule. This is where the structural rule of $MA\Diamond_1$ (mixed associativity) comes in: each application of the rule moves the $\langle x\rangle^1$ subterm one step closer to the top, until we can correctly complete the proof.

### A.3   *Conversion to other type-logical grammars*

As already indicated when justifying the choice for multimodal categorial grammars for the treebank annotation format in Section 2, the multimodal annotation has been designed to be compatible with other modern instantiations of type-logical grammar, such as the Displacement calculus (Morrill *et al.* 2011) and first-order linear logic (Moot 2014). The phenomena discussed in Section B.1 to Section B.3 can be imported into these calculi by simply removing the $\Diamond_0\Box_0$ prefixes since they operate in an associative base logic, whereas an implementation of the multimodal gapping solution of Hendriks (1995), on which our analysis of gapping is based, is presented by Morrill *et al.* (2011).

# B      ADDITIONAL LINGUISTIC PHENOMENA

The full set of rules from Appendix A allows us to treat a number of additional linguistic phenomena. These analyses, or at least the *ideas* behind them, should be relatively unsurprising to people familiar with linguistic analysis in the tradition of the Lambek calculus and its extensions (Moortgat 2011).

## B.1                  *Right-node raising*

Right-node raising (and its rare variant left-node raising) are instances of the structural rule of associativity, as is already implicit in the discussion of the examples by Lambek (1958). We need it to analyse sentences such as the following.

(8)      ses bons et    ses mauvais moments
         its good and its bad        moments

(9)      peut et   parfois     doit accompagner ...
         can   and sometimes must accompany    ...

In example (8), we want to analyse both "ses bons" and "ses mauvais" (a determiner and an adjective, which we would like to assign the formulas $np/n$ and $n/n$ respectively) as $np/\Diamond_0\Box_0 n$ (the reader can verify that we cannot derive $np/n \circ n/n \vdash np/n$ since associativity is not globally available). Similarly, "peut" and "parfois doit" in example (9) should be analysed as $(np\backslash s)/\Diamond_0\Box_0(np\backslash s_{inf})$. We can obtain the desired derivations for example (8) by assigning "et" the type $((np/\Diamond_0\Box_0 n)\backslash(np/n))/(np/\Diamond_0\Box_0 n)$ and combining it with the following derivation for "ses bons" (the derivation for "ses mauvais" is similar).

$$
\cfrac{
  \cfrac{
    \cfrac{ses}{np/n}\,Lex \quad
    \cfrac{
      \cfrac{bons}{n/n}\,Lex \quad
      \cfrac{
        \cfrac{y \vdash \Box n}{\langle y\rangle^0 \vdash n}\,\Box E \; \cfrac{}{}\,Hyp
      }{bons \circ \langle y\rangle^0 \vdash n}
    }{
      \cfrac{ses \circ (bons \circ \langle y\rangle^0) \vdash np}{(ses \circ bons) \circ \langle y\rangle^0 \vdash np}\,MA_r\Diamond_0
    }\,/E
  }{
    \cfrac{
      \cfrac{x \vdash \Diamond_0\Box_0 n}{}\,Hyp \quad (ses \circ bons) \circ \langle y\rangle^0 \vdash np
    }{(ses \circ bons) \circ x \vdash np}\,\Diamond E_2
  }
}{ses \circ bons \vdash np/\Diamond_0\Box_0 n}\,/I_1
$$

B.2                          *Left-node raising*

Very rarely, for a total of nine times in the entire corpus, we need the symmetric rule of left-node raising. In the example below, we have a conjunction of two combinations of two noun post-modifiers $n\backslash n$: "français Aérospatiale" and "italien Alenia".

(10)      ... des    groupes français Aérospatiale et    italien Alenia ...
              of the groups  French  Aérospatiale and Italian Alenia
          'of the French group Aérospatiale and Italian (group) Alenia'

By analysing "et" (and) as $((\Diamond_0\Box_0 n\backslash n)\backslash(n\backslash n))/(\Diamond_0\Box_0 n\backslash n)$ we can use the derivability of $n\backslash n, n\backslash n \vdash \Diamond_0\Box_0 n\backslash n$ (which is derivable given the structural rule $MA_l\Diamond_0$ of Table 4) as follows.

$$
\cfrac{
  \cfrac{x \vdash \Diamond_0\Box_0 n \;\; Hyp}{
    \cfrac{
      \cfrac{
        \cfrac{
          \cfrac{\cfrac{y \vdash \Box_0 n \;\; Hyp}{\langle y\rangle^0 \vdash n}\;\Box E \quad \cfrac{italien}{n\backslash n}\;Lex}{\langle y\rangle^0 \circ italien \vdash n}\;\backslash E \quad \cfrac{Alenia}{n\backslash n}\;L
        }{(\langle y\rangle^0 \circ italien) \circ Alenia \vdash n}\;\backslash E
      }{\langle y\rangle^0 \circ (italien \circ Alenia) \vdash n}\;MA_l\Diamond_0
    }{x \circ (italien \circ Alenia) \vdash n}\;\Diamond E_2
  }
}{italien \circ Alenia \vdash \Diamond_0\Box_0 n\backslash n}\;\backslash I_1
$$

B.3                          *Coordination of multiple arguments*

The product rules $\bullet E$ and $\bullet I$ are used for coordination of multiple arguments (as shown in sentence (11) below, where the two verb arguments $np$ and $pp$ are conjoined, see Section 2.4 of Morrill 2011).

(11)      augmenter [$_{np}$ ses fonds  propres ] [$_{pp}$ de 90 millions de
          increase    [$_{np}$ its equity            ] [$_{pp}$ by 90 million
          francs ] et    [$_{np}$ les quasi-fonds  propres ] [$_{pp}$ de 30
          francs ] and [$_{np}$ its quasi-equity            ] [$_{pp}$ by 30
          millions ]
          million   ]

We can derive these cases by assigning "et" the following formula.

$$((np \bullet pp)\backslash(np \bullet \Diamond_0\Box_0 pp))/(np \bullet pp)$$

Since we can form the $np \bullet pp$ arguments from both combinations of an $np$ and a $pp$ using the $\bullet I$ rule, we can derive "ses fonds propres de ... et les quasi-fonds propres de ..." (abbreviated as $e$ in the proof below) as being of type $np \bullet \Diamond_0 \Box_0 pp$ using an application of the $/E$ rule followed by an application of the $\backslash E$ rule. We can then combine this $np \bullet \Diamond_0 \Box_0 pp$ constituent with the verb "augmenter" (abbreviated as $a$) as follows.

$$
\cfrac{e \vdash np \bullet \Diamond_0 \Box_0 pp \qquad \cfrac{\cfrac{\qquad}{y \vdash \Diamond_0 \Box_0 pp}\ Hyp \qquad \cfrac{\cfrac{\cfrac{\cfrac{a}{((np\backslash s)/pp)/np}\ Lex \qquad \cfrac{\quad}{x \vdash np}\ Hyp}{a \circ x \vdash (np\backslash s)/pp} \qquad \cfrac{\cfrac{z \vdash \Box_0 pp}{\langle z \rangle^0 \vdash pp}\ \Box E}{\ }\ Hyp}{(a \circ x) \circ \langle z \rangle^0 \vdash np\backslash s}\ /E}{\cfrac{a \circ (x \circ \langle z \rangle^0) \vdash np\backslash s}{a \circ (x \circ y) \vdash np\backslash s}\ MA_r \Diamond_0}\ \Diamond E}{\ }\ \bullet E}{a \circ e \vdash np\backslash s}
$$

The $\Diamond_0 \Box_0 pp$ formula allows us to use the right-node raising rule of Section B.1. The proof would be slightly simpler if we assigned the word "augmenter" the formula $(np\backslash s)/(np \bullet pp)$ instead (such an analysis can also be found on page 19 of Morrill 2011). However, since we have already found independent motivation for the right-node raising rules, we have chosen to give the verb the more classical analysis of $((np\backslash s)/pp)/np$.

## B.4 　　　　　　　　　　　　　　*Gapping*

The extraction/infixation rules are used for the analysis of gapping, as shown in sentence (12) below, where the transitive verb "atteindre" is absent from the second clause.

(12)　　Le　salaire horaire　atteint dorénavant　34,06 francs et
　　　　the wages per hour reach　from now on 34.06 francs and
　　　　le　SMIC mensual brut　　　　　　　[$_{tv}$ ] 5756,14 francs.
　　　　the gross minimum monthly wage [$_{tv}$ ] 5756.14 francs.
　　　　'Hourly wages now reach 34.06 francs and the monthly min-
　　　　imum wage 5756.14 francs.'

We use the multimodal approach first proposed by Hendriks (1995) and then advanced by Moortgat (1996). Schematically, the formulas for gapping are of the following form

$$((s/_2 \Box_2 X)\backslash_l (s/_2 X))/(s/\Diamond_1 \Box_1 X)$$

with $X$ being a formula for a verb, for example $X = (np\backslash s)/np$ for a transitive verb.[10] This formula indicates that first a sentence missing a transitive verb to its right is selected (this is the extraction scheme we have seen before, though no longer restricted to right branches), then a sentence missing a transitive verb to its left, but keeping track of the *position* of this missing transitive verb in the sentence – this is implemented using the $l$ and $r$ modes which indicate whether the extracted verb is on the left or on the right of the current node. Finally, we *insert* a transitive verb at the position of this missing transitive verb on the left.

Even though this may seem like a rather roundabout way of achieving the desired sentence – first moving the transitive verb out, then moving it back into its original place – it has the important advantage of allowing us to get the semantics right; we know the verb from the first sentence and can therefore use it in the semantics, whereas a simpler type such as $(s\backslash s)/(s/\Diamond_1\Box_1 X)$ would not allow us to obtain the correct semantics.

In addition, abstracting away from the mode information and the unary connectives, the current analysis is an instantiation of the universal coordination formula $(Y\backslash Y)/Y$ when we choose $Y = s/X$, giving $((s/X)\backslash(s/X))/(s/X)$.

The extraction part of the gapping proof proceeds as shown below; $s$ abbreviates "le salaire horaire" and $f$ abbreviates "34,06 francs".

$$\cfrac{\cfrac{\cfrac{\cfrac{s \vdash np \qquad \cfrac{\cfrac{\cfrac{}{z \vdash \Box_2((np\backslash s)/np)}\,Hyp}{\langle z\rangle^2 \vdash (np\backslash s)/np}\,\Box E \qquad f \vdash np}{\langle z\rangle^2 \circ f \vdash np\backslash s}\,/E}{s \circ (\langle z\rangle^2 \circ f) \vdash s}\,\backslash E}{s \circ (\langle f\rangle^l \circ_2 z) \vdash s}\,I_{2l}}{(s \circ_r \langle f\rangle^l) \circ_2 z \vdash s}\,MA_{2r}}{s \circ_r \langle f\rangle^l \vdash s/_2\Box_2((np\backslash s)/np)}\,/I_1$$

We move the hypothetical $\Box_2((np\backslash s)/np)$ out, but keep track of where

[10] More precisely, the instantiation of the schema we need is

$$((s/_2\Box_2((np\backslash s)/np))\backslash_l(s/_2((np\backslash s)/\Diamond_0\Box_0 np)))/(s/\Diamond_1\Box_1((np\backslash s)/np))$$

with the $\Diamond_0\Box_0 np$ permitting right-node raising (associativity) as we have seen it in Section B.1.

we have used it: from the bottom, we started left of $f$ (leaving $l$ as a unary branch there), then right $(r)$.

Consequently, to get back from the top, we first go right $(r)$ and finally left $(l)$, ending up between $s$ and $f$ as required: we can then insert "atteint" of type $(np\backslash s)/np$, removing the trail of $l$ and $r$ during the process, as follows.[11]

$$
\cfrac{
\cfrac{
\cfrac{
\cfrac{(s \circ_r \langle f \rangle^l) \circ_l (et \ldots) \vdash s/_2((np\backslash s)/np) \quad a \vdash (np\backslash s)/np}{((s \circ_r \langle f \rangle^l) \circ_l (et \ldots)) \circ_2 a \vdash s} \; /E}{((s \circ_r \langle f \rangle^l) \circ_2 a) \circ (et \ldots) \vdash s} \; MC_{2l}^{-1}}{(s \circ (\langle f \rangle^l \circ_2 a)) \circ (et \ldots) \vdash s} \; MA_{2r}^{-1}}{s \circ (\langle a \rangle^2 \circ f) \circ (et \ldots) \vdash s} \; I_{2l}^{-1}
$$

B.5                *Quoted speech*

We need some special rules to treat past-perfect quoted speech, as shown in sentence (14) below. The parenthesized sentence is argument of the past participle "ajouté" and, in addition, this argument is discontinuous.

(13)      [$_s$ L'indice composite (...) a    baissé      de 0,3% en
           [$_s$ the index composite      has descended      0.3% in
           novembre ], a    annoncé    mardi    31 décembre le
           November ], has announced Tuesday 31 December the
           département du commerce.
           Department of Commerce.
           'The composite index fell 0.3% in November, announced the
           Department of Commerce on Tuesday December 31st.'

(14)      [$_{sl}$ Les conservateurs], a    ajouté le    premier ministre ...,
           [$_{sl}$ the Conservatives], has added the Prime    Minister,
           [$_{sr}$ "ne sont pas des opportunistes qui    virevoltent d'une
           [$_{sr}$ "    are not      opportunists who flip-flop    from one
           politique à l'autre    ]
           policy      to another ]

The solution is essentially to analyse the entire verb group missing the $s$ argument "a ajouté $np$" as $s_{main}\backslash_3 s_{main}$, the structural rules the

---

[11] The $-1$ as superscript to the rule names, e.g. in $I_{2l}^{-1}$, indicates that we apply the structural rules from *in situ binding* section of Table 4 in the "inverse" sense, i.e. bottom-up.

allow this entire group to move to the required position in the final string.

To illustrate this basic idea, we show how the structural rules for quoted speech allow us to derive "a ajouté $np$" (for some $np$) as $s_{main} \backslash_3 s_{main}$.

$$
\cfrac{
  \cfrac{a}{(s/np)/(np \backslash s_{ppart})} Lex \quad
  \cfrac{
    \cfrac{}{x \vdash s} Hyp \quad \cfrac{\text{ajouté}}{s \backslash_3 (np \backslash s_{ppart})} Lex
  }{x \circ_3 \text{ajouté} \vdash np \backslash s_{ppart}} \backslash E
}{
  \cfrac{
    \cfrac{a \circ (x \circ_3 \text{ajouté}) \vdash s/np}{
      \cfrac{
        \cfrac{(a \circ (x \circ_3 \text{ajouté})) \circ np \vdash s}{
          \cfrac{(x \circ_3 (a \circ \text{ajouté})) \circ np \vdash s}{
            \cfrac{x \circ_3 ((a \circ \text{ajouté}) \circ np) \vdash s}{(a \circ \text{ajouté}) \circ np \vdash s \backslash_3 s} \backslash I
          } MA_3
        } MC_3
      }{} 
    } /E \quad \cfrac{}{np \vdash np} /E
  }{}
}
$$

# REFERENCES

Anne ABEILLÉ, Lionel CLÉMENT, and Alexandra KINYON (2000), Building a treebank for French, in *Proceedings of the Second International Language Resources and Evaluation Conference*, pp. 87–94, Athens.

Abhishek ARUN and Frank KELLER (2005), Lexicalization in crosslinguistic probabilistic parsing: the case of French, in *Proceedings of the 43rd Annual Meeting of the Association for Computational Linguistics (ACL 2005)*, pp. 306–313, Ann Arbor, Michigan.

Srinivas BANGALORE and Aravind JOSHI (2011), *Supertagging: Using Complex Lexical Descriptions in Natural Language Processing*, MIT Press, Cambridge, Massachusetts.

Raffaella BERNARDI and Richard MOOT (2003), Generalized quantifiers in declarative and interrogative sentences, *Logic Journal of the IGPL*, 11(4):419–434.

André BITTAR (2010), *Building a TimeBank for French: A Reference Corpus Annotated According to the ISO-TimeML Standard*, Ph.D. thesis, Université Paris Diderot.

Johan BOS, Stephen CLARK, Mark STEEDMAN, James R. CURRAN, and Julia HOCKENMAIER (2004), Wide-coverage semantic representation from a CCG parser, in *Proceedings of the 20th International Conference on Computational Linguistics (COLING-2004)*, pp. 1240–1246, Geneva.

Johan BOS, James R. CURRAN, and Edoardo GUZZETTI (2007), The Pronto QA system at TREC-2007: harvesting hyponyms, using nominalisation patterns, and computing answer cardinality, in E. M. VOORHEES and L. P. BUCKLAND, editors, *The Sixteenth Text REtrieval Conference, TREC 2007*, pp. 726–732, Gaitersburg, Maryland.

Johan BOS and Katja MARKERT (2005), Recognising textual entailment with logical inference, in *Proceedings of the 2005 Conference on Empirical Methods in Natural Language Processing (EMNLP 2005)*, pp. 628–635.

Wojciech BUSZKOWSKI and Gerald PENN (1990), Categorial grammars determined from linguistic data by unification, *Studia Logica*, 49:431–454.

Marie CANDITO, Benoît CRABBÉ, Pascal DENIS, and François GUÉRIN (2009), Analyse syntaxique du français : des constituants aux dépendances, in *Proceedings of Traitement Automatique des Langues Naturelles (TALN)*, Senlis.

Marie CANDITO and Djamé SEDDAH (2012), Le corpus Sequoia : annotation syntaxique et exploitation pour l'adaptation d'analyseur par pont lexical, in *Proceedings of Traitement Automatique des Langues Naturelles (TALN)*, pp. 321–334, Grenoble.

Bob CARPENTER (1991), Categorial grammars, lexical rules and the English predicative, in Robert LEVINE, editor, *Formal Grammar: Theory and Practice*, number 2 in Vancouver Studies in Cognitive Science, pp. 168–242, University of British Columbia Press, Vancouver.

Stephen CLARK and James R. CURRAN (2004), Parsing the WSJ using CCG and log-linear models, in *Proceedings of the 42nd annual meeting of the Association for Computational Linguistics (ACL-2004)*, pp. 104–111, Barcelona.

Stephen CLARK and James R. CURRAN (2007), Wide-coverage efficient statistical parsing with CCG and log-linear models, *Computational Linguistics*, 33(4):493–552.

Matthieu CONSTANT, Isabelle TELLIER, Denys DUCHIER, Yoann DUPONT, Anthony SIGOGNE, and Sylvie BILLOT (2011), Intégrer des connaissances linguistiques dans un CRF : application à l'apprentissage d'un segmenteur-étiqueteur du français, in *Proceedings of Traitement Automatique des Langues Naturelles (TALN)*, Montpellier.

Ane DYBRO-JOHANSEN (2004), *Extraction Automatique de Grammaires à Partir d'un Corpus Français*, Master's thesis, Université Paris 7.

Bruno GUILLAUME and Guy PERRIER (2012), Semantic annotation of the French Treebank with modular graph rewriting, in *Proceedings of the Proceedings of META-RESEARCH Workshop on Advanced Treebanking (LREC'12)*, pp. 14–21, Istanbul.

Petra HENDRIKS (1995), Ellipsis and multimodal categorial type logic, in Glyn MORRILL and Richard T. OEHRLE, editors, *Proceedings of Formal Grammar 1995*, pp. 107–122, Barcelona.

Julia HOCKENMAIER and Mark STEEDMAN (2005), CCGbank: users's manual, Technical report, Department of Computer and Information Science, University of Pennsylvania.

Julia HOCKENMAIER and Mark STEEDMAN (2007), CCGbank, a corpus of CCG derivations and dependency structures extracted from the Penn Treebank, *Computational Linguistics*, 33(3):355–396.

Joachim LAMBEK (1958), The mathematics of sentence structure, *American Mathematical Monthly*, 65:154–170.

Anaïs LEFEUVRE, Richard MOOT, Christian RETORÉ, and Noémie-Fleur SANDILLON-REZER (2012), Traitement automatique sur corpus de récits de voyages pyrénéens : une analyse syntaxique, sémantique et temporelle, in *Proceedings of Traitement Automatique des Langues Naturelles (TALN)*, Grenoble.

Roger LEVY and Galen ANDREW (2006), Tregex and Tsurgeon: tools for querying and manipulating tree data structures, in *5th International Conference on Language Resources and Evaluation (LREC 2006)*, Genoa.

David M. MAGERMAN (1994), *Natural Language Parsing as Statistical Pattern Recognition*, Ph.D. thesis, University of Pennsylvania.

Michael MOORTGAT (1996), In situ binding: a modal analysis, in Paul DEKKER and Martin STOKHOF, editors, *Proceedings 10th Amsterdam Colloquium*, pp. 539–549, ILLC, Amsterdam.

Michael MOORTGAT (2011), Categorial type logics, in Johan VAN BENTHEM and Alice TER MEULEN, editors, *Handbook of Logic and Language*, chapter 2, pp. 95–179, North-Holland Elsevier, Amsterdam.

Michael MOORTGAT and Richard MOOT (2001), CGN to Grail: extracting a type-logical lexicon from the CGN annotation, *Language and Computers*, 37(1):126–143.

Richard MOOT (2010a), Automated extraction of type-logical supertags from the Spoken Dutch Corpus, in Srinivas BANGALORE and Aravind JOSHI, editors, *Complexity of Lexical Descriptions and its Relevance to Natural Language Processing: A Supertagging Approach*, chapter 12, pp. 291–312, MIT Press, Cambridge, Massachusetts.

Richard MOOT (2010b), Semi-automated extraction of a wide-coverage type-logical grammar for French, in *Proceedings of Traitement Automatique des Langues Naturelles (TALN)*, Montreal.

Richard MOOT (2012), Wide-coverage semantics for spatio-temporal reasoning, *Traitement Automatique des Languages*, 53(2):115–142.

Richard MOOT (2014), Extended Lambek calculi and first-order linear logic, in Claudia CASADIO, Bob COECKE, Michael MOORTGAT, and Philip SCOTT, editors, *Categories and Types in Logic, Language, and Physics: Essays dedicated to Jim Lambek on the Occasion of this 90th Birthday*, number 8222 in Lecture Notes in Artificial Intelligence, pp. 297–330, Springer, Heidelberg.

Richard MOOT and Mario PIAZZA (2001), Linguistic applications of first order multiplicative linear logic, *Journal of Logic, Language and Information*, 10(2):211–232.

Richard MOOT and Christian RETORÉ (2006), Les indices pronominaux du français dans les grammaires catégorielles, *Lingvisticae Investigationes*, 29(1):137–146.

Richard MOOT and Christian RETORÉ (2012), *The Logic of Categorial Grammars: A Deductive Account of Natural Language Syntax and Semantics*, number 6850 in Lecture Notes in Artificial Intelligence, Springer, Heidelberg.

Glyn MORRILL (1994), *Type Logical Grammar*, Kluwer Academic Publishers, Dordrecht.

Glyn MORRILL (2011), *Categorial Grammar: Logical Syntax, Semantics, and Processing*, Oxford University Press, Oxford.

Glyn MORRILL, Oriol VALENTÍN, and Mario FADDA (2011), The Displacement calculus, *Journal of Logic, Language and Information*, 20(1):1–48.

Van Tien NGUYEN (2012), *Méthode d'Extraction d'Informations Géographiques à des fins d'Enrichissement d'une Ontologie de Domaine*, Ph.D. thesis, Université de Pau et des Pays de l'Adour.

Richard T. OEHRLE (2011), Multi-modal type-logical grammar, in Robert BORSLEY and Kersti BÖRJARS, editors, *Non-transformational Syntax: Formal and Explicit Models of Grammar*, chapter 6, pp. 225–267, Wiley-Blackwell.

Benoît SAGOT (2010), The Lefff, a freely available and large-coverage morphological and syntactic lexicon for French, in *Proceedings of the Seventh International Conference on Language Resources and Evaluation (LREC'10)*, Valletta.

Noémie-Fleur SANDILLON-REZER (2013), *Apprentissage de Grammaires Catégorielles: Transducteurs d'Arbres et Clustering pour Induction de Grammaires Catégorielles*, Ph.D. thesis, Bordeaux University.

Natalie SCHLUTER and Josef VAN GENABITH (2008), Treebank-based acquisition of LFG parsing resources for French, in *Proceedings of the Sixth International Language Resources and Evaluation (LREC'08)*, Marrakech.

Stuart SHIEBER, Yves SCHABES, and Fernando PEREIRA (1995), Principles and implementation of deductive parsing, *Journal of Logic Programming*, 24(1–2):3–36.

Willemijn VERMAAT (2005), *The Logic of Variation. A Cross-Linguistic Account of wh-question Formation*, Ph.D. thesis, Utrecht Institute of Linguistics OTS, Utrecht University.

# 7

# A syntactic component for Vietnamese language processing

*Phuong Le-Hong*[1], *Azim Roussanaly*[2], *and Thi Minh Huyen Nguyen*[1]
[1] VNU University of Science, Hanoi, Vietnam
[2] LORIA, Université de Lorraine, Nancy, France

*Keywords: language, parsing, segmentation, syntactic component, tagging, tree-adjoining grammar, Vietnamese*

## ABSTRACT

This paper presents the development of a grammar and a syntactic parser for the Vietnamese language. We first discuss the construction of a lexicalized tree-adjoining grammar using an automatic extraction approach. We then present the construction and evaluation of a deep syntactic parser based on the extracted grammar. This is a complete system that produces syntactic structures for Vietnamese sentences. A dependency annotation scheme for Vietnamese and an algorithm for extracting dependency structures from derivation trees are also proposed. This is the first Vietnamese parsing system capable of producing both constituency and dependency analyses. It offers encouraging performance: accuracy of 69.33% and 73.21% for constituency and dependency analysis, respectively.

1              INTRODUCTION

Natural language processing (NLP) often depends on a syntactic representation of text. Software that can generate such a representation is usually composed of both a grammar and a parser for a given language.

For decades, NLP research has mostly concentrated on English and other well-studied languages. Recently there has been increased interest in languages for which fewer resources exist, notably because of their growing presence on the Internet. Vietnamese, which is among the top 20 most spoken languages (Paul *et al.* 2014), is one such language attracting increased attention. Obstacles remain, however, for NLP research in general and grammar development in particular: Vietnamese does not yet have vast and readily available constructed linguistic resources upon which to build effective statistical models, nor does it have reference works upon which new ideas may be experimented.

Moreover, most existing NLP research concerning Vietnamese has been focused on testing the applicability of existing methods and tools developed for English or other Western languages, under the assumption that their logical or statistical well-foundedness might offer cross-language validity; whereas assumptions about the structure of a language are usually made in such tools, and must be amended to adapt them to different linguistic phenomena. For an isolating language such as Vietnamese, techniques developed for inflectional languages cannot be applied "as is".

Our goal is to develop a syntactic parser for the Vietnamese language. We believe that a wide-coverage grammar that incorporates rich statistical information would contribute to the development of basic linguistic resources and tools for automatic processing of Vietnamese written text.

Syntactic parsing is a fundamental task in natural language processing. For Vietnamese, there have been few published works dealing with this problem. This paper presents the construction and evaluation of a deep syntactic parser based on Lexicalized Tree-Adjoining Grammars (LTAG) for the Vietnamese language.

The remainder of the paper is organized as follows. The next section introduces some preliminary concepts of different types of syntactic representation, a brief introduction of the Vietnamese language and the tree-adjoining grammar formalism. Section 3 then presents the construction of a tree-adjoining grammar – the first part of the syntactic component. This grammatical resource is extracted automatically from the Vietnamese treebank. Next, Section 4 discusses the construction of a deep parser based on the extracted grammar. The parser is evaluated in Section 5. Section 6 concludes the paper and suggests some directions for future work.

## 2 PRELIMINARIES

### 2.1 *Syntactic representation*

Constituency structure and dependency structure are two types of syntactic representation of a natural language sentence. While a constituency structure represents a nesting of multi-word constituents, a dependency structure represents dependencies between individual words of a sentence. The syntactic dependency represents the fact that the presence of a word is licensed by another word which is its governor. In a typed dependency analysis, grammatical labels are added to the dependencies to mark their grammatical relations, for example *subject* or *indirect object*.

Recently, there have been many published works on dependency analysis for well-studied languages, such as English (Kübler *et al.* 2009) or French (Candito *et al.* 2009b). The dependency parsers developed for these languages are usually probabilistic and trained on corpora available in the language of interest. We can classify the architecture of such parsers into two main types:

- parsers that employ a machine learning method on dependency corpora extracted automatically from treebanks and that directly produce dependency parses (Nivre 2003, McDonald and Pereira 2006, Johansson and Nugues 2008, Candito *et al.* 2010);
- parsers that rely on a sequential process where constituency parses are produced first and then dependency parses are extracted (Candito *et al.* 2009b, de Marneffe *et al.* 2006).

This second type is motivated by the fact that dependency corpora are not readily available for many languages, as in the case of Vietnamese. In such an architecture, we need a module which takes as input constituency parses given by a constituency parser and converts these parses into typed dependency parses as illustrated in Figure 1 and Figure 2 for the English sentence "*A hearing is scheduled on the issue today*" (Nivre and McDonald 2008).

### 2.2 *A brief overview of Vietnamese*

In this section we present some general characteristics of the Vietnamese language; these are adopted from Hạo (2000), Hữu *et al.* (1998) and Nguyen *et al.* (2006).

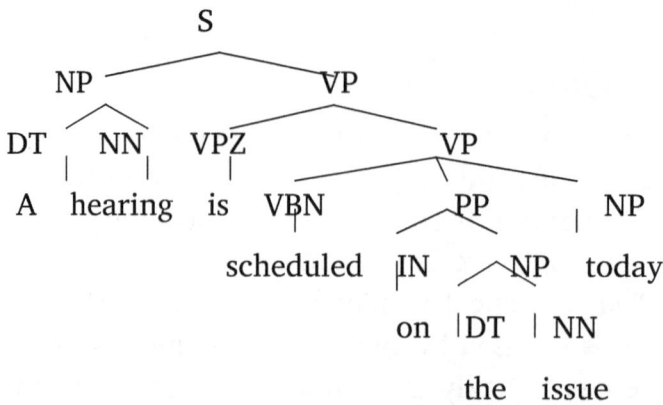

Figure 1: Constituency analysis of an English sentence

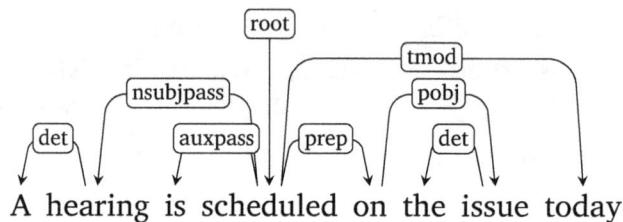

Figure 2: Dependency analysis of an English sentence

Vietnamese belongs to the VietMuong group of the Mon-Khmer branch, which in turn belongs to the Austro-Asiatic language family. Vietnamese is also similar to languages in the Tai family. The Vietnamese vocabulary features a large number of Sino-Vietnamese words which are derived from Chinese (Alves 1999). This vocabulary was originally written with Chinese characters that were used in the Vietnamese writing system, but like all written Vietnamese, is now written with the Latin-based Vietnamese alphabet that was adopted in the early 20th century. Moreover, by being in contact with the French language, Vietnamese was enriched not only in vocabulary but also in syntax by the calque (or loan translation) of French grammar. Thus, for example, the Subject-Verb-Object structure gained prevalence over the natively more common Theme-Rheme construction.

Vietnamese is an isolating language,[1] which means that it is characterized by the following traits:

- it is a monosyllabic language;
- its word forms never change, unlike occidental languages that use morphological variations (e.g. plural form, conjugation);

---

[1] It is noted that Chinese is also isolating; Chinese is classified in a branch of Sino-Tibetan language family.

- hence, all grammatical relations are manifested by word order and function words.

Vietnamese has a special unit called "tiếng" that corresponds at the same time to a syllable with respect to phonology, a morpheme with respect to morpho-syntax, and a word with respect to sentence constituent creation. For convenience, we call these "tiếng" syllables. The Vietnamese vocabulary contains:

- simple words, which are monosyllabic (e.g. *mưa* (rainy) *nắng* (sunny));
- reduplicated words composed by phonetic reduplication (e.g. *trắng* (white) – *trăng trắng* (whitish))
- compound words composed by semantic coordination (e.g. *quần* (trousers), *áo* (shirt) – *quần áo* (clothes))
- compound words composed by semantic subordination (e.g. *xe* (vehicle), *đạp* (to pedal) – *xe đạp* (bicycle));
- some compound words whose syllable combination is no longer recognizable (e.g. *bồ nông* (pelican))
- complex words phonetically transcribed from foreign languages (e.g. *cà phê* (coffee), from the French *café*).

The issue of syntactic category classification for Vietnamese is still in debate in the linguistic community. That lack of consensus is due to the unclear limit between the grammatical roles or syntactic functions of many words as well as the very frequent phenomenon of syntactic category mutation, by which a verb may for example be used as a noun, or even as a preposition. Vietnamese dictionaries (Hoàng 2002) use a set of 8 parts of speech proposed by the Vietnam Committee on Social Sciences (1983).

As for other isolating languages, the most important syntactic information source in Vietnamese is word order. The basic word order is Subject–Verb–Object. There are prepositions but no postpositions. In a noun phrase the main noun precedes the adjectives and the genitive follows the governing noun. These phenomena are subsumed under the term "head-initiality".

The other syntactic means are function words, reduplication, and, in the case of spoken language, intonation.

From the point of view of functional grammar, the syntactic structure of Vietnamese follows a topic-comment structure. It belongs to the class of topic-prominent languages as described by Li and Thompson (1976). In those languages, topics are coded in the surface structure and they tend to control co-referentiality (e.g. *Cây đó lá to nên tôi không thích* (*Tree that leaves big so I not like*), which means *This tree, its leaves are big, so I don't like it*); the topic-oriented "double subject" construction is a basic sentence type (e.g. *Tôi tên là Nam, sinh ở Hà Nội* (*I name be Nam, born in Hanoi*), which means *My name is Nam, I was born in Hanoi*), while such subject-oriented constructions as the passive and "dummy" subject sentences are rare or non-existent (e.g. *There is a cat in the garden* should be translated as *Có một con mèo trong vườn* (*exist one <animal-classifier> cat in garden*)).

## 2.3                    *Tree-adjoining grammars*

In the TAG formalism (Joshi and Schabes 1997), the grammar is defined by a set of elementary trees. A TAG parsing system rewrites nodes of trees rather than symbols of strings as in context-free grammars (CFG). The nodes of these trees are labelled with nonterminals and terminals. Starting from the elementary trees, larger trees are derived using composition operations of substitution and adjunction. In the case of an adjunction, the tree being adjoined has exactly one leaf node that is marked as the foot node (marked with an asterisk). Such a tree is called an *auxiliary tree*. Elementary trees that are not auxiliary trees are called *initial trees*. Each derivation starts with an initial tree. Substituting a tree $\alpha$ in a tree $\beta$ simply replaces a frontier substitution node in $\beta$ with $\alpha$, under the convention that the non-terminal symbol of the substitution node is the same as the root node of $\alpha$. Only initial trees and derived trees can be substituted in another tree. Adjoining an auxiliary tree $\beta$ at some node $n$ of a derived tree $\gamma$ proceeds as follows: the sub-tree $t$ of $\gamma$ rooted by $n$ is removed from $\gamma$, and $\beta$ is substituted for it instead, where $t$ is substituted in the foot node of $\beta$. In the final derived tree, all leaves must have terminal labels.

In TAG, the derived tree does not give enough information to determine how it was constructed. The derivation tree is an object that specifies uniquely how a derived tree was constructed. The root of a derivation tree is labelled by a sentence-type initial tree. All other nodes in the derivation tree are labelled by auxiliary trees in the case of adjunction or initial trees in the case of substitution. We use the following convention when depicting a derivation tree: trees that are adjoined to their parent tree are linked by a solid line to their parent, and trees that are substituted are linked by a dashed line.

In order to represent natural languages, TAGs are enriched with additional linguistic conventions or principles. First, a TAG for natural languages is *lexicalized* (Schabes 1990), which means that each elementary tree has a lexical anchor (usually unique, but in some cases, there is more than one anchor). Second, the elementary trees of a lexicalized TAG (LTAG) represent extended projections of lexical items (the anchors) and encapsulate all syntactic arguments of the lexical anchor; that is, they contain slots (nonterminal leaves) for all arguments. Furthermore, elementary trees are minimal in the sense that only the arguments of the anchor are encapsulated; all recursion is factored away. This amounts to the *condition on elementary tree minimality* from Frank (2002).

Because of these principles, in linguistic applications, combining two elementary trees corresponds to the application of a predicate to an argument (in case of substitution) or to the addition of modifiers (in case of adjunction). The derivation tree then reflects the predicate-argument structure of the sentence. This is why most approaches to semantics in TAG use the derivation tree as an interface between syntax and semantics.

Figure 3 gives a simple Vietnamese TAG and an analysis of a sentence. The first half of the figure shows the elementary trees of the grammar and the second half shows the derived tree and its corresponding derivation tree, where the notation < anchor > represents the elementary tree corresponding to a lexical anchor. A derivation tree in TAG specifies how a derived tree was constructed.

TAG has several advantages over CFG. First, it provides an extended domain of locality. Second, the adjunction operation permits us to model long-distance relationships in single elementary trees due to the factoring of recursion.[2] Third, TAG derivation trees show semantic dependencies between entities in a sentence, as the tree branches rep-

---

[2] These two properties follow from the mathematical properties of TAGs. TAGs belong to the class of mildly context-sensitive grammars. Context-free languages form a proper subset of tree-adjoining languages (TALs), which in turn form a proper subset of context-sensitive languages.

## Elementary trees

```
   NP          S          NP      NP        NP        NP
   |          / \         |      / \        |        / \
   Np      NP↓  VP        P     M  NP*      Nu     NP*  N
   |           / \        |     |           |          |
 Giang      V  NP↓ NP↓   tôi   một         quả        cam
            |
           cho
```

## Derived tree

```
              S
            /   \
          NP     VP
          |     / \
          Np   V  NP    NP
          |    |  |    / \
        Giang cho P   M   NP
                  |   |   / \
                 tôi một NP   N
                         |    |
                         Nu  cam
                         |
                        quả
```

## Derivation tree

```
              <cho>
            /   |   \
    <Giang>  <tôi>  <quả>
                     / \
               <một>  <cam>
```

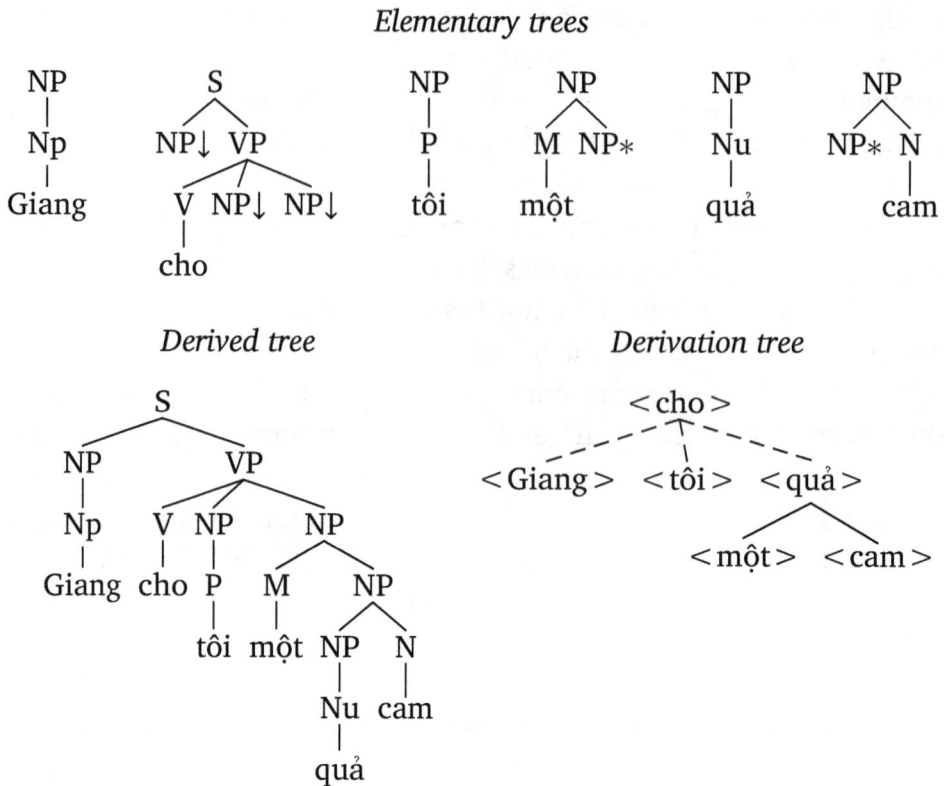

Figure 3: A TAG analysis of the sentence "Giang cho tôi một quả cam" (*Giang gave me an orange*)

resent their combination type (dashed or continuous line for substitution or adjunction, respectively, in Figure 3). In addition, in LTAG, lexical entries naturally capture constraints associated with lexical items, which is not possible in CFG. TAG and LTAG are formally equivalent; however, from the linguistic perspective, LTAG is the system we shall be concerned with in this paper.

## 3          GRAMMAR EXTRACTION

Since the development of hand-crafted grammars is a time-consuming and labour-intensive task, many studies on automatic and semi-automatic grammar development have been carried out during recent decades. A semi-automatic approach to building a large computational grammar is to rely on a formal language capable of describing the target grammar, e.g. a meta-grammar formalism. Many meta-grammar engineering environments were developed to support the construction of large computational grammars for natural language. Most of them were used to build large grammars for occidental languages. A typical example is the XMG (eXtensible MetaGrammar) system which supports rapid prototyping of tree-based grammars (Crabbé *et al.* 2013). An alternative approach for obtaining grammars is to extract grammars from a treebank containing syntactically annotated sentences. This is the approach that we chose to rapidly develop a large computational grammar for Vietnamese.

We present in this section a system that automatically extracts lexicalized tree adjoining grammars from treebanks. We first discuss in detail the extraction algorithms and compare them to previous work. We then report the first results for LTAG extraction for Vietnamese, using the recently released Vietnamese treebank.

## 3.1                              *Extracting grammars from treebanks*

There has been much work done on extracting treebank grammars in general and LTAG grammars in particular from annotated corpora, but all of these works are for common languages. Xia *et al.* (2000) and Xia (2001) developed the uniform method of grammar extraction for English, Chinese and Korean. Chiang (2000) developed a system for extracting an LTAG grammar from the English Penn Treebank and used it for statistical parsing with LTAG. Chen and Vijay-Shanker (2000) and Chen *et al.* (2006) extracted TAGs and there are other works based on Chen's approach such as Johansen (2004) and Nasr (2004) for French, and Habash and Rambow (2004) for Arabic. Neumann (2003) extracted lexicalized tree grammars for English from the English Penn Treebank and for German from the NEGRA treebank. Bäcker and Harbusch (2002) extracted an LTAG grammar for German – also from the NEGRA corpus – and used it for supertagging. Kaeshammer (2012) presented a grammar and a lexicon for PLTAG using the German Tiger corpus. Finally, Park (2006) extracted LTAG grammars for Korean from Korean Sejong Treebank.

## 3.2                              *Vietnamese treebank*

Recently, a group of Vietnamese computational linguists has been involved in developing a treebank for Vietnamese (Nguyen *et al.* 2009). This is the treebank we used for our extraction system.

Table 1: Some Vietnamese treebank tags

| No. | Category | Description |
|---|---|---|
| 1. | S | simple declarative clause |
| 2. | VP | verb phrase |
| 3. | NP | noun phrase |
| 4. | PP | preposition phrase |
| 5. | N | common noun |
| 6. | V | verb |
| 7. | P | pronoun |
| 8. | R | adverb |
| 9. | E | preposition |
| 10. | CC | coordinating conjunction |

The construction of a Vietnamese treebank is a branch project of a national project which aims to develop basic resources and tools for Vietnamese language and speech processing.[3] The raw texts of the treebank are collected from the social and political sections of the Youth online daily newspaper. The corpus is divided into three sets corresponding to three annotation levels: word-segmented, POS-tagged and syntax-annotated set. The syntax-annotated corpus, a subset of the POS-tagged set, is currently composed of 10 471 sentences (225 085 tokens). Sentences range from 2 to 105 words, with an average length of 21.75 words. There are 9314 sentences of length 40 words or less. The tagset of the treebank has 38 syntactic labels (18 part-of-speech tags, 17 syntactic category tags, 3 empty categories) and 17 function tags. For details, please refer to Nguyen *et al.* (2009).[4] The meanings of the tags that appear in this paper are listed in Table 1.

3.3                    *Extraction algorithms*

In general, our work on extracting an LTAG grammar for Vietnamese follows closely the method of grammar extraction originally proposed by Xia (2001). The extraction process has three steps: first, phrase-structure trees are converted into LTAG derived trees; second, the derived trees are decomposed into a set of elementary trees conforming to their three predefined prototypes; and third, invalid extracted elementary trees are filtered out using linguistic knowledge.

---

[3] The VLSP project, http://vlsp.vietlp.org:8080/demo/.
[4] All the resources are available at the website of the VLSP project.

### 3.3.1                               Building LTAG derived trees

The phrase structures in the Vietnamese treebank follow the English Penn Treebank (PTB) bracketed style format which are not suitable for LTAG extraction due to two reasons. First, the PTB trees do not distinguish heads, arguments and adjuncts as required in derived trees of an LTAG. Second, for each PTB tree, it is not trivial to recover a derivation tree generating it if it is not in a proper format of derived tree.

Therefore, we first have to convert the phrase structures of the treebank into derived trees by augmenting them with additional information needed for extraction.

In this step, we first classify each node in a phrase-structure tree as one of three types: head, argument or modifier. We then build a derived tree by adding intermediate nodes so that at each level of the tree, the nodes satisfy exactly one of the following relations (Xia 2001):

- *predicate-argument relation*: there is one (or more) node(s), where one is the head, and the rest are its arguments;
- *modification relation*: there are exactly two nodes, where one node is modified by the other;
- *coordination relation*: there are exactly three nodes, in which two nodes are coordinated by a conjunction.

In order to find heads of phrases, we have constructed *a head percolation table* (Magerman 1995; Collins 1997) for the Vietnamese treebank. This table is used to select the head child of a node. In addition, we have also constructed *an argument table* to determine the types of arguments that a head child can take. The argument table helps explicitly mark each sibling of a head child as either an argument or an adjunct according to the tag of the sibling, the tag of the head child, and the position of the sibling with respect to the head child. Together with *the tagset table*, these three tables constitute the Vietnamese treebank-specific information that is required for the extraction algorithms.

Since the conjunction structures are different from the argument and modifier structures, we first recursively bracket all conjunction groups of a treebank tree by Algorithm 1 and then build the full derived tree for the resulting tree by Algorithm 2. A conjunction group

Algorithm 1:    **Data**: A syntactic tree $T$.
ProcessConj($T$)   **Result**: $T$ whose conjunction groups are processed.

**for** $K \in T.\text{children}$ **do**
    **if** *IsPhrasal*($K$) **then**
        $K \leftarrow$ ProcessConj($K$);

$(\mathscr{C}_1, \ldots, \mathscr{C}_k) \leftarrow$ ConjGroups($T.\text{children}$);
**for** $i = 1$ *to* $k$ **do**
    **if** $\|\mathscr{C}_i\| > 1$ **then**
        InsertNode($T, \mathscr{C}_i$);

**if** $k > 2$ **then**
    **for** $i = k$ *downto* $3$ **do**
        $\mathscr{L} \leftarrow \mathscr{C}_{i-1} \cup c_{i-1} \cup \mathscr{C}_i$;
        $T' \leftarrow$ InsertNode($T, \mathscr{L}$);
        $\mathscr{C}_{i-1} \leftarrow T'$;

**return** $T$;

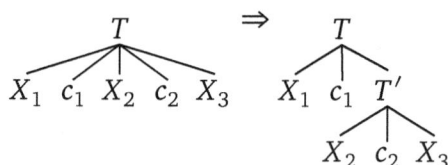

Figure 4: Transformation of conjunction groups

is a group of coordinating words or phrases connected by one or more coordinating conjunction. The form of a conjunction group is either "A and B" or "A or B".[5] Figure 4 shows a tree with conjunction groups before and after being processed by Algorithm 1 where $c_i$ are coordinating conjunctions and $X_i$ are conjunction groups. Figure 5 shows a realisation of Algorithm 2 where $A_i$ are arguments of the head child $H$ of $T$ and $M_i$ are modifiers of $H$. These two algorithms use the function InsertNode($T, \mathscr{L}$) to insert an intermediate node between a node $T$ and a list of its child nodes $\mathscr{L}$. This new node is a child of $T$, has the same label as $T$ and has $\mathscr{L}$ as the list of its children. The function IsPhrasal($X$) checks whether $X$ is a phrasal node or not.[6] The function

---

[5] In the treebank, there are no conjunctions which use the coordinating punctuation; that is, a structure like "A, B and C" is not present.

[6] A phrasal node is defined to be a node which is not a leaf or a preterminal. This means that it must have two or more children, or one child that is not a leaf.

**Data**: A tree $T$ whose conjunction groups have been processed.

Algorithm 2:
BuildDerivedTree($T$)

**Result**: A derived tree whose root is $T$.

**if** *(not IsPhrasal($T$))* **then**
    | **return** $T$;

$H \leftarrow$ HeadChild($T$);
**if** *not IsLeaf($H$)* **then**
    **for** $K \in T.\texttt{children}$ **do**
        | $K \leftarrow$ BuildDerivedTree($K$);

    $\mathscr{A} \leftarrow$ ArgNodes($H, \mathscr{L}$);
    $\mathscr{M} \leftarrow$ ModNodes($H, \mathscr{L}$);
    $m \leftarrow \|\mathscr{M}\|$;
    **if** $m > 0$ **then**
        | $\mathscr{L} \leftarrow \{H\} \cup \mathscr{A}$;
        | $T' \leftarrow$ InsertNode($T, \mathscr{L}$);

    $(M_1, M_2, \ldots, M_m) \leftarrow \mathscr{M}$;
    **for** $i \leftarrow 1$ **to** $m - 1$ **do**
        | $\mathscr{L} \leftarrow \{M_i, T'\}$;
        | $T'' \leftarrow$ InsertNode($T, \mathscr{L}$);
        | $T' \leftarrow T''$;

**return** $T$;

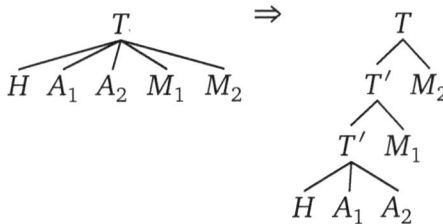

Figure 5: An example of derived tree realisation

ConjGroups($\mathscr{L}$) returns $k$ groups of components $\mathscr{C}_i$ of $\mathscr{L}$ which are separated by $k - 1$ conjunctions $c_1, \ldots, c_{k-1}$, which have a special POS tag in the treebank (CC).

    Algorithm 2 uses several simple functions. The HeadChild($X$) function selects the head child of a node $X$ according to a head percolation table. The function IsLeaf($X$) checks whether a node $X$ is a

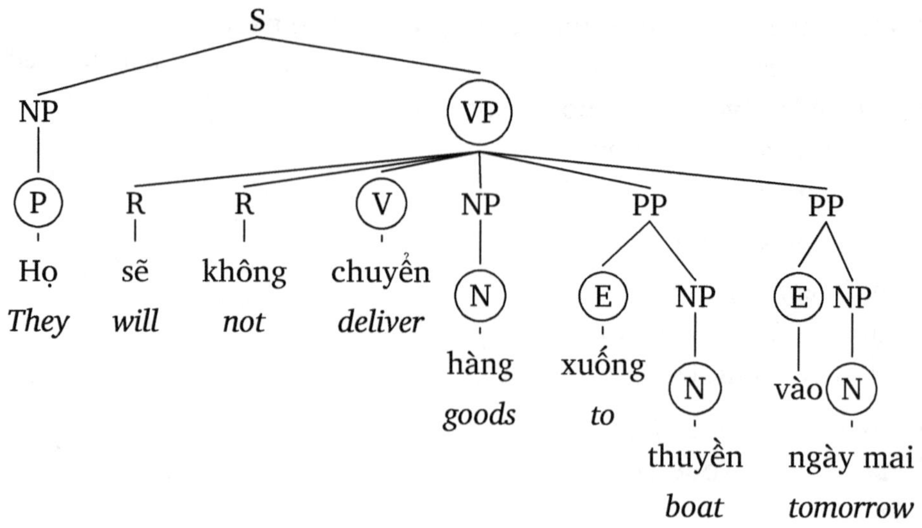

Figure 6: A parse tree of the Vietnamese treebank

leaf node or not. The functions ArgNodes($H, \mathscr{L}$) and ModNodes($H, \mathscr{L}$) each return a list of nodes which are arguments and modifiers, respectively, of a node $H$. The list $\mathscr{L}$ contains all sisters of $H$.

For example, Figure 6 shows the phrase structure of a sentence extracted from the Vietnamese treebank "*Họ sẽ không chuyển hàng xuống thuyền vào ngày mai.*" (They will not deliver the goods to the boat tomorrow.) The head children of phrases are circled.

The derived tree of the sentence once processed by Algorithm 2 is shown in Figure 7, wherein the inserted nodes are marked by the quotation mark symbol (').

3.3.2     Building elementary trees

At this step, each derived tree is decomposed into a set of elementary trees. The recursive structures of the derived tree are factored out and will become auxiliary trees, and the remaining non-recursive structures will be extracted as initial trees.

Extracted elementary trees fall into one of three prototypes as determined by the relation between the anchor and other nodes, as shown in Figure 8. The extraction process involves copying nodes from the derived tree for building elementary trees. The result of the extraction process is three sets of elementary trees: $\mathscr{S}$ contains spine trees, $\mathscr{M}$ contains modifier trees and $\mathscr{C}$ contains conjunction trees.

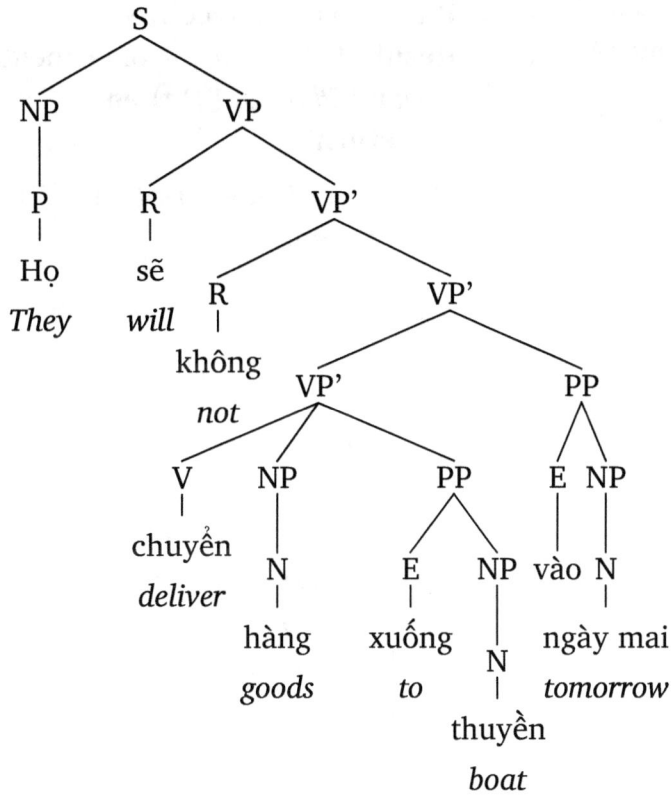

Figure 7: The derived tree of the treebank tree in Figure 6

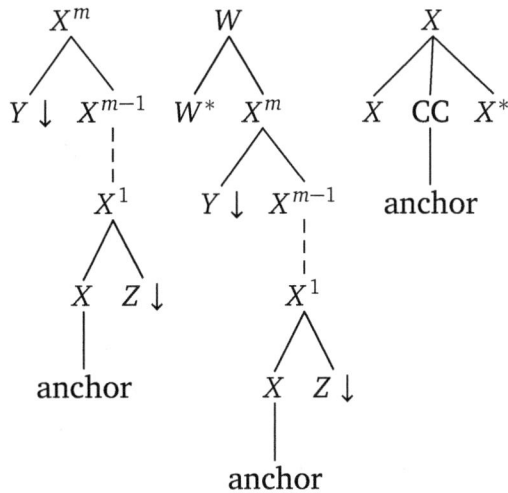

Figure 8: Prototypes of spine trees and auxiliary trees

Algorithm 3:
BuildElementaryTrees($T$)

**Data:** $T$ is a derived tree.

**Result:** Sets $\mathcal{S}, \mathcal{M}, \mathcal{C}$ of elementary trees.

**if** *(not IsPhrasal($T$))* **then**
   | **return** ;

$\{H_0, H_1, \ldots, H_n\} \leftarrow$ HeadPath($T$);
$ok \leftarrow$ false;
$P \leftarrow H_0$;
**for** $j \leftarrow 1$ ***to*** $n$ **do**
   | $\mathcal{L} \leftarrow$ Sisters($H_j$);
   | **if** $|\mathcal{L}| > 0$ **then**
   |   | Rel $\leftarrow$ GetRelation($H_j, \mathcal{L}$);
   |   | **if** Rel $=$ Coordination **then**
   |   |   | $\mathcal{C} \leftarrow \mathcal{C} \cup$ BuildConjTree($P$);
   |   | **if** Rel $=$ Modification **then**
   |   |   | $\mathcal{M} \leftarrow \mathcal{M} \cup$ BuildModTree($P$);
   |   |   | **if** $j = 1$ **then**
   |   |   |   | $\mathcal{S} \leftarrow \mathcal{S} \cup$ BuildSpineTree($P$);
   |   |   |   | $ok \leftarrow$ true;
   |   | **if** Rel $=$ Argument **then**
   |   |   | **if** *not ok and not IsLinkNode($P$)* **then**
   |   |   |   | $\mathcal{S} \leftarrow \mathcal{S} \cup$ BuildSpineTree($P$);
   |   |   |   | $ok \leftarrow$ true;
   | **else**
   |   | **if** *not IsLinkNode($P$) and IsPhrasal($P$)* **then**
   |   |   | $\mathcal{S} \leftarrow \mathcal{S} \cup$ BuildSpineTree($P$) ;
   | $P \leftarrow H_j$;

To build elementary trees from a derived tree $T$, we first find the head path[7] $\{H_0, H_1, \ldots, H_n\}$ of $T$. For each parent $P$ and its head child $H$, we get the list $\mathcal{L}$ of sisters of $H$ and determine the relation between $H$ and $\mathcal{L}$. If the relation is coordination, a conjunction tree will

---

[7] A *head path* starting from a node $T$ in a derived tree is the unique path from $T$ to a leaf node where each node except $T$ is the head child of its parents. Here $H_0 \equiv T$ and $H_j$ is the parent of its head child $H_{j+1}$. A node on the head path is called a *link node* if its label is the same as that of its parent.

```
NP  NP      NP        NP    VP        VP         PP          VP
 |   |       |         |   ╱ ╲      ╱ ╲        ╱ ╲         ╱ ╲
 P   N       N         N   R  VP*   R  VP*     E  NP↓     VP* PP
 |   |       |         |   |        |          |             ╱ ╲
Họ  hàng   ngày mai  thuyền sẽ    không      xuống          E  NP↓
                                                               |
                                                              vào
```

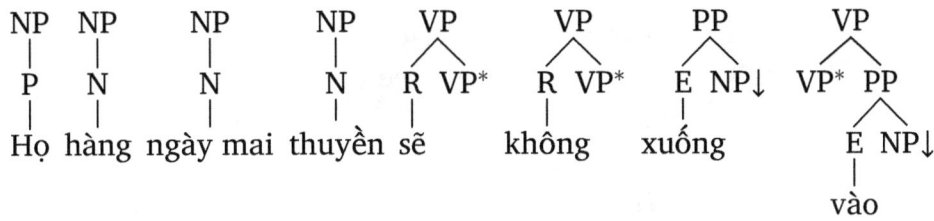

Figure 9: Extracted elementary trees

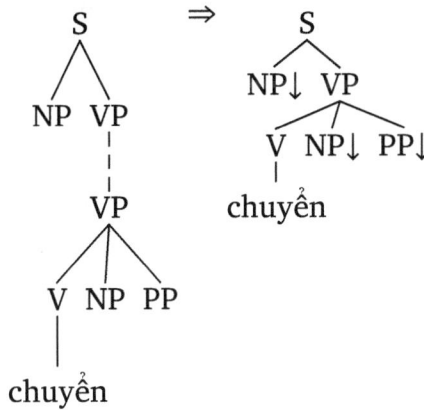

```
        S          ⇒          S
       ╱ ╲                    ╱ ╲
     NP   VP               NP↓   VP
           |                    ╱|╲
          VP                   V NP↓ PP↓
        ╱ | ╲                  |
       V  NP PP              chuyển
       |
     chuyển
```

Figure 10: Merge link nodes to get a spine tree

be extracted; if the relation is modification, a modifier tree will be extracted; otherwise, the relation is predicate-argument and a spine tree will be extracted. Algorithm 3 shows the complete extraction algorithm. This algorithm uses additional functions as follows:

- BuildSpineTree($T$) which creates a spine tree;
- MergeLinkNodes($T$) which merges all link nodes of a spine tree into one node (see Figure 10 for an example);
- BuildModTree($T$) which creates a modifier tree;
- BuildConjTree($T$) which creates a conjunction tree.

As an example, from the derived tree shown in Figure 7, nine trees are extracted by algorithms as shown in Figure 9 and Figure 10.

### 3.3.3          Filtering out invalid trees

Annotation errors may be present in any particular treebank. The errors in parse trees will result in incorrect elementary trees. An elementary tree is called invalid if it does not satisfy some linguistic requirement. We have constructed some linguistic rules for filtering out invalid elementary trees. For example, in Vietnamese, an adjective (or an adjectival phrase) can be an argument of a noun (or a noun phrase); however, it must always be to the right of the noun. For instance, in

**Algorithm 4:**
**BuildSpineTree($T$)**

**Data:** $T$ is a derived tree.
**Result:** A spine tree.
$T_c \leftarrow$ Copy($T$);
$P \leftarrow T_c$;
$H \leftarrow$ NULL;
**repeat**
$\quad\Big|\quad$ $H \leftarrow$ HeadChild($P$);
$\quad\Big|\quad$ $\mathcal{L} \leftarrow$ Sisters($H$);
$\quad\Big|\quad$ **if** $|\mathcal{L}| > 0$ **then**
$\quad\Big|\quad\quad\Big|\quad$ Rel $\leftarrow$ GetRelation($H, \mathcal{L}$);
$\quad\Big|\quad\quad\Big|\quad$ **if** Rel = Argument **then**
$\quad\Big|\quad\quad\Big|\quad\quad\Big|\quad$ **for** $A \in \mathcal{L}$ **do**
$\quad\Big|\quad\quad\Big|\quad\quad\Big|\quad\quad\Big|\quad$ BuildElementaryTrees($A$);
$\quad\Big|\quad\quad\Big|\quad\quad\Big|\quad\quad\Big|\quad$ $A$.children $\leftarrow \emptyset$;
$\quad\Big|\quad\quad\Big|\quad\quad\Big|\quad\quad\Big|\quad$ $A$.type $\leftarrow$ Substitution;
$\quad\Big|\quad\quad\Big|\quad$ **else**
$\quad\Big|\quad\quad\Big|\quad\quad\Big|\quad$ **for** $A \in \mathcal{L}$ **do**
$\quad\Big|\quad\quad\Big|\quad\quad\Big|\quad\quad\Big|\quad$ $P$.children $\leftarrow P$.children $\setminus A$;
$\quad\Big|\quad$ $P \leftarrow H$;
**until** *(H = NULL)*;
**return** MergeLinkNodes($T_c$);

**Algorithm 5:**
**BuildModTree($T$)**

**Data:** $T$ is a derived tree
**Result:** a modifier tree
$T_c \leftarrow$ Copy($T$);
$H \leftarrow$ HeadChild($T_c$);
$H$.children $\leftarrow \emptyset$;
$H$.type $\leftarrow$ Foot;
$M \leftarrow$ Modifier($H$);
$T' \leftarrow$ BuildSpineTree($M$);
**if** $|M$.children$| > 1$ **then**
$\quad\Big|\quad$ BuildElementaryTrees($M$);
$M \leftarrow T'$;
**return** $T_c$;

**Data:** $T$ is a derived tree.
**Result:** A conjunction tree.
$T_c \leftarrow \text{Copy}(T)$;
$H \leftarrow \text{HeadChild}(T_c)$;
BuildElementaryTrees($H$);
$K \leftarrow \text{Coordinator}(H)$;
BuildElementaryTrees($K$);
$H$.children $\leftarrow \emptyset$;
$H$.type $\leftarrow$ Foot;
$K$.children $\leftarrow \emptyset$;
$K$.type $\leftarrow$ Substitution;
**return** $T_c$;

Algorithm 6:
BuildConjTree($T$)

the noun phrase *cô gái đẹp* (*beautiful girl*), the adjective *đẹp* (*beautiful*) must go after the noun *cô gái* (*girl*). Thus if there is an adjective on the left of a noun of an extracted spine tree, the tree is invalid and it must be filtered out.

3.4          *Comparison with previous work*

As mentioned above, our approach for LTAG extraction follows the uniform method of grammar extraction proposed by Xia (2001). Nevertheless, there are some differences between our design and implementation of extraction algorithms and that of Xia.

First, in the step in which we build the derived tree, we first recursively bracket all conjunction groups of the tree before fully bracketing the arguments and modifiers of the resulting tree. We think that this approach is easier to understand and implement since conjunction structures are different from argument and modifier structures. Second, in the elementary tree decomposition step, we do not split each node in the derived tree into the top and bottom parts as was done in Xia's approach of Xia. In our implementation, the nodes are directly copied to build extracted trees. Third, the tree extraction process is separated into functions; each function builds a particular type of elementary tree; and these functions can call each other to repeat the extraction process for the subtrees whose roots are not yet visited. In spite of using recursive functions, our extraction algorithms are carefully designed to avoid redundant or repeating function calls:

| Category | Original tags | Tags in $G_2$ |
|---|---|---|
| noun phrases | NP/WHNP | NP |
| adjective phrases | AP/WHAP | AP |
| adverbial phrases | RP/WHRP | RP |
| preposition phrases | PP/WHPP | PP |
| clauses | S/SQ | S |

Table 2: Some tags in the Vietnamese treebank tagset are merged into a single tag

| Type | # of trees | # of templates |
|---|---|---|
| $G_1$ | **46 382** | **2317** |
| Spine trees | 24 973 | 1022 |
| Modifier trees | 21 309 | 1223 |
| Conjunction trees | 100 | 72 |
| $G_2$ | **46 102** | **2113** |
| Spine trees | 24 884 | 952 |
| Modifier trees | 21 121 | 1093 |
| Conjunction trees | 97 | 68 |

Table 3: Two LTAG grammars extracted from the Vietnamese treebank

each node is assured to be visited one time. The "divide and conquer" approach seems to be reasonably efficient and is easy to optimise.

### 3.5      *An LTAG for Vietnamese*

We ran extraction algorithms on the Vietnamese treebank and extracted two treebank grammars. The first one, $G_1$, uses the original tagset of the treebank. The second one, $G_2$, uses a reduced tagset, where some sets of tags in the treebank are consolidated, as shown in Table 2. The grammar $G_2$ is smaller than $G_1$ and it is presumed that the sparse data problem is less severe when $G_2$ is used.

We count the number of elementary trees and tree templates. The sizes of the two grammars are in Table 3. Recall that a template is an elementary tree without the anchor word.

There are 15 035 unique words in the treebank and the average number of elementary trees that a word anchors is around 3.07. We also count the number of context-free rules of the grammars where the rules are simply read off the templates in an extracted LTAG. The extracted grammars $G_1$ and $G_2$ have 851 and 727 context-free rules, respectively.

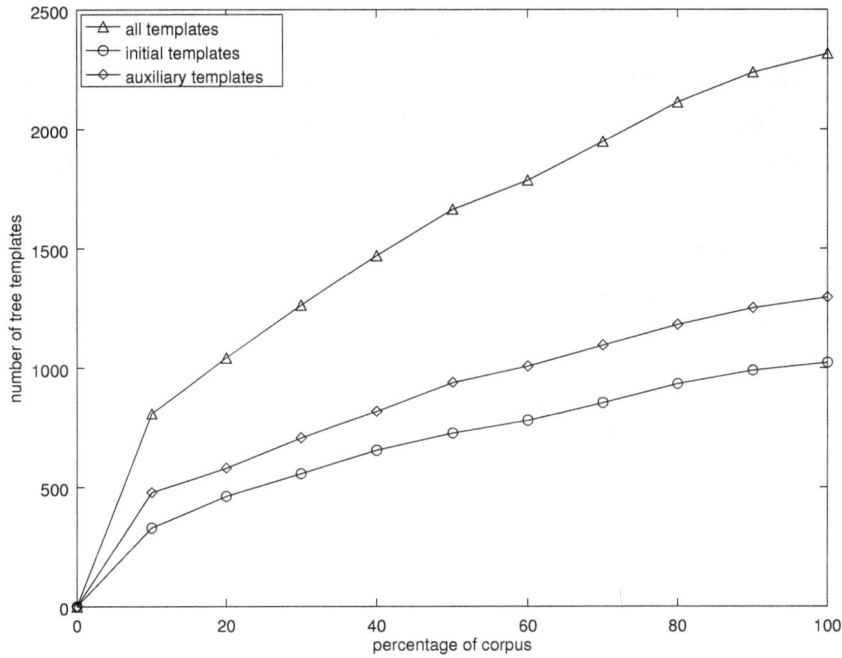

Figure 11: The growth of tree templates

In order to evaluate the coverage of the Vietnamese treebank, we count the number of extracted tree templates with respect to the size of the treebank. Figure 11 shows that the number of templates converges very slowly as the size of the corpus grows, implying that there are many unseen templates. This experiment also implies that the size of the current Vietnamese treebank is not large enough to cover all the grammatical templates of the Vietnamese language.

We have developed a software package[8] that implements the presented algorithms for extracting an LTAG for Vietnamese. The software is written in the Java programming language and is freely distributed under the GNU/GPL license. The software is very efficient in term of extraction speed: it takes only 165 seconds to extract the entire grammar $G_1$ on an ordinary personal computer.[9] It should be straightforward to extend the software in order to extract LTAGs from treebanks of other languages since the language-specific information is intentionally factored out of the general framework. In order to use the software on a treebank of a given language, a user would need to provide the treebank-specific information for that language: a tagset, a head percolation table, and an argument table.

---

[8] http://mim.hus.vnu.edu.vn/phuonglh/softwares/vnLExtractor
[9] On an Intel Core 2 Duo CPU U9600 with 4GB RAM.

3.6                          *Summary*

In this section, we have presented a system that automatically extracts LTAGs from treebanks. The system has been used to extract an LTAG for the Vietnamese language from the recently released Vietnamese treebank. The extracted Vietnamese LTAG covers the corpus; that is, the corpus can be seen as a collection of derived trees for the grammar and can be used to train statistical LTAG parsers directly.

The number of templates extracted from the current Vietnamese treebank converges slowly. This implies that there are many new templates outside the corpus and the current Vietnamese treebank is not large nor typical enough to cover all the grammatical templates of the Vietnamese language.

We are currently experimenting with extracting a French LTAG from a French treebank (Abeillé *et al.* 2003). We also plan to compare quantitatively syntactic structures of French and Vietnamese. We believe that a quantitative comparison of the two grammars may reveal interesting relations between them.

4                  PARSER CONSTRUCTION

We present in this section the construction of a deep syntactic parser for Vietnamese. Our parser is able to produce both constituency and dependency analyses for a given sentence.

4.1                    *Preprocessing pipeline*

Before being parsed, a text is fed to a chain of preprocessing modules including a sentence segmenter, a word tokenizer and a tagger. In particular, we have integrated the following preprocessing modules into the parser:

- **vnSentDetector** – a sentence detector which segments a text into sentences;

- **vnTokenizer** – a tokenizer which segments sentences into words or lexical units (Le-Hong *et al.* 2008);

- **vnTagger** – a part-of-speech tagger which tags each word of a sentence with its most appropriate syntactic category (Le-Hong *et al.* 2010).

We have adapted an LTAG parser developed at the LORIA[10] laboratory to construct a deep syntactic parser for Vietnamese. This parser was initially used to parse French text (Roussanaly *et al.* 2005). Given a sentence, the parser outputs all possible constituency parses and their corresponding derivation trees. The most important improvement we made to the parser is the refactoring and introduction of general interfaces and modules for preprocessing tasks (sentence detection, word segmentation, POS tagging) which naturally depend on specific languages. We have also enriched the parser by adding a supplementary module which extracts dependency parses from constituency parses given by the parser.[11] This module implements the dependency analysis extraction algorithm which will be described in the next subsections.

4.2                          *Dependency annotation schema*

There exist many schema for dependency annotation. Examples include the Stanford Dependency (SD) annotation scheme (de Marneffe *et al.* 2006), created via an automated conversion of the English Penn Treebank; the PARC 700 scheme (King *et al.* 2003), inspired by functional structures of lexical functional grammars; and the GR scheme (Caroll *et al.* 1998) or EASy (Paroubek *et al.* 2005) for French. Recently, McDonald *et al.* (2013) presented a universal treebank with homogeneous syntactic dependency annotation for six languages: German, English, Swedish, Spanish, French and Korean. The multiplicity of these different annotation schema is due to different linguistic and practical choices. We prefer defining an annotation scheme of surface dependency for the Vietnamese language which can be not only convertible to different standards cited above but also enlargeable to finer dependency schema if necessary. The current scheme contains 13 grammatical relations representing principal functional dependencies between Vietnamese words. All these dependencies use the syntactic categories defined in the Vietnamese treebank (Nguyen *et al.* 2009) and they are divided into three groups.

The first group, *arg*, represents the relationship between a head word and its argument. There are two types of arguments: subject

---

[10] http://www.loria.fr/
[11] http://mim.hus.vnu.edu.vn/phuonglh/softwares/vnLTAGParser

(*subj*) or object (*obj*). It is worth noting that Vietnamese is a topic-prominent language where sentences are structured around topics rather than subjects and objects. In many cases, we cannot identify the subject and the object of a Vietnamese sentence by their respective positions. The distinction between subject and object of a Vietnamese sentence is thus not a trivial task, expecially in an automatic process. Therefore, at the moment, we do not distinguish the two relations *subj* and *obj* in our evaluations. The second group, *mod*, represents modification relations of a word and its head word (or its governor). According to the syntactic category of the modifier, we distinguish nine modification relations named *modN* (nominal modifier), *modM* (numeral modifier), *modA* (adjective modifier), *modR* (adverbial modifier), *modE* (prepositional modifier), *modV* (verbal modifier), *modL* (determinant modifier), *modP* (pronominal modifier) and *modC* (subordinating coordination modifier). The third group, *coord*, represents dependencies of each lexical head of two coordinating phrases on the conjunction.

Having defined a dependency annotation scheme for Vietnamese, we now propose an algorithm for automatically extracting dependency analyses from TAG derivation trees.

### 4.3               *Dependency relation extraction*

It has been shown that the TAG formalism shares many important similarities with the dependency grammar formalism (Rambow and Joshi 1994). A derivation tree of TAG can be converted superficially into a dependency tree in the case of lexicalized grammars (Kallmeyer and Kuhlmann 2012). The main idea is to transform each derivation operation into a dependency relation. A derivation operation between a source tree $t_1$ and a target tree $t_2$ results in a dependency relation between the head word of $t_1$ as governor and the head of $t_2$ as dependent word.

The dependency analysis corresponding to the analysis in Figure 3 is shown in Figure 12. We see that the derivation tree can be transformed into the dependency tree by a simple transformation in which each node of the derivation tree (representing an elementary tree) is replaced with its lexical node. Here, we want to extract typed dependencies where each one is labelled by a grammatical relation following the annotation scheme defined above. We thus need to consider the

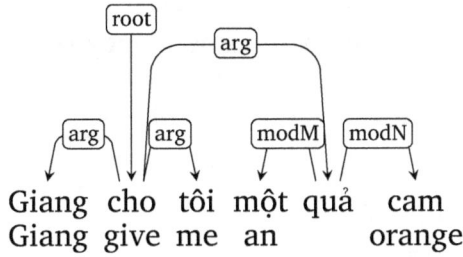

Figure 12: Dependency tree corresponding to the analysis in Figure 3

operation done at each node of the derivation tree. If it is a substitution, a relation of type *arg* will be created; if it is an adjunction, a relation of type *mod* will be created and its label can be determined by examining the syntactic category of the concerned word at the lexical node of the derivation tree.

Figure 13: Examples of coordination auxiliary trees

The most difficult case is the construction of coordination relations where we must consider three related nodes and two combination operations at the same time since an auxiliary tree for conjunctions in TAG has a specific form having a substitution node and a foot node, as illustrated in example trees in Figure 13. We propose an algorithm for the automatic extraction of dependency relations from a derivation tree given by a constituency parser. The algorithm ExtractRelations($N$) (Algorithm 7) shows the extraction procedure in detail.

This algorithm uses some supplementary functions as follows. The function LexicalNode($N$) returns the lexical head of a node of an input derivation tree $N$, while the function POSNode($N$) returns the part-of-speech of a lexical head. The functions IsSubst() and IsAdj() are called at each node of the derivation tree to verify whether the node is about a substitution or an adjunction. Finally, the function NewRelation(type, $w_1, w_2$) creates and returns a new relation of type type between two lexical units $w_1$ and $w_2$.

Algorithm 7:
ExtractRelations($N$)

**Data:** A derivation tree $N$.

**Result:** A set $\mathscr{R}$ of dependency relations.

$w_n \leftarrow$ LexicalNode($N$);

$t_n \leftarrow$ POSNode($N$);

**for** $K \in N.\texttt{children}$ **do**

    $w_k \leftarrow$ LexicalNode($K$);

    $t_k \leftarrow$ POSNode($K$);

    **if** $K.IsSubst()$ **then**

        **if** $t_n = $ CC **then**

            $\mathscr{R} \leftarrow \mathscr{R} \cup$ NewRelation($\texttt{coord}, w_n, w_k$);

        **else**

            $\mathscr{R} \leftarrow \mathscr{R} \cup$ NewRelation($\texttt{arg}, w_n, w_k$);

    **else**

        **if** $K.IsAdj()$ **then**

            **if** $t_k \in \{$A, N, R, V, E, L, M, P, C$\}$ **then**

                $\mathscr{R} \leftarrow \mathscr{R} \cup$ NewRelation($\texttt{mod}t_k, w_n, w_k$);

            **if** $t_k = $ CC **then**

                $\mathscr{R} \leftarrow \mathscr{R} \cup$ NewRelation($\texttt{coord}, w_k, w_n$);

    *// Recursively extract relations from tree $K$;*

    ExtractRelations($K$);

**return** $\mathscr{R}$;

For example, the application of this algorithm on the input derivation tree in Figure 1 results in the following relations: *arg*(cho,Giang), *arg*(cho,tôi), *arg*(cho,quả), *modM*(quả,một), *modN*(quả,cam).

## 5    PARSER EVALUATION

In this section, we evaluate the parser on a test corpus. The parser performance is considered in two versions, with and without using part-of-speech (POS) tagging.

The grammar used to evaluate the parser is an LTAG extracted from the Vietnamese Treebank (Nguyen *et al.* 2009) containing 10 163 sentences (225 085 words, about 22.14 words per sentence on average). Figure 14 shows the distribution of the number of sentences ac-

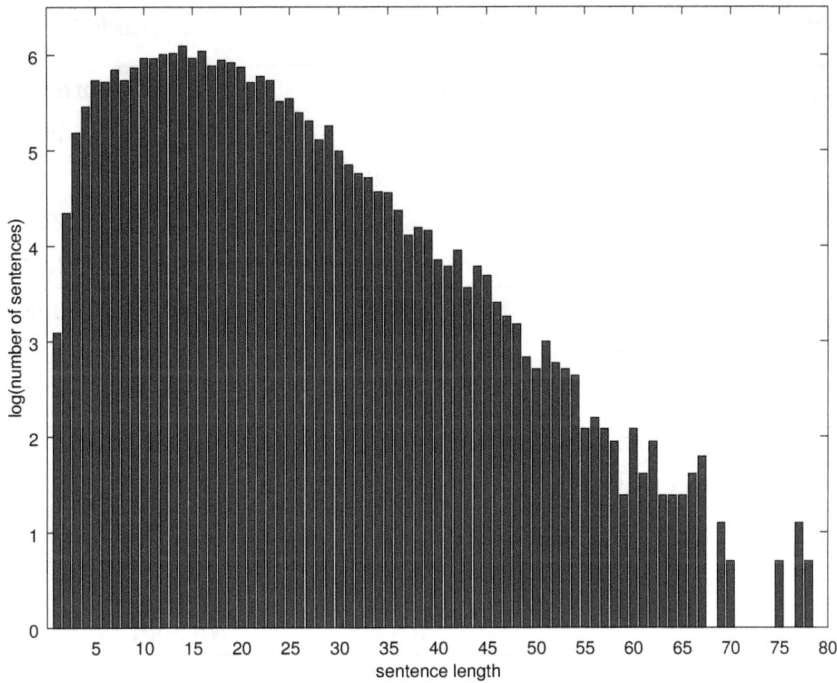

Figure 14: The distribution of the number of sentences according to their length

cording to their lengths. We see that most of the sentences have a length between 5 and 30 words.

We choose a subset of the treebank containing 8808 sentences of length 30 words or less as an evaluation corpus. This corpus is divided into two sets: a training set (95% of the corpus, 8367 sentences) and a test set (5% of the corpus, 441 sentences). We use **vnLExtractor** to extract an LTAG for Vietnamese from the training set. This grammar contains 35 655 elementary trees instantiated from 1658 tree templates. The size of this grammar is shown in Table 4.

Table 4: Size of the LTAG extracted from the training corpus

| Type | Number of trees | Number of templates |
|---|---|---|
| Spine trees | 19 708 | 741 |
| Modifier trees | 15 868 | 860 |
| Conjunction trees | 79 | 57 |
| **Total** | **35 655** | **1658** |

To evaluate the parser, we make use of two measures: *tree accuracy* (or *T*-accuracy) and *dependency accuracy* (or *D*-accuracy).[12]

_____

[12] In computing these scores, unanalyzable sentences and punctuations are not taken into account.

Table 5: Performance of the constituency analysis without or with POS tagging

| T-accuracy | All | | ≤ 10 words | |
|---|---|---|---|---|
| | No POS | POS | No POS | POS |
| Precision | 67.98 | 69.15 | 71.28 | 71.60 |
| Recall | 68.40 | 69.52 | 71.39 | 72.30 |
| F-measure | 68.19 | **69.33** | 71.33 | **71.95** |
| Complete match | 13.00 | 16.67 | 17.57 | 20.69 |
| Average crossing | 2.66 | 2.39 | 1.80 | 1.69 |
| No crossing | 23.00 | 27.78 | 29.73 | 32.76 |
| Fewer than three crossings | 55.00 | 54.17 | 68.92 | 65.52 |
| Tagging accuracy | 87.72 | 95.25 | 87.34 | 95.43 |

Table 6: Performance of the dependency analysis without or with POS tagging

| D-accuracy | With type | | Without type | |
|---|---|---|---|---|
| | No POS | POS | No POS | POS |
| Precision | 70.83 | 71.81 | 74.02 | 73.21 |
| Complete match | 15.87 | 20.00 | 23.37 | 25.45 |

When there are multiple parse trees for a sentence (which is very often the case even with short sentences), we choose one of *the derivation trees whose derived trees have smallest number of nodes* because these parses correspond to the most specific tree.[13]

### 5.1        *Performance without POS tagging*

First, the parser is evaluated without using a POS tagger. That is, the module **vnTagger** is not integrated into the parser. In this setting, each word occurrence of an input sentence is tagged with all possible tags that have been assigned to it in the training set. Unknown words are tagged as common nouns (label N). We first evaluate the performance of the constituency analysis. The results are shown in Table 5.[14]

In addition to the familiar precision and recall ratios, other measures are reported to help analyze the results:[15]

---

[13] In case of equality by this criterion, we take the first result returned by the parser.

[14] The presented evaluation results are calculated automatically by EVALB, a tool used frequently for the evaluation of syntactic constituency analysis which is distributed freely at http://nlp.cs.nyu.edu/evalb/.

[15] The *F*-measure is the harmonic mean of precision and recall and is computed as $F = 2\frac{PR}{P+R}$.

- Complete match ratio is the percentage of sentences where recall and precision are both 100%. About 13% of the test sentences match completely. The complete match ratio for sentences of 10 words or less is 17.57%.
- The average crossing ratio is the number of constituents crossing a test constituent divided by the number of sentences of the test corpus.
- The no crossing ratio is the percentage of sentences which have zero crossing brackets. There are 23% of the test sentences that do not have any crossing (29.73% for the sentences of 10 words or less). There are 55% (respectively 68.92%) of the test sentences which have fewer than three crossings.
- The tagging accuracy is the percentage of correct POS tags (without punctuations). It is interesting to note that the tagging accuracy declines slightly when shorter test sentences are used.

The performance of dependency analysis is evaluated in two versions: with and without type. In the first version, two typed dependencies $type_1(u_1, v_1)$ and $type_2(u_2, v_2)$ are considered equal if three corresponding parts of these dependencies are all equal, that is $type_1 \equiv type_2, u_1 \equiv u_2, v_1 \equiv v_2$. In the second version, we compare only two pairs of concerned words without using their dependency types. The $D$-accuracy of the two evaluations are given in Table 6.[16] Table 7 shows the system's performance for each dependency type.

We see that the parser works perfectly on coordination structures, as they are inherently unambiguous in both the grammar and the extraction algorithm. The performance on the dependencies of type *argument* is much better than that of type *modifier*. These results justify a higher ambiguity of the adjunction operation of the LTAG formalism (which is related to auxiliary trees) in comparison with the substitution operation (which is related to initial trees).

We observe that the parser could not parse about 16.6% of the test corpus. We believe that there may be two main reasons that some sentences can not be analysed. First, there is an insufficient coverage of the underlying LTAG grammar used by the parser. That is, the gram-

---

[16] Note that when evaluating the accuracy of a dependency analysis, we do not need to compute precision or recall ratios since they are equal: the number of relations given by the parser always matches the number of correct relations.

Table 7: Performance of dependency analysis by type without or with POS tagging

| Type | Precision | | Recall | | F-measure | |
|---|---|---|---|---|---|---|
| | No POS | POS | No POS | POS | No POS | POS |
| *arg* | 87.57 | 87.18 | 79.02 | 80.95 | 83.08 | 83.95 |
| *coord* | 100.00 | 100.00 | 100.00 | 100.00 | 100.00 | 100.00 |
| *modA* | 48.57 | 59.09 | 62.96 | 65.00 | 54.84 | 61.90 |
| *modC* | 46.67 | 66.67 | 43.75 | 60.00 | 45.16 | 63.16 |
| *modE* | 50.00 | 35.71 | 56.52 | 35.71 | 53.06 | 35.71 |
| *modL* | 72.73 | 100.00 | 47.06 | 50.00 | 57.14 | 66.67 |
| *modM* | 80.00 | 81.82 | 53.33 | 75.00 | 64.00 | 78.26 |
| *modN* | 50.00 | 58.54 | 66.67 | 68.57 | 57.14 | 63.16 |
| *modR* | 64.10 | 47.06 | 60.98 | 42.11 | 62.50 | 44.44 |
| *modV* | 52.63 | 58.33 | 62.50 | 87.50 | 57.14 | 70.00 |

mar extracted from the training corpus does not contain the syntactic structure (elementary trees) of a given sentence to be parsed. Secondly, our heuristic choice of tagging all the new words as a common noun may effectively introduce errors prior to the analysis, which may result in analysis failures. We have not yet thoroughly investigated these causes.

The ambiguity and the duration of parsing are strongly dependent on the length of sentences, as shown in Figure 15. It seems that the number of parses has an exponential growth with respect to the length of the sentence.[17]

5.2          *Performance with POS tagging*

The results reported in the previous subsection make possible a preliminary evaluation of the grammar and the performance of the parser. Nevertheless, the condition under which the experimentation is carried out is rather harsh since the parser has to try all possible syntactic categories of each word of an input sentence. The experiments in this subsection are closer to real use conditions, in that each sentence is first processed by a tagger to remove POS-tagging ambiguity – each word is assigned a unique tag. We have thus a sole sequence of

---

[17] For some considerably long sentences, the parser could not give any result after a fixed time-out predefined at 3 minutes. We limit the sentence length to 15 words in the experiments with the symbolic parser.

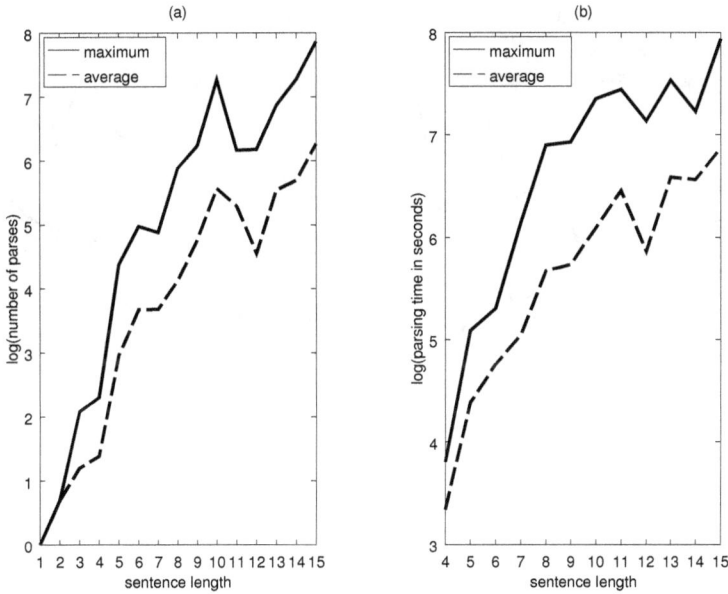

Figure 15: The ambiguity (a) and duration (b) of analysis, average and maximum, according to the length of sentences

words/tags and it is used as input to the syntactic parser. The tagging is done by the **vnTagger** module.

We proceed with the evaluation of this parser version in a similar way as presented for the previous version without POS tagging. We first give constituency parsing results, then dependency parsing results and finally the ambiguity and duration of the parsing.

The $T$-accuracy of the system is shown in Table 5. By integrating a POS tagger, the tagging accuracy is greatly improved, from 87.72% to 95.25%.[18] This helps improve all the scores of the system, notably the complete match ratio, from 13.00% to 16.67% (and that for sentences of length 10 words or less improves to 20.69%).

The dependency analysis performance both with and without type is shown in Table 6 and the performance of particular dependency types is shown in Table 7.

We see that the performance of the system is improved slightly in comparison with the system without tagging. However, the most important benefit of the parser with the integrated tagger is a strong reduction of analysis ambiguity and time, shown in Figure 16. The tag-

---

[18] Recall that the test corpus only contains sentences of 30 words or less.

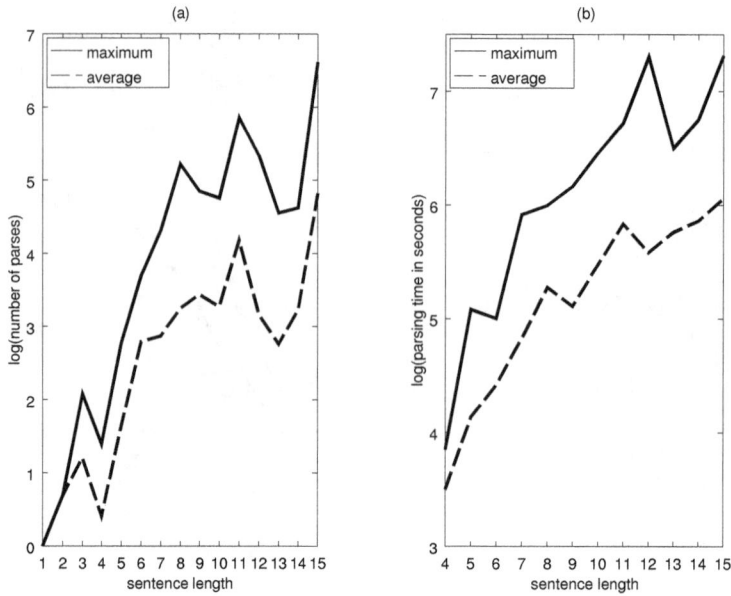

Figure 16: The ambiguity (a) and duration (b) of analysis, average and maximum, with an integrated tagger

ger helps reduce analysis ambiguity fivefold on average and reduces analysis duration three times in comparison with the required time of the parser without prior tagging. Nevertheless, we observe that the integration of the tagger results in a higher number of sentences that the parser could not parse, to 40% of the test corpus. This result is to be expected because in this version the parser uses only a syntactic category (the most probable POS) given by the tagger for each word. (We note also that the precision of the tagger at sentence level is about 32% (Le-Hong *et al.* 2010); that is, the tagger can give correct tags for all the words of a sentence to be parsed only one third of the time).

## 5.3                    *Discussion*

In the previous section, we evaluated a syntactic analysis system based on LTAG for Vietnamese. The best results obtained are 73.21% (dependency accuracy, or D-accuracy) and 69.33% (*F*-measure of constituency accuracy, or T-accuracy, measured by EVALB) on a test corpus.

It is worth noting that these are the first results of syntactic analysis of Vietnamese based on LTAG. To our knowledge, to date there have been few published works on the syntactic analysis of Vietnamese. The most complete report on parser performance for Vietnamese is an empirical study of applying probabilistic CFG parsing models by Collins (2003); its best result on constituency analysis is 78% $T$-accuracy on a test corpus, while there is no result reported for dependency analysis. Concerning the constituency parsing result, their parser is slightly better than ours. However, these results are not directly comparable since the parsing models are trained and tested on a different corpus.

Our first results of the syntactic parsing of Vietnamese are rather good although they are still significantly weaker than parsing results for well-studied languages like English (whose $T$-accuracy is 91.10% (Carreras *et al.* 2008) and whose $D$-accuracy is 92.93% (Koo and Collins 2010) on the Penn Treebank) or French ($T$-accuracy is 86.41% (Candito *et al.* 2009a) and $D$-accuracy is 85.55% on a French treebank (Candito *et al.* 2010)). However, we can improve our results by correcting three main sources of errors identified by the experiments; we examine each such type of error presently.

The principal source of parsing errors is the selection of parse. When there are multiple parses for a sentence, only the parse whose derivation tree contains the fewest nodes is selected. Although the returned tree corresponds to the most specific analysis, it is obvious that this selection method is purely heuristic and fragile. However, the use of a probabilistic parser does not improve significantly the parsing accuracy. We think that the parameters of the statistical parser are currently not optimised for parsing Vietnamese or the Vietnamese grammar is not large enough in order for the statistical parser to be effective. Consequently, optimising parameters of the statistical parsing model could help improve the parsing performance.

The second source of parsing errors is the POS tagging. In the experiments with a tagger integrated, we use only the most confident prediction generated by **vnTagger** as input to the parser. We have seen that the tagger often makes errors at the sentence level; perfectly tagged sentences are rare. A tagging error may effectively introduce one or more parsing errors. An improvement in tagging performance is thus another necessary condition to improve the performance of the parser.

The third source of parsing errors concerns the coverage of the grammar used in the experiments. In general, the proportion of test sentences having at least one word that the grammar does not recognize is rather high, at about 15%. Consequently, the parser could not build the correct analysis for these sentences. A straightforward solution to this problem is to enlarge the coverage of the LTAG grammar, which in turn necessitates an enlargement of the Vietnamese treebank. However, developing such a corpus is an expensive and labour-intensive task. In addition, this may lead to the typical problem of a symbolic syntactic parser: the tradeoff between its performance and its efficiency. This is an interesting problem in itself, which we shall investigate in future works.

# 6 CONCLUSION

In this article, we have presented a complete syntactic component for Vietnamese language processing. The component comprises two essential resources: a lexicalized tree-adjoining grammar for Vietnamese and a set of software tools that are chained together to produce syntactic structures from Vietnamese raw text. The grammar is extracted automatically from a treebank by an efficient algorithm. The software includes necessary modules for detecting sentence boundaries, tokenizing word units, part-of-speech tagging and syntactic parsing. This syntactic component is the first system capable of generating both constituency and dependency analyses for the language with encouraging performance.

Syntactic dependency representation of natural sentences has gained a wide interest in the natural language processing community and has been successfully applied to many problems and applications such as machine translation (Ding and Palmer 2004), ontology construction (Snow *et al.* 2005) and automatic question answering (Lin and Pantel 2001). A primary advantage of dependency representation is its natural mechanism for representing discontinuous constructions or long distance dependencies which are common in Vietnamese. We think that the presence of a good dependency schema and a dependency parser for Vietnamese will be very helpful in a wide range of tasks for Vietnamese processing.

We have seen in recent years a rapid increase of research on data-driven dependency parsers, especially the rise of statistical methods in natural language processing where dependency annotated corpora exist. These parsers use one of two predominant paradigms for data-driven dependency parsing which are often called graph-based and transition-based dependency parsing. However, the constituency parser and dependency parser developed in this work are currently purely symbolic in that they do not make use of any probabilistic evidence to discriminate good parses from bad ones for a given sentence, regardless of its grammaticality. An initial investigation of statistical dependency parsing for Vietnamese has shown encouraging results (Nguyen *et al.* 2013). We believe that there is room to improve the performance of dependency parsers in general and of our dependency parser in particular by employing a hybrid approach: use elementary trees of an lexicalized tree-adjoining grammar as good syntactic features in a statistical dependency parser. This is an interesting problem that we plan to work on in the future.

## ACKNOWLEDGEMENTS

This research is funded by the Vietnam National University, Hanoi (VNU) under project number QG.15.04. Any opinions, findings and conclusion expressed in this paper are those of the authors and do not necessarily reflect the view of VNU.

We are grateful to our three anonymous reviewers for their insightful comments, which helped us improve the quality of the article in terms of both presentation and content. Finally, we thank the copy editors of the Journal of Language Modelling for their great job on the manuscript.

## REFERENCES

Anne ABEILLÉ, Lionel CLÉMENT, and François TOUSSENEL (2003), Building a treebank for French, in Anne ABEILLÉ, editor, *Treebanks: Building and Using Parsed Corpora*, volume 20 of *Text, Speech and Language Technology*, pp. 165–187, Springer Netherlands.

Mark ALVES (1999), What's so Chinese about Vietnamese?, in *Proceedings of the Ninth Annual Meeting of the Southeast Asian Linguistics Society*, pp. 221–224, University of California, Berkeley, USA.

Jens BÄCKER and Karin HARBUSCH (2002), Hidden Markov model-based supertagging in a user-initiative dialogue system, in *Proceedings of TAG + 6*, pp. 269–278, Universita di Venezia, Italy.

Marie CANDITO, Benoît CRABBÉ, and Djamé SEDDAH (2009a), On statistical parsing of French with supervised and semi-supervised strategies, in *Proceedings of EACL 2009 Workshop on Computational Linguistic Aspects of Grammatical Inference*, pp. 49–57, Athens, Greece.

Marie CANDITO, Benoît CRABBÉ, and Pascal DENIS (2010), Statistical French dependency parsing: treebank conversion and first results, in *Proceedings of LREC 2010*, pp. 19–21, Valletta, Malta.

Marie CANDITO, Benoît CRABBÉ, Pascal DENIS, and François GUÉRIN (2009b), Analyse syntaxique du français : des constituants aux dépendances (Syntactic Parsing of French: from constituents to dependencies), in *Actes de Traitement Automatique des Langues*, pp. 40–49, Senlis, France.

John CAROLL, Ted BRISCOE, and Antonio SANFILIPPO (1998), Parser evaluation: a survey and a new proposal, in *Proceedings of LREC 1998*, Granada, Spain.

Xavier CARRERAS, Michael COLLINS, and Terry KOO (2008), TAG, dynamic programming, and the perceptron for efficient, feature-rich parsing, in *Proceedings of CoNLL 2008*, pp. 9–16, Manchester, UK.

John CHEN, Srinivas BANGALORE, and K. VIJAY-SHANKER (2006), Automated extraction of tree-adjoining grammars from treebanks, *Natural Language Engineering*, 12(3):251–299.

John CHEN and K. VIJAY-SHANKER (2000), Automated extraction of TAGs from the Penn treebank, in *Proceedings of the Sixth International Workshop on Parsing Technologies*.

David CHIANG (2000), Statistical parsing with an automatically extracted tree adjoining grammar, in *Proceedings of ACL*, pp. 456–463, Morristown, New Jersey, USA.

Michael COLLINS (1997), Three generative, lexicalised models for statistical parsing, in *Proceedings of ACL*, pp. 16–23, Association for Computational Linguistics, Stroudsburg, Pennsylvania, USA.

Michael COLLINS (2003), Head-driven statistical models for natural language parsing, *Computational Linguistics*, 29(4):589–637.

Benoît CRABBÉ, Denys DUCHIER, Claire GARDENT, Josheph Le ROUX, and Yannick PARMENTIER (2013), XMG: eXtensible MetaGrammar, *Computational Linguistics*, 39(3):591–629.

Marie-Catherine DE MARNEFFE, Bill MACCARTNEY, and Christopher D. MANNING (2006), Generating typed dependency parses from phrase structure parses, in *Proceedings of LREC 2006*, pp. 449–454, Genoa, Italy.

Yuan DING and Martha PALMER (2004), Synchronous dependency insertion grammars: a grammar formalism for syntax-based statistical machine translation, in *Workshop on Recent Advances in Dependency Grammars*, pp. 90–97, Geneva, Switzerland.

Robert FRANK (2002), *Phrase structure composition and syntactic dependencies*, MIT Press, Boston, USA.

Nizar HABASH and Owen RAMBOW (2004), Extracting a tree-adjoining grammar from the Penn Arabic treebank, in *Actes de Traitement Automatique des Langues*, pp. 50–55, Fez, Morocco.

Cao Xuân HẠO (2000), *Vietnamese – Some Questions on Phonetics, Syntax and Semantics (in Vietnamese)*, NXB GD, Hanoi, Vietnam.

Phê HOÀNG (2002), *Vietnamese Dictionary*, NXB DN, Danang, Vietnam.

Đạt HỮU, Trí Dõi TRẦN, and Thanh Lan ĐÀO (1998), *Basis of Vietnamese (in Vietnamese)*, NXB GD, Hanoi, Vietnam.

Ane-Dybro JOHANSEN (2004), *Extraction des grammaires LTAG à partir d'un corpus étiquetté syntaxiquement*, Master's thesis, Université Paris 7, Paris, France.

Richard JOHANSSON and Pierre NUGUES (2008), Dependency-based syntactic-semantic analysis with PropBank and NomBank, in *CoNLL 2008: Proceedings of the Twelfth Conference on Computational Natural Language Learning*, pp. 183–187, Manchester, UK.

Aravind K. JOSHI and Yves SCHABES (1997), Tree Adjoining Grammars, in Grzegorz ROZENBERG and Arto SALOMAA, editors, *Handbooks of Formal Languages and Automata*, pp. 69–123, Springer-Verlag, New York, USA.

Miriam KAESHAMMER (2012), *A German treebank and lexicon for tree-adjoining grammars*, Master's thesis, Universitat des Saarlandes, Saarlandes, Germany.

Laura KALLMEYER and Marco KUHLMANN (2012), A formal model for plausible dependencies in lexicalized tree adjoining grammar, in *Proceedings of TAG + 11*, pp. 108–116, Paris, France.

Tracy Holloway KING, Richard CROUCH, Stefan RIEZLER, Mary DALRYMPLE, and Ronald M. KAPLAN (2003), The PARC 700 dependency bank, in *Proceedings of 4th International Workshop on Linguistically Interpreted Corpora*, pp. 1–8, Budapest, Hungary.

Terry KOO and Michael COLLINS (2010), Efficient third-order dependency parsers, in *Proceedings of ACL*, pp. 1–11, Uppsala, Sweden.

Sandra KÜBLER, Ryan McDONALD, and Joakim NIVRE (2009), *Dependency parsing*, Morgan & Claypool Publishers.

Phuong LE-HONG, Thi Minh Huyen NGUYEN, Azim ROUSSANALY, and Tuong Vinh HO (2008), A hybrid approach to word segmentation of Vietnamese texts, in *Proceedings of LATA, LNCS 5196*, pp. 240–249, Springer.

Phuong LE-HONG, Azim ROUSSANALY, Thi Minh Huyen NGUYEN, and Mathias ROSSIGNOL (2010), An empirical study of maximum entropy approach for part-of-speech tagging of Vietnamese texts, in *Actes de Traitement Automatique des Langues*, pp. 50–61, Montreal, Canada.

Charles N. LI and Sandra A. THOMPSON (1976), Subject and topic: a new typology of language, in *Subject and topic*, pp. 457–489, London/New York: Academic Press.

Dekang LIN and Patrick PANTEL (2001), Discovery of inference rules for question answering, *Natural Language Engineering*, 7(4):343–360.

David M. MAGERMAN (1995), Statistical decision-tree models for parsing, in *Proceedings of ACL*, pp. 276–283, Stroudsburg, Pennsylvania, USA.

Ryan MCDONALD, Joakim NIVRE, Yvonne QUIRMBACH-BRUNDAGE, Yoav GOLDBERG, Dipanjan DAS, Kuzman GANCHEV, Keith HALL, Slav PETROV, Hao ZHANG, Oscar TÄCKSTRÖM, Claudia BEDINI, Nuria Bertomeu CASTELLÓ, and Jungmee LEE (2013), Universal dependency annotation for multilingual parsing, in *Proceedings of ACL*, pp. 92–97, Sofia, Bulgaria.

Ryan MCDONALD and Fernando PEREIRA (2006), Online learning of approximate dependency parsing algorithms, in *Proceedings of EACL*, pp. 81–88, Trento, Italy.

Alexis NASR (2004), *Analyse syntaxique probabiliste pour grammaires de dépendances extraites automatiquement*, Habilitation à diriger des recherches, Université Paris 7, Paris, France.

Günter NEUMANN (2003), A uniform method for automatically extracting stochastic lexicalized tree grammar from treebank and HPSG, in Anne ABEILLÉ, editor, *Treebanks: Building and Using Parsed Corpora*, volume 20 of *Text, Speech and Language Technology*, pp. 351–365, Springer Netherlands.

Phuong Thai NGUYEN, Luong Vu XUAN, Thi Minh Huyen NGUYEN, Van Hiep NGUYEN, and Phuong LE-HONG (2009), Building a large syntactically-annotated corpus of Vietnamese, in *Proceedings of the 3rd Linguistic Annotation Workshop, ACL-IJCNLP*, pp. 182–185, Suntec City, Singapore.

Thi Luong NGUYEN, My Linh HA, Viet Hung NGUYEN, Thi Minh Huyen NGUYEN, and Phuong LE-HONG (2013), Building a treebank for Vietnamese dependency parsing, in *The 10th IEEE RIVF*, pp. 147–151, IEEE, Hanoi, Vietnam.

Thi Minh Huyen NGUYEN, Laurent ROMARY, Mathias ROSSIGNOL, and Xuan Luong VU (2006), A lexicon for Vietnamese language processing, *Language Resources and Evaluation*, 40(3–4).

Jaokim NIVRE and Ryan MCDONALD (2008), Integrating graph-Based and transition-Based dependency parsers, in *Proceedings of ACL-08*, pp. 950–958, ACL, Columbus, Ohio, USA.

Joakim NIVRE (2003), An efficient algorithm for projective dependency parsing, in *Proceedings of the 8th International Workshop on Parsing Technologies (IWPT 03)*, pp. 149–160, Nancy, France.

Jungyeul PARK (2006), Extraction of tree adjoining grammars from a treebank for Korean, in *Proceedings of COLING-ACL Student Research Workshop*, pp. 73–78, Morristown, New Jersey, USA.

Patrick PAROUBEK, L. G. POUILLOT, I. ROBBA, and Anne VILNAT (2005), EASY: Campagne d'évaluation des analyseurs syntaxiques (EASY Evaluation compagne of syntactic parsers), in *Actes de Traitement Automatique des Langues*, pp. 3–12, Dourdan, France.

Lewis M. PAUL, Gary F. SIMONS, and Charles D. Fennig (EDS.) (2014), *Ethnologue: Languages of the World, Seventeenth edition*, SIL International, Dallas, Texas, USA.

Owen RAMBOW and Aravind JOSHI (1994), A formal look at dependency grammars and phrase-structure grammars, with special consideration of word-order phenomena, in *Current Issues in Meaning-Text Theory*, pp. 1–20, Pinter, London, UK.

Azim ROUSSANALY, Benoît CRABBÉ, and Jérôme PERRIN (2005), Premier bilan de la participation du LORIA à la campagne d'évaluation EASY, in *Actes de Traitement Automatique des Langues*, pp. 49–52, Dourdan, France.

Yves SCHABES (1990), *Mathematical and computational aspects of lexicalized grammars*, Ph.D. thesis, University of Pennsylvania, Pennsylvania, USA.

Rion SNOW, Dan JURAFSKY, and Andrew Y. NG (2005), Learning syntactic patterns for automatic hypernym discovery, in *Advances in Neural Information Processing Systems*, pp. 1297–1304, Vancouver, Canada.

VIETNAM COMMITTEE ON SOCIAL SCIENCES, editor (1983), *Vietnamese Grammar (in Vietnamese)*, NXB KHXH, Hanoi, Vietnam.

Fei XIA (2001), *Automatic grammar generation from two different perspectives*, Ph.D. thesis, University of Pennsylvania, Pennsylvania, USA.

Fei XIA, Martha PALMER, and Aravind JOSHI (2000), A uniform method of grammar extraction and its applications, in *Proceedings of the joint SIGDAT conference on empirical methods in NLP and very large corpora*, pp. 53–62, Morristown, New Jersey, USA.

# Permissions

The contributors of this book come from diverse backgrounds, making this book a truly international effort. This book will bring forth new frontiers with its revolutionizing research information and detailed analysis of the nascent developments around the world.

We would like to thank all the contributing authors for lending their expertise to make the book truly unique. They have played a crucial role in the development of this book. Without their invaluable contributions this book wouldn't have been possible. They have made vital efforts to compile up to date information on the varied aspects of this subject to make this book a valuable addition to the collection of many professionals and students.

This book was conceptualized with the vision of imparting up-to-date information and advanced data in this field. To ensure the same, a matchless editorial board was set up. Every individual on the board went through rigorous rounds of assessment to prove their worth. After which they invested a large part of their time researching and compiling the most relevant data for our readers.

The editorial board has been involved in producing this book since its inception. They have spent rigorous hours researching and exploring the diverse topics which have resulted in the successful publishing of this book. They have passed on their knowledge of decades through this book. To expedite this challenging task, the publisher supported the team at every step. A small team of assistant editors was also appointed to further simplify the editing procedure and attain best results for the readers.

Apart from the editorial board, the designing team has also invested a significant amount of their time in understanding the subject and creating the most relevant covers. They scrutinized every image to scout for the most suitable representation of the subject and create an appropriate cover for the book.

The publishing team has been an ardent support to the editorial, designing and production team. Their endless efforts to recruit the best for this project, has resulted in the accomplishment of this book. They are a veteran in the field of academics and their pool of knowledge is as vast as their experience in printing. Their expertise and guidance has proved useful at every step. Their uncompromising quality standards have made this book an exceptional effort. Their encouragement from time to time has been an inspiration for everyone.

The publisher and the editorial board hope that this book will prove to be a valuable piece of knowledge for researchers, students, practitioners and scholars across the globe.

# List of Contributors

**Igor Yanovich**
Universität Tübingen

**Andrzej Wiśniewski and Joanna Urbańska**
Institute of Psychology, Adam Mickiewicz University, Poznań

**Paweł Łupkowski, Mariusz Urbański, Katarzyna Paluszkiewicz, Natalia Żyluk, Andrzej Gajda and Bartosz Marciniak**
Institute of Psychology, Adam Mickiewicz University, Poznań
Reasoning Research Group, Adam Mickiewicz University, Poznań

**Wojciech Błądek, Agata Juska, Anna Kostrzewa, Dominika Pankow and Oliwia Ignaszak**
Reasoning Research Group, Adam Mickiewicz University, Poznań

**Dea Bankova, Bob Coecke and Dan Marsden**
Quantum Group, University of Oxford

**Martha Lewis**
ILLC, University of Amsterdam

**Katya Alahverdzhieva and Alex Lascarides**
School of Informatics, University of Edinburgh, UK

**Dan Flickinger**
Center for the Study of Language and Information, Stanford University, USA

**Mark-Jan Nederhof and Fahrurrozi Rahman**
School of Computer Science University of St Andrews United Kingdom

**Richard Moot**
CNRS (LaBRI), Bordeaux University

**Phuong Le-Hong and Thi Minh Huyen Nguyen**
VNU University of Science, Hanoi, Vietnam

**Azim Roussanaly**
LORIA, Université de Lorraine, Nancy, France

# Index

CPSIA information can be obtained
at www.ICGtesting.com
Printed in the USA
LVHW060117010222
709877LV00005BA/279

9 781639 871230